The Nazareth Route

Jesus' Spirituality of Challenge and Vulnerability

Cecil Hargreaves

Published by

MELROSE
BOOKS

An Imprint of Melrose Press Limited
St Thomas Place, Ely
Cambridgeshire
CB7 4GG, UK
www.melrosebooks.com

FIRST EDITION

Cover designed by Catherine McIntyre

ISBN 978-1-906050-44-3

Printed and bound in Great Britain by:
Biddles 24 Rollesby Road, Hardwick Industrial Estate
King's Lynn. Norfolk PE30 4LS

Much in mind in the writing

of the following pages was

CATRIONA

whose vitality, love and laughter

taught us to go for the things

that matter most

For JEREMY, DOUGAL and RICHARD

in gratitude for many route-findings in the hills over the years,

shared and much enjoyed.

CONTENTS

CONTENTS (cont.)

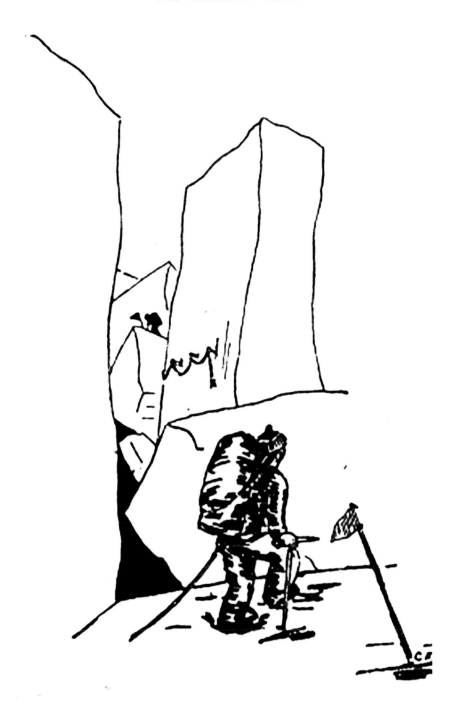

Illustration by Charles Evans

INTRODUCTION

As this book's subtitle shows, challenge and that form of vulnerability which consists in a willingness to get hurt and wounded if necessary are two topics on which this book focuses. The book may also be said to be about human dilemma in general.

The book starts with the story of Jesus' sermon in the Nazareth synagogue on *Isaiah* Chapter 61 and its prophetic message about justice for the oppressed. He is faced by the dilemma of receiving from his hearers first of all acclamation for his challenging message and theme but later on having to face from them anger, rejection and physical threats when his hearers discovered that Jesus was saying that he himself embodied Isaiah's prophetic voice and message, adding that he knew that they would not listen to him, just as Jews had always rejected their own prophets. So Jesus faces the dilemma of experiencing both acclamation and rejection, his challenge causing his rejection and making him exposed to wounding, danger and vulnerability, a prospect that he came to accept as his vocation. Later, of course, he was to call his followers to accept a like vocation of challenge and facing getting wounded and being hurt in their own lives and situations, their own cultures and national settings.

So the book leads into a study, in many chapters, of Jesus' own spirituality of challenge and vulnerability, and attempts to record and recall some of Jesus' modern followers who have taken Jesus' pattern of life in Galilee and Judaea (what I have called *The Nazareth Route*) as what they would hope to make the pattern of their own lives. The book aims to describe as many as twenty or thirty people in modern times across the world who, in the opinion of others, can be seen to be now, or recently have been seen to be, among Jesus' modern Nazareth 'route-makers' and 'route-finders'. For example, the book naturally includes something on Archbishop Desmond Tutu who played such a major part in challenging and campaigning against the system of apartheid in South Africa in the 1980s when it was being imposed, but who as a result was left exposed to many death-threats and much wounding for him and his family.

Remembering the dilemmas which Jesus faced, the final chapter of the present book is entitled 'Four Current Dilemmas in Human Route-finding'. It touches on the extremes of both religious extremism and the outright denials of much modern cynicism: also on sensuality and the celebration of the senses, the claims of both justice and compassion, and of both competition and sharing. And in others of the later chapters various other individual figures are focussed on for whom the challenge or the vulnerability takes different forms.

Here are four examples, out of the twenty or thirty people mentioned above, of the sort of Nazareth route-makers on whom the book focuses, following on the mention of Desmond Tutu.

M.M. Thomas in India was a giant among Christian route-makers in the second half of the twentieth century. As a lay-theologian with a background in economic and political studies and with an active commitment within the Mar Thoma Church he was able to carry his route-making into secular realms and into new ways of thought for his generation. One of his books was called *Secular Ideologies of India and the Secular Meaning of Christ*. His theology of humanness led to a stress on and a deep challenging concern for oppressed human beings whose experience of life was depersonalised and dehumanised. His writings came out of an Asian awareness of the stark facts of world poverty, coupled with the spirituality of 'hope, love and sacrifice' (his own words) to which he aspired. He wrote a notable article in 1969 on 'The Pattern of Christian Spirituality'. He knew much both about challenge and about entering into the wounded stateness and vulnerability of the world's marginalised people.

Among those focused on in the book is the Chinese and Taiwanese theologian Choan-Seng Song. Although he uses the phrase 'A Parable of People's Political Theology' as the sub-title of one of his books, it is the wounded state, powerlessness and pain that stand out as the overall focus of his writing, and as the main emphasis in his Nazareth route-making. He writes about God's loving involvement in human life having its 'painful' and 'radically disturbing' aspects. He uses the concept and phrase 'pain-love' as being the deepest verbal expression of the word 'love', relating it to Calvary's weakness made powerful. He says that 'in the Chinese language the words "love" and "pain" are interchangeable', and that what a mother feels for her child is properly described as 'pain-love'.

Though modern theology in the West, say through Jürgen Moltmann's phrase 'the grief of the Father, the love of the Son and the drive of the Spirit', in his book *The Crucified God*, is not without those who touch on this aspect of human understandings of God, it is Asian theologians such as C.S. Song who seem to spell it out in a specially explicit way. Many will hear in his theology an echo of the Japanese Kazoh Kitamori's 1946 book *Theology of the Pain of God*. (The latter speaks of how his book was being written in times, for his country, of defeat in war and of pain.) C.S. Song, in one of his books, *The Tears of Lady Meng*, writes: '…powerlessness can transform into powerfulness through the power of tears and that is the power of love and truth'. Christian writing on vulnerability goes deep here.

In western countries in the last decades of the twentieth century talk was also of pain. Henri Nouwen's book *The Wounded Healer* in 1979 was written from the conviction that would-be helpers of other people, in an age when there have been many wounded, rootless and dislocated people, can best offer help, and get a hearing as helpers, by passing on to them something about the helper's own wounded state, vulnerability and fragility. That conviction was based on Jesus' own significance and reality as wounded healer. Nouwen's book is given a place in the present book.

Also mentioned is Esther de Waal and her 1997 book *Living with Contradiction*. She may be described perhaps as tackling the pain of contradiction and tensions. But there is also a distinct element of challenge in what she writes. She wants to sound a note of warning and challenge about our human tendency often to try and avoid facing and tackling our inner tensions, conflicts and contradictions. She writes, in the preface to her book, of life's 'tensions', in the facing of which, she says, she 'needed all the help' she could get. She writes later: 'we all stand in need of healing' and 'unless we attend to our inner conflicts and contradictions, not only will we find ourselves torn apart by our inner divisions, but also we shall very likely inflict wounds on those around us'.

Not all of *The Nazareth Route* is directly about challenge and vulnerability. One chapter has the heading 'Artistic and Other Approaches to Biblical Meaning'. Another chapter describes the contemporary figure of a young priest in Nablus and the adjoining area in Palestinian lands, whose father was a carpenter in modern Nazareth. Further passages in the book describe not only a young couple in modern Britain making their choices, but also the late Gillian Rose, the philosopher, route-making between the claims of reason and the claims of love. Among many other people described, mention is made of the Iona Community and of what one member of it sums up as its wild-goose aim to follow a way of 'holy restlessness'.

1

JESUS' NAZARETH SERMON AND A SOUTH AFRICAN HOUSE GROUP'S READING OF IT

I have always found the story in Chapter 4 of the *Gospel of Luke* about Jesus' words to the congregation in the Nazareth synagogue one of the most extraordinary and striking stories in the Gospels.

Following his reading of a scriptural reading from the later chapters of the *Book of Isaiah* (The Lord 'has sent me to announce good news to the poor... and to let the broken victims go free...'), Jesus proceeded to apply the words to himself and to say in effect that the way in which God had blessed his own preaching, teaching and healing in neighbouring places had shown that the words written in *Isaiah* were coming true and being fulfilled. 'Today in your hearing this text has come true.' At this, we read, 'there was general approval; they were astonished that words of such grace should fall from his lips'. But then Jesus added some words very critical of Nazareth, comparing it and its people unfavourably with certain people on the Mediterranean coast and in Syria; and that 'roused the whole congregation into fury; they leapt up, drove him out of the town, and took him to the brow of the hill on which it was built, meaning to hurl him over the edge', though he 'walked straight through the whole crowd and went away'.

So in spite of the initial welcome and approval, there we have the rejection of him. In spite, too, of the fact, recorded in the Gospels about this stage in Jesus' activities in Galilee, that in neighbouring places Jesus' teaching was being widely acclaimed, people saying that 'unlike the scribes', the class of Jewish religious teachers, 'he taught with a note of authority'.[1]

Here, from early in the story of Jesus' activities in Galilee, we find that the Nazareth route as experienced by Jesus was indelibly marked both by the authoritativeness and the vulnerability with which he responded to the demands and the challenges which the route brought for him. I use the many-syllabled word 'authoritativeness' rather than 'authority', because the latter can bear 'authoritarian' connotations which 'authoritativeness' does not have.

But the above paragraphs are simply my own reactions to the biblical story and my 'reading' of it. How do readers and Christians across the world 'read' the story? How do those who are not church leaders, biblical scholars or theologians 'read' it?

The Zulu house group

In 1999 a book entitled *The Academy of the Poor*[2] by Gerald West, Associate Professor in the School of Theology in the University of Natal, included a transcript of a house group discussion and study in 1988 – six years before the end of the apartheid period ending in 1994 – on part of the biblical passage in *Luke* described above. The house group was in Amawoti settlement near Pietermaritzburg and Durban. This present chapter includes

---

1. *Luke* 4.14-30, *Mark* 1.22 (REB)
2. Gerald West. Sheffield Academic Press 1999 pp.143-153

a record of the discussion, originally in Zulu but translated in the transcript into English.

The settlement was a community of about 100,000, one of South Africa's very many 'informal shack settlements'. Gerald West in his book is keen to show what goes on in such bible study groups in many places among 'a whole range of readers'. He says that the range overall includes largely illiterate readers and members from African Independent Churches, in the townships and settlements: also unemployed youth: also the disabled and unemployed: activist union workers in local civic structures who are disillusioned with the church: and those engaged as social workers in the community. Special mention is made of the important group of the 'rural black women' who are among those oppressed in race, class and gender, but who also play vital roles in the community and 'support the church with their presence, faith and finances'. So there are many in all those just mentioned who are poor and marginalised, though it also implied that those with some resources and knowledge about the Bible are also invited to join in the study groups. In fact the Amawoti house group, refreshingly, seemed to have a good proportion of very vocal and articulate members who pressed their questions in a very determined way, in an attempt to see how a particular phrase in the biblical passage related to modern life and their local situation.

The precise wording of the biblical verses studied by the house group (*Luke* Chapter 4.16-22 in the *Revised English Bible*) is:

> 'Jesus came to Nazareth, where he had been
> brought up, and went to the synagogue on the
> Sabbath day as he regularly did. He stood up to
> read the lesson and was handed the scroll of the
> prophet *Isaiah*. He opened the scroll and found the
> passage which says,

"The spirit of the Lord is upon me
because he has anointed me; he has sent me to
announce good news to the poor; to proclaim
release for prisoners and recovery of sight for
the blind; to let the broken victims go free, to
proclaim the year of the Lord's favour."

He rolled up the scroll, gave it back to the
attendant, and sat down; and all eyes in the
synagogue were fixed on him. He began to
address them: "Today," he said, "in your hearing
this text has come true." There was a general
approval; they were astonished that words of such
grace should fall from his lips.'

There will not be found in the house group's discussion
such questions as whether this synagogue-event in *Luke,* Chapter
4, ever actually happened, historically; that is, questions that come
up in many modern school A-level 'religious studies' classes. It is
interesting to note however on that point that in the sixth chapter
of the Gospel of *Mark* there is a shorter reference to that whole
synagogue-event outlined earlier in this present chapter. In *Mark*
the account is of Jesus going to 'his home town' (Nazareth), and
of how on the Sabbath 'he began to teach in the synagogue', of
how 'the large congregation who heard him asked in amazement.
"Where does he get it from? What is this wisdom he has been
given?"' But *Mark* also adds how they went on to 'turn against
him', saying to each other 'is he not the carpenter, the son of Mary,
the brother of James, Joses and Juda and Simon?' Saying in effect,
'He's putting on airs: he's just one of us.'[3] So *Luke's* account of both
acclamation and rejection is backed up by *Mark's* account, though
the matter is shorter. But if, in the Amawoti house group, no one
examines that question of whether the event really happened, or
looks for backing in another Gospel for the account, yet what I do

---

3. *Mark* 6. 1-6 (REB)

notice especially in the house group is that they find plenty of time to look at apparently obscure references in the biblical passage to 'the year of Jubilee', that is 'the year of the Lord's favour', which modern bodies across the world such as the Jewish Association for Business Ethics in their 'money and morals' programme, and the Christian Justice Group's study on 'Markets and Morals', have in recent years focussed on as critically important for today.

Nine people took part in the house group session, which was just one in their series of meetings held on a regular, weekly basis. The nine are named as Mbuso, Philani, Phumzile, Zithulele, Sandile, Nomonde, Dombi, Sara and Sipho – the last named being 'the facilitator' who guided the course of the discussion. No detailed description of their individual backgrounds is given, but even a digest may show that they brought a variety of diverse and important contributions to the discussion. Some of the participants were well-educated or trained in knowledge of the Bible. Many were not. Faith was what they had in common. Three of them in particular could be tough speakers and questioners, though with a clear background of faith: the three clearly had a strong social concern. One stands out as keen to explore the meanings of particular words in a biblical passage. Another obviously as a very practical person, wanting a focus on action and being task-orientated (whatever the terms used): but, again, with a clear background of faith, expressed in definite and not vague terms. One or two were perhaps victims of especial poverty for whom making articulate statements was not easy: but one of them joined in cheerfully through the medium of a small joke. And one was splendidly keen to stress the importance of relationships, and of winning the trust of people with whom one wanted to share good news. And so on.

The digest of the group's discussion

Sipho, after prayer, spoke about Jesus' sermon on 'describing the purpose of his coming to earth'. 'Why do you think Christ came to earth?' he asked the group. There was a silence till Dombi said, 'To show us the way to heaven.'

Dombi then read the passage: *Luke* 4.16-22. There were some initial exchanges then about Jesus in the synagogue, the passage's mention of standing and sitting down for the lesson and the address. One member of the group was interested in Jesus being able to read, but did this mean he had been to school? The group got on to verses 18 and 19 and in fact spent nearly all their time on the different phrases there, as found in the *Isaiah* ch. 61 passage in the lesson read, and applied by Jesus to his own calling. Their discussion touches mainly on half a dozen searching questions, the first of which is put to the group by Sipho.

Who are the poor?

The conversation was opened by some sensitive sharing of experiences. The poor are those who need hope, and if you preach to them they will follow you. The rich are comfortable as they are, so they are not interested in Jesus' bringing of good news to the poor. But it is only some rich people who don't respond to God. That led on to more observations about the rich and the poor, and whether it is wrong to be rich. It seems to have been generally agreed that 'it is not wrong to be rich, but rich people are proud', and keep to themselves and are not interested in the poor. One member expressed it strongly and said, 'If you are rich you have no time for God, and "me" is on the chair or throne of your life.' Another supplied a brief statistic, referring to the fact that 'only ten families in our community are rich, and have electricity'. Mbuso drew attention to the whole phrase 'good news to the poor', and commented that Jesus being poor

6

was able to be a bringer of good news to the poor and would be listened to. This started some talk about how much money Jesus had as a carpenter working with his father; and how he surely did not come to give money to people in a set-up where crops must have mattered most. And he was poor in the sense of being given food by different families when travelling round speaking to and helping people.

Are there not two senses of the word 'poor'?

This was a point occupying some time. Philani and Sipho both raise the question. While Jesus did not come to give money to people or mainly to give food, it was important to remember that he definitely came to bring blessing to those who were without spiritual resources. Mbuso said, 'You can be rich for this world, but poor on the side of God,' and Philani adds, 'If you are rich spiritually you will always be happy and praising God, no matter what your situation is.' But the group did not just stop at this point; it seemed to go deeply into related issues, such as 'which is more important, then, trying to help people who are materially needy or trying to help people who have no spiritual resources?' Most members wanted to say, 'Both are equally important. God cares for everybody. All are equal in his sight.' (An issue of course that surfaces across the world, wherever people want to take sides between 'service' and 'evangelism'.) Sandile added the observation that some people were poor spiritually and poor materially, the latter often because their money goes on drink, like the people of Amaotama (a particularly poor part of Amawoti). Sipho added the comment that in the past the Church has understood the biblical phrase 'the poor' to mean only the spiritually poor, because 'the leaders of the Church were rich and not part of the poor people'. But now, he said, there has been a change and some parts of the Church, especially first in South America where there is a lot of oppression, have understood 'the poor' to mean both the physically poor and the spiritually poor. The discussion led on naturally to the following issue.

Why are people poor?

As a sign of the group's ability to let blunt, straight questions be asked, the following question was addressed to two members of the group: 'Why are you poor, Zithulele?' 'Why are you poor, Nomonde?' The transcript says that in fact at least one of those two was embarrassed and made uncomfortable by the question. One of them just said, 'I don't have the money to buy what's needed' and 'how can you plan when you are poor?' The other's response was a laughing response, with a little joke uttered, of a sort that implied that she thought the idea of poor people ever being actually helped to a better life was simply unbelievable. However, there were suggestions later on from other members of the group, related to the point about making plans that were more positive, and making clear that some help over and tackling of the problems had been effectively taking place. Sipho was later to sum up as follows some of the answers that the group had listed as being contributory causes of poverty. Some families don't try to plan ahead. Or educational facilities are not available, which, for all except ten rich families, would be caused through bad or mistaken government. Or social and other forms of oppression leave some in poverty. Comments from individual members varied considerably. Some families were in a position to sell some cattle, one said, to tide over families in the provision of schooling, though where to get the latter apart from South Africa? Or once one was educated that would mean a more secure job, and not being easily tired, and would help to avoid unemployment. Dombi's line was 'we must pray for God to help the poor', though that prompted an immediate response from a member (otherwise obviously free of any cynicism), that individual effort was also required, and 'there is no manna today'.

Who is Jesus referring to when he talks about good news and release for prisoners?

When this phrase was discussed, one of the sharpest comments came from Philani, who, so the transcript tells us, had been attacked by activist Inkatha vigilantes the previous night. She said, 'What! Is Jesus going to release them?' And the group is said to have replied, 'No, we wouldn't like it if Jesus released them.' Another member mentioned someone from Amawoti who had been detained by the South African Defence Force as a criminal two days earlier. And there, said one member, Jesus would release him 'because he hadn't really committed a crime, but was just being exploited'. Further discussion centred on the thought that, for example, the people in prison to whom Jesus was referring were those who couldn't pay their debts, who owed people money. 'They were slaves. These are the poor, these are the ones Jesus was going to set free.' 'Jesus told them that they would be free. By educating people you make people aware of oppression and slavery.' At this stage several members of the group emphasised that the meaning of 'prisoners' here was extended in the prophetic passage being quoted, and in the phrase that followed 'prisoners', to 'broken victims' ('the oppressed') as included in those who were to be set free. One person asked directly 'what does oppression mean for us in South Africa today?' Various answers suggested that there was a chain of oppression starting with any of us oppressing ourselves, 'when you don't want to listen': going on to people being oppressed by other human beings, and one member adding that such human beings were oppressed by Satan. Mbuso summed it up: oppression comes from Satan, then from the government, then from different political parties, then some rich people, and local business folk. Philani also at one point put the challenge direct. 'Did Jesus come to tell people to riot?' with Sandile responding, 'No, but to make them realise what their situation is and to tell the rich people to forgive those who owed them debts.' In response to what the prophetic message says about 'recovery of sight for the blind', there was a general agreement that this included spiritual blindness, and on 'the importance of helping people to see and also to act', as part of Jesus' challenge and good news. There seems to have been only passing reference to the physical healing of the blind, though issues about Satan perhaps healing people as well as making them blind seemed to be current topics locally.

How do you preach good news to the poor?

This question about ways of 'proclaiming' was briefly looked at, and pressed further by 'how can you preach the Bible at Amaotama?', known as we mentioned as a particularly poor part of Amawoti. 'Telling them the word of God,' was one answer, and another 'tell them about doomsday', in relation to criminality and other social factors. Philani agreed that one can't give money to people there or 'they might just buy gavine' (homemade cane spirits) 'and that is making the problem worse'. But nor can we just give food. Reference was made to the saying, 'Give a man a fish and you feed him for one day. If you teach him to fish, you will feed him for the rest of his life', since 'that was part of the Gospel'. Philani's remark that 'they must know you before you can preach. They must trust you,' seemed of particular importance.

How can we change the injustice that is causing the poverty?

As a way of tackling the last clause of the prophetic passage from *Isaiah* – 'to proclaim the year of the Lord's favour' – Sipho suggested that the group look at verses in *Isaiah* ch. 58, coming just before *Isaiah* ch. 61. He explained that by the year of the Lord's favour the Jews meant what they called 'jubilee years' or 'sabbaticals' every seventh year and especially in the seven-times-seven-year fixed on as each 50th year. These years were regarded as memorials of God's Exodus-deliverance of the Jews from Egypt and as continuing acts of mercy between Jew and Jew, displayed by delivering people from debts or slavery or restoring them to land originally theirs but taken from them. It all aimed to stop the rich from getting richer and the poor from getting poorer. But, said Sipho, the verses in *Isaiah* ch.58 give us a clue to what 'God's favour' means in the prophetic message: it means 'a doing away with injustice and the yoke of oppression' and it also means 'giving food, shelter and clothes'. (Sandile added 'This is the practical Gospel' as Jesus takes over the prophetic message.) This in *Isaiah* ch.58 verses 6-8 – which the group then read – certainly talks of 'sharing your food with the hungry' and 'taking the homeless poor into your house', but is described centrally as the 'fasting' or self-giving that the Lord wants from us rather than only traditional patterns of fasting: it is the way to changing injustice and to sharing the vulnerability of the oppressed.

All this 'jubilee' talk of people being 'set free' from this and that seemed too idealistic to one or two in the group. Mbuso and Sandile said: 'It's unbelievable!' But Sipho replied, 'If Christ came to do this, did he finish doing it? No, not completely. But Jesus started, and we must continue.' He added, 'Yes, our help is sometimes harmful,' which prompted Sara in the group, who had said nothing all along, to put in an example of her experience: 'A tramp asked me for money. I offered to go with him and buy some tea and food, but he refused, he just wanted money.' But Sipho, agreeing with the difficulties, said that the *Isaiah* prophecy spoke of helping with what is needed. In fact, the group mainly turned to how much help was possible in their situation, and positive discussion followed. It was agreed that some charities in flood and relief situations helped to get needy people themselves to work on the problems and to feel that they too have made a contribution and not just passively received 'charity'. Lessons had been learnt about how it was not just no good, but harmful, to give building materials in some cases without helping a person to build the house. There were indeed right ways of giving help, and mention was made of various projects and organisations which, learning by experience, were channels of help.

The group discussion was followed by the group making a poster in which they compiled the most important things that they had learnt. This was put up on the wall of the local Ilimo Project office:-

Jesus came

- For the rejected and neglected people
  He came with the answer to their problem

God's kingdom

- Is where God's project is carried out:
  - good news is coming for the poor
  - the oppressed are liberated
- Is people who build people

In Amawoti, we see God's kingdom when:-

- the community is organised
  - they use good ways to meet needs
- they make changes
  - the leaders are servants of the community

Those who are familiar with books such as *Faith in the Poor* by Bob Holman,[4] about the very large housing estate scheme

4. Lion publishing, Sandy Lane West, Oxford, England. 1998

Easterhouse of around 40,000 people on the edge of Glasgow, will be aware that phenomena somewhat comparable to Gerald West's 'academy of the poor' are to be found in Great Britain.

Finally, one point may be mentioned following this chapter's central description of the Amawoti experience; it is this. That in the *Gospel of Luke* the context of, and the lead-up to, the Nazareth story in the Gospel's Chapter 4, are contained in *Luke* Chapter 3's relating of the baptism of Jesus by John the Baptist in the river Jordan. In its closely packed and profound verse 22 we read that when Jesus had been baptised 'the Holy Spirit descended upon him in bodily form like a dove. And a voice came from Heaven "you are my Son, the Beloved; with you I am well pleased"' (NRSV). Those words echo both *Psalm* 2 verse 7 and *Isaiah* 42 verse 1. *Psalm* 2 verse 7 had long been a very well known phrase among Jews because the verse was used traditionally when a new Jewish king was being enthroned, commissioned and given authority under God. The words had been repeated each year at the celebration of the anniversary of the king's accession. *Psalm* 2.7 summed up messianic and royal salutations. And *Isaiah* 42.1 summed up the Jewish prophetic conviction from exile days in Babylon that God's chosen one would be a servant-like figure suffering with God's people: the *Isaiah* verse hears God calling him 'my chosen, in whom my soul delights'. (NRSV)

So the significance of the voice from heaven was that Jesus was being declared authoritative by God, and was being called to a vocation of service and vulnerability.

A footnote about Nazareth in modern times

Anyone for whom the Nazareth synagogue story comes across strongly, and is seen to be of particular importance in forming our picture of the Jesus of history, will be intrigued to find that modern Christian churches and congregations in Nazareth in quite modern times have had a special festival day each year remembering the event. It has gone by the name of the Feast of the Precipitation (a name derived of course from the hill-top cliff or precipice in the story). To commemorate Jesus being taken to the brow of the hill, there has been a procession up to the hilltop.

Najwa Farah, the Palestinian-Arab writer and poet, herself born in Nazareth of Nazarene parents and who grew up as a girl in the years before the second world war, in her striking book *A Continent called Palestine*[5] writes of girlhood memories: 'In the afternoon of the feast day, young men and women in summer clothes walked up the steep rocky hill on the south side of Nazareth overlooking the plain of Esdraelon [Jezreel]. It was the season of green almonds and the walkers would take some with them as they climbed up and back...' She describes also how, a little later in the year than the festival, the Feast of the Transfiguration was celebrated, including there also a visit up Mount Tabor, one of the proposed probable sites of the Gospel's event, not too many miles from Nazareth and a distant part of the Nazareth landscape. 'The road to the summit had many hairpin bends and before the coming of the car, people went up there on horseback.' The book tells also of how many Christian processions there would be during the year in Nazareth, with its many different worshipping communities reflecting a range of Christian traditions. Nazareth's population, she says, was a third Muslims, a third Greek Orthodox, and a third 'what we call Western Christian communities, comprising Protestant, Greek Catholic, and Latin/Roman Catholic'.

Najwa Farah's descriptions include many happy times, not least among Nazareth's many orchards and gardens, with Nazareth being famed for its apricots: and in walks on Sunday afternoons in the surrounding hills, with the picking of flowers like anemones and cyclamen in spring. But descriptions also of

---

5. SPCK London 1996 p.21

unhappy and anguished times as the years went on, and after 1948. She was in Nazareth when the Israeli forces came in 1948, and describes how the Arab population in Galilee mostly fled to Syria and Jordan: and expresses strongly the huge Palestinian-Arab sense of injustice at the United Nations' partition resolution of November 1947; this not only gave the Jews what would be the largest share of the country as part of the recommendation for the creation of a Jewish state, but meant, in Arab eyes, that the Arabs were being made to pay the price for this act of reparation to the Jews after the horrific and massive Jewish experience of the Holocaust. For the price, of course, was the dispossessing of many of the Arabs and their expulsion from their ancestral lands.

Najwa Farah was also in the West Bank in 1967 when the Israelis occupied considerable areas of West Bank land, in defiance of the United Nations' Resolution 242. She was in Beirut, too, in 1982, during that further invasion into the Lebanon. These blows, she writes, followed on after the Palestinian Arabs' background of having been ruled by the colonialism of the very authoritarian Ottoman Empire and the Turkish government in the preceding centuries. So, in all the 20th century experiences of refugee existence, there were many anxious times of travel and routes taken by Nazareth people, as well as by their fellow Arabs, meaning that the phrase 'the Nazareth route' in those times meant too often a deeply painful route.

In closing this chapter, one cannot fail to include a word about Najwa's honesty at one point in her telling of her story about the Feast of Precipitation already touched on. Added to what I inserted above about the walkers up the hill usually picking some green almonds off the almond trees, as they climbed up and later returned, she has these eight words about the walkers – 'regretting what was done to Jesus, I hope.' Those wistful words seemed to me, when I read them, as being a very striking brief recognition that the natural and happy taking home of some treasured fruit might well have made participants on the special day forget, at least for a moment, the poignancy of Jesus' humiliation and rejection in the first century event. Her brief realistic touch at that point seemed to me typical of her book's whole realistic approach, for there is no painting of a sentimentally-coloured picture.

2

A VISIONARY 'LETTER TO HEBREWS' ON JESUS' ROUTE-MAKING SPIRITUALITY

A Letter to Hebrews, written by someone who was a visionary of great depth, is one of the most remarkable books in the *New Testament*. Its primary theme is the Sonship of Christ ('God has spoken to us in his Son' comes in the *Letter's* second verse) and the vocation of Christ's followers, and of all human beings, to sonship ('God is treating you as sons' comes in the book's later chapters).[6] This theme of Christ the Son is specially developed in the senses of Christ the Pioneer and Route-maker through human existence, Christ the Priest who pioneers the way for humanity through the darkness of evil and perversity on into reconciliation and peace, and Christ the Mediator of the Covenant of faithfulness and trust between God and humanity.

The book has in some ways an intricate pattern and style, theological and textual matters alternating with much simpler passages: but these latter form one of the book's main, and practical purposes and aims, which is being a letter of encouragement for a group of folk who had apparently lost their early confident

---

6. *Hebrews* 1.2 and 12.5 (REB)

Christian belief. And one of the great things about *Hebrews* seems to be the visionary depth of it all, which catches the reader's attention almost immediately at the very beginning: '…the Son is the radiance of God's glory and the exact representation of his being, sustaining all things by his powerful word…'.[7] And this is still visible near the close of the book when the writer is exhorting his readers to recover their faith, and doing it in ringing tones:- 'It is not to the tangible, blazing fire of Sinai that you have come, with its darkness, gloom and whirlwind… No, you have come to Mount Zion, the city of the living God, the heavenly Jerusalem, to myriads of angels, to the full concourse and assembly of the firstborn who are enrolled in heaven, and to God the judge of all, and to the spirits of good men made perfect, and to Jesus the mediator of a new covenant…'.[8]

What I have called 'visionary depth' is more than rhetorical and poetic power. It has come across to me in something of a recurring way, at intervals, over many years. It is a long time ago now since I heard a sister of a religious community, in the course of an address which she was giving, urging her audience not to miss the message of faith and hope that the *Letter* gave us at many points of its thirteen chapters. She told us not to miss '*Hebrews*' great message of faith and hope, and its exhortation 'to see the unseen invisible things that lie beyond earthly life'. She quoted four verses from the *Letter's* 11th chapter[9] where past Jewish heroes and their faith had focussed on faith in what was unseen: the last of those four verses telling of how Moses 'was resolute, as one who saw the invisible God'. And she urged us to see the force of *Hebrews'* emphasis throughout on a 'not yet… but already' presentation, beginning early on, with reference to

---

7. *Hebrews* 1.3 (New International Version)

8. *Hebrews* 12.18-24 (REB)

9. *Hebrews* 11.3, 11.7, 11.13, 11.27 (REB)

human beings: 'we do not yet see everything in subjection to them, but we do see Jesus, who for a little while was made lower than the angels, now crowned with glory and honour because of the suffering of death, so that by the grace of God he might taste death for everyone'.[10] *Hebrews'* visionary qualities may also be described as its distinctive sense of an eternal perspective.

As already mentioned, two of the *Letter's* descriptions of Jesus are of him as the Pioneer, and the High Priest; with a third major description being that of him as the Mediator of the Covenant of faithfulness and trust between God and humanity. Two other descriptions linked to those, and ones that are focussed on strongly in the *Letter*, are those of The Tried and Tested Enabler of a Suffering Humanity through his journey through human existence, and, touched on above, 'the Son': both of those latter descriptions enabling Jesus to be the ideal High Priest and Mediator of the Covenant of trust.

The two descriptions of Jesus as The Pioneer ('pioneer of salvation' for humanity, and 'the pioneer of faith')[11] come near the beginning of *Hebrews* or near the end; surely significantly, thus indicating a primary theme occurring in, or underlying, the whole letter. (Instead of the word 'pioneer', some English versions of the Bible have preferred the words 'leader' or 'captain'.) The word 'pioneer' surely catches the strength of meaning here, since the *Letter* makes much of those who, 'by faith', were forerunners of Jesus – Moses, Abraham, Isaac, Joseph, Moses, Gideon, Barak, Samson, Jephthah, David, Samuel and other stalwart leaders – and their leadership was marked especially by their initiative in pioneering a way through fierce opposition in the service of God's purposes.[12]

---

10. *Hebrews* 2.8-9 (NRSV)

11. *Hebrews* 2.10, 12.2

12. *Hebrews* Ch.11

A second description of Jesus which receives strong emphasis in the *Letter* is that of the Tried and Tested Enabler of a Suffering Humanity. If Jesus was to be proclaimed for what he is as an enabler of humanity, says the *Letter*, enabling it to face suffering and death, he must first have experienced suffering and death himself and been through the test of that himself. One of the events in the past history of the Jews to which they looked back was called by them 'the Akedah' or the Test, referring to the times of testing in the desert under Moses, and the word became a big theme in their belief and view of life. So the *Letter*, writing of Jesus, says: – '...in bringing many sons to glory it was fitting that God ... should make the pioneer of their salvation perfect through sufferings', and again: '...because he himself has passed through the test of suffering, he is able to help those who are in the midst of their test'.[13] In the same chapter the *Letter* says: – 'we see Jesus... crowned now with glory and honour because he suffered death, so that, by God's gracious will, he should experience death for all mankind'.[14]

A third, and major, description of Jesus in the *Letter* is that of him as the Mediator of the Covenant of Trust and Faithfulness between God and Humanity. In the *Old Testament* the Covenant is seen as having a sacrificial side to it, with the sprinkling of blood: the sacrifice being understood as a sealing and a ratifying of the coming together of God and humanity, and of their belonging together in mutual trust and faithfulness. But the central focus is on how a covenant and a coming together in trust and faithfulness are possible. Towards the end of the *Letter*, it comes out strongly that this is the central focus in the covenant theme; – 'Let us be

---

13. *Hebrews* 2.10, 2.18 (REB)

14. The Revised English Bible's rendering of *Hebrews* 2.9

firm and unswerving in the confession of our hope, for the giver of the promise is to be trusted'.[15]

A fourth, and central, description of Jesus in the *Letter* is that of Christ the High Priest, making real and accessible to humanity the expiation of sin by his sacrificial life and death, and by all the reconciling blessing that he brings. This theme permeates the whole *Letter*, from the end of Chapter 4 onwards. It brings a message generally and for any reader, but in the particular context in which the *Letter* was written, it forms the foundation of the *Letter's* plea to its original readers to be confident that they can and should put behind them the past and its failures and discouragements, national and personal, and make a new start.

At the heart of this section of the *Letter l,* i.e. verses in *Hebrews* Chapter 10, where we find a distinctive approach to, and understanding of, the Atonement: Jesus' decisive activity on the Cross is seen as his saying to the Father: 'I have come to do your will.'[16] One twentieth century interpretation of this passage was this:- 'Christ did the will of God as a Son and not as a servant, not through fear or constraint but out of spontaneous and unlimited love. This is what God had looked for from the beginning of the world and had never seen ... The human will of Christ was tested to the uttermost; and in his death it was found flawless and complete in its self-offering to the Father.'[17]

From earliest Christian times it has been customary to describe the Eucharist or Holy Communion service as a sacrifice. The *Didache* was a short manual (more fully entitled 'The Teaching of the Lord through the Twelve Apostles') discovered in Constantinople in the 19th Century, and assigned by scholars

---

15. *Hebrews* 10.23 (REB)

16. *Hebrews* 10.7 and the whole passage from verse 5 to verse 10.

17. Stephen Neill. *Bible Words and Christian Meanings*. SPCK London 1970.

to a very early period, possibly before the end of the first century A.D. It is about Christian life, worship and ministry, and contains the following passage: 'On every Lord's Day gather yourselves together and break bread and give thanks, first confessing your transgressions that your sacrifice may be pure.' This passage about Christian worshippers' sacrifice is clearly an addition to an understanding of the Eucharist as a memorial of Christ's sacrifice. *A Letter to Hebrews*, in its focus on Christ as High Priest, makes clear the basic nature of Christ's sacrificial Priesthood and the worshippers' sacrifice in the Eucharist. The worshippers' sacrifice is summed up in the *Letter's* final chapter: 'through Jesus let us continually offer up to God a sacrifice of praise'.[18] Jesus' sacrifice is described very fully. His priestly work goes on for ever, a continual offering of himself to the Father on behalf of humanity: 'He has entered heaven itself, to appear before God on our behalf.'[19]

There has been much discussion and controversy - especially in the twentieth century - as to whether it is in line with scriptural understanding of the phrase 'eucharistic sacrifice', and our understanding of the phrase in relation to eucharistic observance in church. Many of us would want to avoid any encouragement to seeing eucharistic devotion as including the idea of a repetition of Christ's sacrifice being made real in the church service. But that does not mean that we are left with any sense of the absence of Christ the High Priest, in all the fullness of his sacrificial activity, in the eucharistic observance: our sacrifice of praise joins with Christ's presence in the service, for 'we have been consecrated, through the offering of the body of Jesus Christ once for all'.[20]

---

18. *Hebrews* 13.15 (REB)

19. *Hebrews* 9.24 (REB)

20. *Hebrews* 10.10 (REB)

3

SOME MODERN DESCRIPTIONS OF JESUS

There are many modern descriptions of the historical Jesus of Galilee and Judaea currently circulating. Here are a few brief excerpts from the writings of four leading recent figures from the worlds of scholarship, theology, biblical studies, spirituality and church leadership:

Hugh Montefiore was a theologian of wide interests including the world of science, and a biblical scholar, with years early on in parish ministry; he was later Bishop of Birmingham:

> 'It seems sufficiently certain that Jesus worked
> as a carpenter until his thirties, when he joined
> the holiness movement of his cousin John…' but
> 'he did not merely resort with those who were
> religiously respectable, but in particular with
> "outsiders" and "the unloved".[21]

Samuel Rayan, who died at the end of the twentieth century, was an Indian Jesuit, and a widely known leader in the realms of Indian Christian theology and spirituality, with a strong social concern:

---

21. *Credible Christianity* (Mowbray 1993) p.75

'Jesus experienced the kingdom' (the Kingdom of
God) 'as pressing upon him and upon history...
The community was embodied in Jesus' own
person. He was its seed. He experienced himself
as socially potent, as enshrining the harvest
of a new humanity... The mysticism of the
Fourth Gospel is historical mysticism, and its
contemplation fixes on the glory of God as
revealed in Jesus' love for and service to the
people.'[22]

Alan Webster was a former Dean of St Paul's Cathedral in
London, with many years' ministry in parishes and in theological
training in his earlier years. He shared in, and gave leadership in,
many initiatives for change in the life of the church:

'Within the Church's search for truth in word and
deed stands the figure of Jesus Christ, so radical,
elusive and powerful. His story and his presence
continue to inspire and surprise. He refuses to be
neatly classified or convincingly explained. In the
Gospels each generation discovers new truths.'[23]

Geza Vermes is a noted Jewish scholar and writer with
academic appointments in the history of Judaism and the first
century Palestinian world. Beginning life as a Catholic in Eastern
Europe, he later returned to the faith of his ancestors:

'Jesus was the just man, the zaddick, the helper
and healer, the teacher and leader, against a
background of Galilean Judaism... He takes his
place in the venerable company of the devout and
of the ancient hasidim... He was an unsurpassed

---

22. *Jesus and the Father* in the journal *Jeevadhara* (Alleppey, Kerala,
India May 1974) p.244: and *Jesus and the Poor in the Fourth Gospel*
in *Readings in Indian Christian Theology* (Indian SPCK 1993) p.107.

23. *Reaching for Reality* (SPCK 2002)

master of the art of laying bare the inmost core of
spiritual truth and of bringing every issue back to
the essence of religion, the existential relationship
of man and man, and man and God... There
is manifest disparity between Jesus and other
hasidim. Jesus stood head and shoulders above the
others.' [24]

For me, many of the phrases in the above quotations are
unmistakably striking. They gather up many points in the picture
of Jesus which we find in the *Gospels* about his life and teaching,
death and resurrection in first-century Galilee and Judaea. Jesus
and the unloved, Jesus and the splendid surprises of events
and sayings. The combination of how he spoke with power and
authority in the eyes of those who listened to him and movingly
(and disturbingly) to his immediate followers about how he
himself wanted to be a servant of others, and wanted them to
have the same outlook. Then Jesus' constant talk of the kingdom
of God, the fullness of a rule or a kingdom, where new standards
and values would be sovereign. And that word 'existential' in the
last quotation, and the phrase about Jesus bringing every issue
in human existence to focus on relating to God and relating
to others.

Further different angles of viewpoint

The variety of those who have their descriptions of Jesus is of
course very wide indeed. There are descriptions coming from
specialist historians in Judaism and in the Palestinian Judaism
of the first-century Christian era. There are fresh archaeological
excavations and discoveries: also the many diverse researches
on social, economic, religious and political aspects of that same
first-century Jewish Palestinian world into which Jesus was born;

---

24. *The Changing Faces of Jesus* Allen Lane. Penguin Press. 2000

most of them providing what may well be a single-phrase, single-formula title for Jesus, such as 'The Prophet of Social Change', 'The Teacher of the Wisdom of God', 'The Charismatic Healer and Counsellor', 'The Prophet of the Ultimate Fulfilment of God's Purposes'.

We have also been fortunate over the last twenty years to have books on this theme from a wider field than before: e.g. *Faces of Jesus in Latin America*, *Asian Faces of Jesus*, *Faces of Jesus in Africa*, adding to what was previously literature mainly from the west and north of the world. That addition has shown how the words of the Gospels, and of the *Bible* as a whole, are being interpreted in contexts and situations that in many respects (see Chapter 10 for more on 'the wider fields' referred to) are post-colonial situations. We have also had overall the expression of new and often radical styles of interpretation of the Bible that may, for instance, apply highly controversial criteria concerning the authenticity of many sayings ascribed to Jesus in the *Gospels*. Nor should we forget that there are those, perhaps many, in the world who would just want to continue asking the old questions such as 'did any figure such as the received Jesus of Nazareth figure ever actually and historically exist?' And all those in the post-modern world who want to get right away from the old religious 'grand narratives' drawn up from the Bible in ages long past. The above sorts of issues are looked at further, though still briefly, in Chapter 8.

Inherited Jewish memories of Jesus

Although a mainstream of possible clues to the identity of the historical Jesus are undoubtedly to be looked for in a focus on the first-century Palestinian Jewish world into which Jesus was born, the central emphasis of this small book is rather different. It is on the historical heritage from past Jewish history which Jesus will have received as a Jew. By heritage I mean the whole Jewish background of national experience, memories, tradition, symbols and imagery from the days of Abraham onwards. For these too provide many possible clues to the identity of the historical Jesus, and they are clues sometimes perhaps liable to get side-lined today.

The approach by heritage is of course not wholly a new approach. Many in the early Christian church saw a significant pre-figuring of the figure of Jesus in figures in the *Old Testament*, and a not inconsiderable group of biblical interpreters today stress the importance of seeing the whole authorised 'canon' of the books of the Bible as belonging firmly together, and as best interpreted when one part is seen in relation to another, with major themes weaving in and out through them.

The pages that follow adopt just a very simple form of heritage approach. It takes as basic the nomadic journeying of Abraham, starting with his long protracted travel from Ur in what we now call southern Iraq, to Haran in Northern Syria, and then down as far as Beersheba, almost to the borders of northern Arabia. Even though he will probably have been making use of some ancient trade-routes, Abraham's route-finding, route-making and route-following are highlighted in the biblical accounts. The simple form of heritage approach suggested here follows the stories of Abraham and some of his descendants, and picks out what are taken to be three distinctive or defining features of early Hebrew history. The three are as follows: first, as in Abraham's journeying above, a long national experience and history of pioneering in one form or another, often in the form of route-making in unknown or hostile territory. Secondly a long experience of somehow having a gift for spotting something which could be turned to good account and used; in other words a knack for spotting provision, and coming to be experienced in that; or spotting of things that, in a modern parlance, might be called providential. Thirdly, a long expcrience of coming across strange paradoxes on their travels, developing into an insight into the significance of paradox. A few more examples, of course, need to be given of what have been described as these three distinct Hebrew features. They are certainly of continuing significance in the *Bible*.

The Hebrew experience of pioneering

A good symbol of Abraham's pioneering and his nomadic life is bound to be tents, the constant mention of tents and his living in tents. These seem to have been the symbol of Abraham and his descendants in desert times that was a continuing element in the Jewish mind, from early days right through to about eighteen centuries later when Christian writers were providing our *New Testament* writings in the Christian era. In an early chapter in *Genesis* (12.8) we read of how Abraham 'moved on to the hill-country east of Bethel... and pitched his tent...' and (the later, written) records of the oral folk-lore of the time are full of how he lived in tents. Then, eleven centuries later, they remain a central symbol. *Hosea* the prophet, in his message challenging his contemporaries about the dishonesty and luxurious dwellings in their culture and society, appealed to them to hear God, saying to them 'I have been the Lord your God since your days in Egypt: I shall make you live in tents yet again...' (12.9). And the writer of *A Letter to Hebrews* in the *New Testament*, another eight centuries later than that, wrote how Abraham settled in the promised land, 'living in tents with Isaac and Jacob', adding that he had 'left home in trust and faith without knowing where his journey would take him', as one mid-20th century translation put it (Ronald Knox).

As a symbol of the Hebrew desert years, one might of course just as well choose rocks. (Tents perhaps came to mind because of the close link with Abraham, the patriarchal figure.) The Jews continued to think of God in terms of 'rock and refuge'.

It is worth remembering, in connection with deserts, that one recent traveller in a truck across the Sahara desert in Morocco, said afterwards that it had made him realise that the desert area turned out to be three quarters mainly rock and only one quarter mainly sand.

The focus on route-making was triggered off for me by two passages written in the last decade or two by two theologians writing about the significance of the Crucifixion. Each of them, separately, suggested that, for those who find it helpful to have some illustration or 'model' of what Jesus was doing on the cross, the figure of a mountain-climbing route-finder or route-maker might provide the nearest approach. That is (though the wording is mine and not theirs) someone who punishingly but vigorously pioneers a way up an apparently impenetrable barrier or rock face for himself or herself, and for others to use in the future.[25] That the same metaphor or symbolism can be extended to the issue of Jesus' historical identity as well as to a route-making on the cross seems to me a possible and worthwhile approach.

The approach via heritage rather than by first-century Palestinian-Jewish historical evidence and modern researching including stimulating excavations on social, economic, religious and political aspects of the first century Jewish Palestinian world into which Jesus was born, is not of course to discount the importance of the latter. In both types of approach attention to history and to heritage is evident and obvious. But there is perhaps a danger of the heritage approach getting somewhat side-lined, since it does not contain quite the excitement of, say, modern archaeological excavations in the Nazareth neighbourhood, and it could get dismissed lightly as an approach that has long received major attention in some sense, and as just working in an already

---

25. Paul Fiddes *Past Event and Present Salvation* DLT 1989 p.136 and Vernon White *Atonement and Incarnation* Cambridge University Press 1991 p.53.

well-worked field. But I think that here too, on the heritage side, there is more 'digging' to be done.

Long distances, long centuries of pioneering

For striking lines of poetry on what now gets called (in admiring or in critical tones) the 'grand narratives' of Hebrew ancestral journeying, Edwin Muir's mid-twentieth century verse seems to catch the atmosphere, and for a very good reason. Brought up in the Orkneys in his rural farming setting and its long horizons surrounding him, he also had a good knowledge of the *Bible*. His poems *Abraham* and *The Succession* have the true wild country feel.[26] He wrote about people in the various Middle East regions through which Abraham travelled:

> 'Legendary Abraham,
> The old Chaldaean wanderer,
> First among these people came,
> Cruising above them like a star
> That is in love with distances
> And has through age to calmness grown,
> Patient in the wilderness
> And untarrying in the sown...'

[from *The Succession*]

Or again:

> 'The rivulet-loving wanderer Abraham
> Through waterless wastes tracing his fields of
>   pasture
> Led his Chaldaean herds and fattening flocks
> With the meandering art of wavering water
> That seeks and finds, yet does not know its way.
> He came, rested and prospered, and went on,

---

26. *Edwin Muir. Collected Poems.* Faber and Faber 1960 p.221 and p.263

Scattering behind him little pastoral kingdoms,
And over each one its own particular sky,
Not the great rounded sky through which he
        journeyed,
That went with him but when he rested
        changed…'

[from *Abraham*]

There is no space here to add more than a very
few lines also of Muir's description of Jesus'
route-making within humanity. He wrote of how
Jesus 'courted mortality', and 'schooled himself to
learn his part; a poor man skilled in dialectic art'.

[from *The Church*][27]

Abraham's 1000-mile journey from Ur, in what we now
know as southern Iraq, was northwards via the Euphrates
valley to Haran towards the present Turkish border; then due
south right down to Beersheba in the direction of Arabia, after
crossing into the Palestinian land of Canaan. Many parts of all
that journey, especially the earlier parts through the modern-
styled 'Fertile Crescent' and the Euphrates area was in pastoral
land and near a river, and the brief excerpts from Edwin Muir
above reflect this. But there was also much dry, desert country
along the route; down into Canaan only the coveted water of the
river Jordan was a big water-supplier. Modern proposed peace
processes between Israel and the Palestinians have had to include
extensive arrangements for the sharing of water resources. One
of the hopeful water-projects to the south of the area, concerned
with arid-land agriculture and water resource management has
been centring on good and symbolic cooperation between Israeli
researchers and Palestinian and Jordanian hydrologists and water

---

27. *Edwin Muir. Collected Poems.* Faber and Faber 1960 p.221 and
p.263

engineers, the project being affiliated to the University of Negev; it is located, significantly, in Beersheba, Abraham's first major point of settlement. That concluding point is a reminder that just as Abraham would have had to use and to work out routes and trade-routes on foot, so the use and working out of routeing and negotiating of water routes and availability is a big concern. A reminder, in other words, that Abraham in his pioneering acts of movement, moved in a world of routes.

The first exodus and the pioneering desert journey via Sinai

According to the biblical account of Abraham's whole journeying and that movement of the Hebrew people, it took a very considerable number of years. He is thought likely to have arrived in the land of Canaan about 1850 years before the Christian era.

A date about 600 years after that is thought to be the probable date of the first exodus (the second being much later and into Babylon). It was the Exodus out of Egypt after the Hebrews had been in a time of slavery there. Their crossing of the Red Sea at the end of the time of enslavement was a huge and specially remembered moment of liberation for them. That led on to the time of their long, protracted journey 'in the wilderness' and the desert, right up to the crossing of the river Jordan, north of the Dead Sea, into the modern west Bank, west-of-Jordan territory. This was a time of travel for them through much uninterrupted desert-country, confronting hills and rocky areas, and marked by the facing of many difficulties and dilemmas. Though events at 'Mount Sinai' were key events at this time, it has not been easy for analysts of the various biblical accounts of the happenings, and the routes taken there, to tell precisely whether their journey took them down to the more southern parts of Arabia (as traditionally thought) or on a route out of Egypt more immediately south of Palestine, on their way towards the east of the Dead Sea northwards.

Cultural and religious pioneering throughout the *Old Testament*

This took the Jews through a wide range of cultural and religious experiences, which one could say was its own sort of route-making. The background to that route-making, as mentioned earlier, was national past memories. And it is those memories, as a later chapter looks at, that, for instance, Jesus' recorded teaching about the Kingdom of God reflects or echoes. It is also a collective Jewish memory of what is handed down as on its own a general matter of history, quite apart from the Hebrew growth of religious faith. It was a background clearly concerned with both means and ends, both short-term issues and long-term issues, both journey and destination, both present experience and the horizons of promise, both ethical values for the present and those realities that are to do with what is ultimate, future and decisive: dilemma and debate as between 'the two sides' in each of those coupled phrases, seeing how they relate, is clearly the business of route-making and route-finding, and the reason why these latter are central in the biblical story.

Without suggesting 'The Route-maker' as yet another single-phrase description of Jesus, since, as noted earlier, such single-formula-phrases are notoriously inadequate to describe him, one has strong reasons, I believe, to see route-making as a hidden, defining factor underlying all understanding of the Jesus of history, perhaps a kind of DNA-like coil of meaning, threading through his human existence in Galilee and Judaea, emerging from his heritage in Judaism and from within humanity. A coil of guiding and programming (though not a deterministic coil nor one offering to human life a struggle-free or problem-free existence) both through those opposites and dilemmas that are truly contradictory (right and wrong, hope and despair) and between those apparent opposites and dilemmas that are twin, paradoxical reflections of the truth (meaning and love, toughness and sensitivity).

The above approach, and the words above about Jesus 'emerging from his heritage in Judaism', obviously together raise wide issues about the dimensions of Jesus' identity. They relate to the broadly held and centuries-long Christian conviction within the Church, and according to its early authorised propositional statement that Jesus was 'fully God and fully human'.[28] To focus on the Jesus of history, and to see the historical Jesus as giving us deep clues about human existence, as this small book does, is, to my mind, in no way to discount the parallel significance of the Jesus Christ beyond history. For example, a conviction about Christ as 'The Word' and the expression of God's being was there from the near beginning of Christianity.[29] That fits in well with the wording found in phrases in some modern theological thinking, of Christ as a figure who 'emerges from humanity' as 'the fulfilment of man's capacity for God and of God's purpose for man'.[30] The particular approach taken here in this present book does not need, of course, to be tied to any one specific manner of describing how Jesus may be said to be fully divine and fully human.

28. A phrase from the Athanasian Creed about the Church's faith in Christ as printed on p.145 of the Church of England's *Common Worship* publication (2000).

29. 'The Word' translates 'The Logos' in Greek as used in the *New Testament*. The Greek word also had the diverse connotation of 'Expression', 'Meaning', 'Reason' and 'Rationale' in the Greek world of thought.

30. The two latter phrases are quoted by Professor George Newlands in *A New Dictionary of Christian Theology* (SCM 1983 p.107) as a phrase describing the thinking of Norman Pittenger in *The Word Incarnate* (1959).

The Hebrew experience of provision

The Jewish ancestors' desert-period clearly provides a number of instances of their need of provision, such as the need for water and food in the long journey via Sinai. The symbol chosen here, however, to represent provision is another symbol from the series about Abraham in *Genesis*. It is the ram that Abraham unexpectedly discovered caught near him in some thick bushes when he was expecting to have to sacrifice his own son Isaac. The *Bible* uses the words 'it was provided' (*Genesis* ch.22.14 REB). It was a symbol coming at the key moment in Abraham's story and it was a symbol that continued to be remembered by Jews in subsequent centuries.

It has to be admitted that this story proves a stumbling block to many modern readers. They say 'How can I be expected to accept such a primitive story of cruelty and child sacrifice contemplated by a father who is one of the great heroes of the Bible?' And it does have to be accepted that the *Bible* contains stories of early stages in the historical progress of awareness of the truth in humanity. Personally, I find the interpretation of the passage in *Peake's Commentary on the Bible* (a one volume commentary in the middle of the twentieth century by a notable professor of *Old Testament* studies in London University, S.H. Hooke, which was reprinted in 2001)[31] to be the best description of both the realism of the primitive story and of the positive religious and prophetic significance of the story. He says that from the anthropologist's point of view it may be regarded as evidence for the existence of child-sacrifice among the Hebrews at an early period of their settlement in Canaan: but that, alongside that, it may also be recognised as a prophetic protest against this practice which persisted so long in the area. He cites, for the latter, a verse of protest by the biblical prophet *Micah* at the end

---

31. Published by Routledge

of the eighth century before the Christian Era at the time of King Hezekiah: 'Shall I give my firstborn for my transgression, the first of my body for the sin of my soul?'[32] *Peake's commentary* suggests that the anthropological viewpoint and the prophetic viewpoint should both be seen as shedding light on the situation described. A father is pressured by the custom, in a crisis, to sacrifice his child as being thought the only solution available to expiate his sins, with at the same time a pull of loyalty to his son having to be weighed against that, thus creating a tragic dilemma. So the story of the ram can indeed stand, as it did for the Jews, as representing a deep, early, human experience of the Hebrews.

A further objection of a somewhat different nature, but perhaps in the minds of some readers of this present chapter, needs to be mentioned briefly. I have used earlier, in an initial mention of 'provision', the word 'providentially'; and this may seem to some people to depart too much from what they would regard as down-to-earth historical background about Hebrew experience into the realms of religious faith to be of much use to us in a historical search. But distinctions between the realm of history and that of faith, as also between 'the Jesus of history' and 'the Christ of faith', are delicate ones. Some biblical descriptions of experience or of people are simply historical, some simply faith-rooted, and some are a combination of both and lie on the borderland. The line between a simple human experience of unexpected provision and an experience of something as it were providentially provided from outside, that faith glimpses at, is a somewhat blurred line. Imaginative approaches to Jesus' past historical heritage, and to past Jewish experience such as the realm of poets, and of the often poetic and reflective language of spirituality, treasured for its expression of dimensions of reality beyond the historical, seem to belong partly to the realm of experience and partly to the realm

---

32. *Micah* 6.7 REB

of faith. And, with reference to any heavily emphasised 'Jesus of history/Christ of faith' distinction, many *New Testament* scholars have inclined to the view that the distinction is basically not borne out by the *New Testament* as a whole. As one writer states, 'it is not satisfactory to radically distinguish the Christ of faith from the Jesus of history'.[33]

Then again, examples of a providential hand at work in the Joseph stories of later *Genesis* chapters (stories written up centuries later, but with clear traces of a pre-existent foundation going back to ancestral times)[34] show an interweaving of divine grace and human, Jewish, historical experience. Such features in the Jewish national memory can well be claimed to be at least part of good, down-to-earth, historical background.

It is relevant, I think, to touch on the following point. In a modern book entitled *Secular Judaism*[35] the main theme is that there are many non-religious Jews who accept the *Bible* as the central source of 'Jewish collective memory' but who reject any rabbinic monopoly on its interpretation. They are described as wanting to celebrate the festivals and main life cycle events, but in forms adapted to their values; and as perhaps wanting to forge new forms of spirituality. So these forms, irrespective of orthodox religious faith which may follow on and develop early collective memories and experience, are seen as parts of history on their own and to be recognised as such.

---

33. Eduard Schweizer in *Jesus Christ The Man from Nazareth and the Exalted Lord.* Mercer 1967.

34. Claus Westermann. *Joseph* T&T Clark 1996 p.10.

35. Matthew Reisz, Valentine Mitchell 2003, See also article by Yaakov Malkin in the journal *Prospect* November 2003.

The Hebrew experience of paradox

Experience of, and the insight into, the significance of paradox found its basic desert symbol in the burning bush which Moses in his time in the deserts of Midian (*Exodus* 3.6) saw. It was a symbol of pure paradox. It was something that was seen to be on fire but was never destroyed. To Moses it came as a message that for all the fire of oppression and affliction the Israelites had been through in Egypt they were not to be destroyed or forsaken. The symbol clearly remained a powerful one for the Jews through succeeding centuries. It is referred to specifically by Jesus in the *Gospels'* accounts of Jesus' sayings in the *New Testament*.

The focus on paradox is also found frequently in Jewish writings in other centuries following the desert days. It was a noticeable characteristic of the ways of some of the great prophetic writers and figures of the time roundabout the deportation into Babylon. A paradoxical combination of apparent opposites is found in one of the greatest verses in the *Old Testament*, in writings in the tradition of *Isaiah* and where the prophet wrote: 'These are the words of the high and exalted one, who is enthroned forever, whose name is holy: I dwell in a high and holy place and with him who is broken and humble in spirit...' (*Isaiah* 57.15 REB). Paradoxical ways of expression are frequent in the Jewish meditative, poetic and 'wisdom' translations, such as in the *Psalms*. The psalmist is constantly found unable to express the reality of his situation without those frequent passages expressing twin moods where he uses with conviction, in almost one and the same breath, both sentiments such as 'Lord, why do you hide yourself from us? Why stand far off?' and also 'But in you, my rock and refuge, I trust'.

Fortunately, we have had, in our own day, a modern great poet of paradox, R.S. Thomas, who has helped to draw out from the symbol and story of Moses' burning bush further surrounding meanings. One instance is R.S. Thomas' poem *The Bright Field*.[36] Starting from mention of his seeing the sun break through onto a small field, and his going off and forgetting all about it, until later realising it was the pearl of great price, he writes: 'life is not hurrying/ on to a receding future, nor hankering after/ an imagined past. It is the turning/ aside like Moses to the miracle/ of the lit bush, to a brightness/ that seemed as transitory as your youth/ once, but is the eternity that awaits you'. Another, later, 1990 poem of R.S. Thomas', *Counterpoint*, in which the burning bush briefly recurs again, contains these lines at its ending: 'When we are weak, we are/ strong. When our eyes close/ on the world, then somewhere/ within us the bush/ burns. When we are poor/ and aware of the inadequacy/ of our table, it is to that/ uninvited the guest comes. / I think that maybe/ I will be a little surer/ of being a little nearer. / That's all. Eternity/ is in the understanding/ that that little is more than enough'.[37] In many of the latter stanzas of this long poem we get the deep, long-pondered distillation of R.S. Thomas' thoughts on paradox. Some great thinkers and practical leaders, such as the very different figures of Socrates and Winston Churchill, have, I know, described paradox as little more than muddled or escapist thinking that evades coming to a decision. But others, like Plato, with his mystical side, and the 20th century Highland Scots theologian Donald Baillie (according to a positive phrase from an American contemporary),[38] have described paradox less adversely as the antechamber preceding the inner sanctum through which the realm of mystery is truly able to start being entered upon.

---

36. *R.S. Thomas Collected Poems*. Phoenix. P.302. 1993: poem from a collection dated 1975.

37. *Counterpoint*. Bloodaxe. 1990 p.62

38. George B Hall. Article: 'D.M. Baillie: A Theology of Paradox' in *Christ, Church and Society*. T&T Clark. Ed. David Fergusson. 1993 p.85.

R.S. Thomas' words seem to offer an imaginative glimpse into some central realities touched on within this part of the Jewish heritage. And the above three early national experiences and features mainly of early Hebrew heritage can be found to have been among those that set a mark upon the historical world into which Jesus was born. They give us, I believe, many obvious and some half-hidden clues to the significance and identity of the Jesus of history, and to that side of the story of Jesus that consists of his making of routes, for himself and for others, through the journey of human existence.

In Chapter 4 some features and symbols found in Jewish life as it developed in about ten centuries before Christ, but preceding the beginning of the Christian era, will be briefly looked at. But the above three features stand out as undoubtedly and basically significant.

4

JUDAISM:
ITS PERSPECTIVES AND DILEMMAS

Later in this book the figure of Gillian Rose features rather more fully. Here it is just a sentence of hers that is used to give this chapter's title. She, as a Jewish philosopher teaching in Warwick University, wrote '…my Judaism helps me to develop a perspective on quandaries'.

This chapter focuses on Jewish route-making in later centuries than the early, mostly desert years; roughly from 1000 years before the Christian era, and through all the centuries before Jesus was born, when Judaism was taking its much more developed shape. It was the time when Jewish belief and life came to have more institutionalized and structured religious forms of expression through which the nation could be guided through its quandaries and dilemmas.

Here again there were distinctive symbols, which have been clearly and usefully listed for us by scholars.[39] There was the Temple with its holy of holies; the Holy Land; the Torah (that is the law, instruction and guidance passed down through priest

---

39. N.T. Wright. *The New Testament and the People of God* p.226. Fortress 1993

and prophet on everyday matters and on the practical working out of the whole revelation of God's nature and purpose); and the national identity emphasis including injunctions against mixed marriages. All these constituted a strong symbolic framework. These symbols were able to act as something definite, a powerful focus, and were not too complex for people to understand.

However, although those symbols were absolutely central, we cannot fail to mention alongside them some of the rather different sorts of symbol provided by the story tellers of the *Old Testament*, which could come across also with powerful effect from generation to generation of telling. A striking example is the story of Jonathan and his two rocks which comes from the centuries between the early Hebrew centuries and the more developed Judaism time. In the story Jonathan, son of Saul the king, and a heroic and colourful figure, was leading the fight against the Philistines, and on this occasion, accompanied only by his armour-bearer, was making a single-handed attack on the Philistine garrison of Michmash. The pass through which he had to make his way to the Philistine position had on each side of it a prominent rocky crag or column of rock (they had the names Bozez and Senneh), and his dangerous and exposed approach between the rocks, and through them, achieved success for the venture. Interestingly some commentators on the biblical passage remind us that the rocky crags were both helpfully able to provide Jonathan with some cover, as well as leaving him dangerously exposed when passing through. His forcing of a route through the rocks was a powerful symbol of the challenge to find and make a route through dilemmas.

This was just one of the symbols emerging from well-known Hebrew stories enabling the Jews in their route-making, in among the quandaries, problems and dilemmas of their history. From this story, the two rocks became one of many symbols for the Jews, emerging from stories.

Three problem-situations faced in *Old Testament* Jewish history

Here are three historical situations which presented major dilemmas calling for wise route-making.

First, that reflected in the story of the conflict between the twin brothers Jacob and Esau in *Genesis* Chapters 25-27. The story, scripturally, gives the origins of the continued conflict between Israel-Judah and the country of Edom to the south, where Esau's descendants lived. The story stands as a classic, typical story of many other later family disputes. Of Isaac's two sons, Esau was a hunter, Jacob a herdsman. Other stories about land followed, of land disputes and disputes between neighbouring countries. It is a story that has been open to many biblical interpretations, but the 'mainstream', received, Jewish interpretation has been to put all the emphasis on *Genesis* 25.33 which says that Esau had been the first and so the first born of the twins, yet when they were boys, Jacob used a moment when Esau was exhausted from hunting to sell his birthright to him as the condition for being given food by Jacob. That meant that Jacob from then on would be the one to inherit their father's blessing, possessions and land. Fortunately that was not the end of the story. Jacob first secured, by deceit, a further special blessing from his father, and Esau complained bitterly of this further exclusion of him. Yet then, much later, when Jacob experienced a time of weakness, and also went through being himself cheated by his father-in-law, there came a moment when reconciliation was possible. At a moment of meeting again which had been expected to be hostile, Jacob came bringing Esau a gift, saying how gracious God had been to him himself (*Genesis*. 33.11). And they both embraced and hugged one another. From then on, family blessings were to be shared, and not fought over.

Among biblical stories, many of which highlight qualities of fighting and of undoubted bravery in the winning of battles, it seems important not to miss those stories within the narratives of Jewish history that focus on where routes of cooperation rather than simply competition are discovered. And not to miss stories where dilemmas between arguing about prior claims on the land on the one hand and sharing blessings on the other are faced. The story in the paragraph above is the subject of an interesting article from a modern Dutch biblical scholar.[40] Working in India for many years, especially in the Tamil-speaking area, he says he found the Jacob-Esau story of particular relevance. One of the students with whom he read and discussed the story in the late 1980s, listened to it with one of the current great problems of Indian society in mind, the conflict between Tamils and Sinhalese in Sri Lanka. Later, Wielenga used the story when invited to give some lectures in Sri Lanka on church and state. Naturally the story had its relevance there about shared heritages; whether in relation to the claiming of rights by Sri Lankan owners of land or by Tamil separatist protesters.

Secondly, in Jewish history, after an age already too much beset by feuds within families, there began an age where 'kingdom-feuds' were the problem situations and the danger. In the days of the first kings – Saul, David and Solomon – from the end of the 11th century before the Christian era, there was a more or less united monarchy, though not without dissidents. But after Solomon the rift between the more northerly Jews and the southerly ones became more marked, and attempts to find a way through the claims of the two sides failed. So the united monarchy became the divided monarchy, and the separate Kingdoms of Israel and Judah lasted until the end of the 7th century in a divided state and a shared heritage was damaged.

---

40. Bastiaan Wielenga in *The Post-Colonial Bible* ed. R.S. Sugirtharajah. Sheffield 1998.

Thirdly, more than a problem situation arose for the Jews when the super-power exercising imperial rule over the whole region, the Babylonians, deported about 50,000 Jews in Judaea from Jerusalem to the Babylon area (what is today the centre of Iraq). The Jews were deported as rebels endangering the security of the region, had to face a tough desert crossing of over 600 miles, and had to live there with their families in exile in the Euphrates valley for 60 years. The only complete way of describing this period in Jewish history is that it was both a period when the Jews experienced one of their most intense times of suffering, and also a period which saw the flowering of some of the deepest spiritual writings and counsel ever to emerge in the nation's history. These three 'prophets of the exile', as they are known – *Jeremiah*; the later writer in the tradition of the earlier *Isaiah* of Jerusalem, widely seen as a separate author of much of what we know as '*Isaiah* Chapters 40-66'; and *Ezekiel*. Foundations had been firmly laid in the earlier prophetic writers. *Amos* and *Hosea* between them had voiced strong messages about God's justice, called for in contemporary society, and about God's continuing love for his people. *Isaiah* of Jerusalem spoke powerfully of assured hope for the future.

But the prophets of the exile had a message of distinctive profundity which was undoubtedly born out of suffering, able to communicate hope convincingly, and carry conviction in their own times and beyond. Perhaps the simplest way of describing the overall depth of message is to say that they spoke clearly of the real possibilities of them and their fellow countrymen being able to experience for the present and the future three things: caring (God's and among themselves); sharing similarly; and bearing too, which would be the encouragement of the Spirit of God for them.

The route-centred message of the Prophets of the Exile

The 'route' theme was central for them throughout, and the image of a route became a distinctive symbol for them, whether centring on the route into Babylon territory, with the route symbolising exile, suffering and virtual imprisonment away from their own land, or on the other hand centring on the route out towards Jerusalem afterwards, the joy of return, deliverance and hope, discovery of a new start. Typical of the prophetic message throughout, voicing the word of God for his people in this crisis, was the utterance from the *Isaiah* 40-66 chapters: 'Stop dwelling on past events and brooding over days gone by. I am about to do something new. Even in the wilderness I shall make a way, and paths in the barren desert'. Or again, '...Yahweh marches at your head and the God of Israel is your rearguard' and 'saving justice for you will go ahead and Yahweh's glory come behind you'.[41] On the point of the above, *Isaiah* Chapter 40-66's focus on suffering (as already touched on in Chapter 3), there is also, centrally, in these chapters, the big focus particularly on the Jewish individual and community called to be the suffering servant of God: a servant at the same time utterly unflinching in his suffering and yet also vulnerable, and creative, a wounded healer. 'He was despised, shunned by all, pain-racked..., we despised him..., held him of no account..., yet it was our afflictions he was bearing, our pain he endured... he was pierced for our transgressions.[42] This was accompanied by another biblical verse, seeing it all as a divine act and involvement in humanity's tragedies: 'Then the Lord will say: "build up a highway, clear the road, remove all that blocks my people's path. These are the words of the high and exalted One, who is enthroned forever, whose name is holy: I dwell in a

---

41. *Isaiah* 43.18-19 (REB), *Isaiah* 52.12 (New Jerusalem Bible), *Isaiah* 58.8 (NJB)

42. *Isaiah* 53.3-5 (REB)

high and holy place and with him who is broken and humble in spirit, to revive the spirit of the humble, to revive the courage of the broken".[43]

The chapters beginning at Chapter 40 of the book of *Isaiah* followed on faithfully from the earlier *Isaiah* of Jerusalem's message of hope, and his assurance to the Jews 'In calm detachment lies your safety, your strength in quiet trust'.[44] *Isaiah* Chapter 40 onwards ('Comfort my people; bring comfort to them, says your God'...)[45] came to be known as 'The consolation of Israel'.

Jeremiah was the earliest of these three prophets of the exile, and received the call to minister thirty years before the deportation of the exiles to Babylon. He has been called the foundation-prophet of all the time before and during the exile, and after the return to Jerusalem. Though himself still based in Judaea, he sent messages to the exiles after the deportation, urging them to try and not be bitter towards the inhabitants of any city in which they might find themselves. But more than that, he urged them to find sure hope and trust in the long purposes of God; 'these are the words of the Lord... I have dearly loved you from of old, and still I maintain my unfailing care for you... Again you will plant vineyards on the hills of Samaria...'.[46]

The figure of Jeremiah that comes across to the reader of the Bible is often that of a prophet of doom solely, preaching judgement solely. His temperament certainly seems to have been that of a very sensitive person – sensitive to the wrongness and injustices in society, which he saw as bound to bring disaster and destruction to Jerusalem. He expressed his indignation in strong judgements, which caused him to suffer persecution and imprisonment. And

---

43. *Isaiah* 57.14-15 (REB)

44. *Isaiah* 30.15 (REB)

45. *Isaiah* 40.1 (REB)

46. *Jeremiah* 31.2,3,5 (REB)

sensitive in himself, with marked low spirits, a sense of loneliness, and bewilderment over the sufferings of many of those whom he knew. His writings are full of the outpourings of his heart: 'would that... my eyes were a fountain of tears, that I might weep day and night for the slain of my people'.[47] But, as we must surely see it, these things were, in the providence of God, what made him the understanding and effective pastoral counsellor that he was to his fellow Israelites, entering fully into their sufferings. This whole aspect of him, as someone who knew about suffering, is what has made some biblical interpreters ask whether it was not he who was being written about in the description of the suffering servant in *Isaiah*. Another passage also claims special attention. 'Hope of Israel, their saviour in time of trouble,... must you be like a man suddenly overcome, like a warrior powerless to save himself? You are in our midst, Lord, and we bear your name. Do not forsake us.'[48] Was this just a protest that God seemed so slow in causing the downfall of the nation's opponents? Perhaps. But I have been intrigued by the alternative thought that Jeremiah may have been glimpsing wistfully at the possibility that God's purposes for the future could include a coming together of authoritative power and the vulnerability or servant-king element of leadership among the Jews, which the later prophetic authors of *Isaiah* Chapters 40-66 so definitely envisaged in *Isaiah* Chapter 53. It can be added that Jeremiah's sensitivity fits in well with the fact that he was a poet and his writings are full of poetry. (The commentator on *Jeremiah* in *Peake's Commentary* gave, amongst the whole of a very full page, a section headed 'Jeremiah as a poet'. Jeremiah used his poetic passages about the wonders and facts of nature and the natural creation to illustrate the complexities of the human world.)

---

47. *Jeremiah* 9.1 (REB)

48. *Jeremiah* 14.8&9 (REB)

Ezekiel came a little later on the scene, accompanied the exiles into exile, and seems to have been with them there for about twenty years. It is the first few chapters of the book of *Ezra* that give a picture of the later, joyful, return to Jerusalem. But in addition to continuing the prophetic message of the promise and the hope of a return to Jerusalem which Ezekiel gave the Jews personally while with them in exile, he was the one among these prophets who first fully introduced an emphasis on more distant, future horizons and unseen dimensions of ultimate reality that lay ahead on the 'route' stretching on into the future. This was one special contribution that he brought to the perspectives of Judaism. He was visionary, and, over about fifteen chapters in *Ezekiel*, his visions and what has been called his 'unworldly spirituality' unfolded his convictions about realities of 'the end-times' beyond the temporal world, of the glory of God to be known in a cleansed and reformed Temple, and of new spiritual life to be known by God's people in the future. The vision of the new life coming into the valley of dry bones reveals to him the latter dimension.[49]

But alongside this strong glimpse into the eternal future dimension of the whole perspective, Ezekiel also shared with the other prophets of the exile a strong concern with the ethical dimension relating to the past, present and future parts of the 'route'. He not only declares 'I shall judge every one of you Israelites on his record', says the Lord God. 'Repent, renounce all your offences.'[50] But, as well as adding that the Israelites cannot excuse themselves by saying that they have only inherited their sinfulness from their forbears, he has a detailed passage on what the Jews' relationships should be after the return from Babylon, whenever they find 'aliens' living among them in the land to which they return. 'You should distribute this land amongst the

---

49. *Ezekiel* 37.1-14 (REB)
50. *Ezekiel* 18.30,20 (REB)

tribes of Israel and assign it by lot as a share for yourselves and for any aliens who are living in your midst and have children among you. They are to be treated like native-born Israelites and receive with you a share by lot among the tribes of Israel. You are to give the alien his share in whatever tribe he is resident. This is the word of the Lord God.'[51] The principle that blessings are things to be shared and not hoarded emerges again, and very explicitly, in *Ezekiel*.

A modern comment

The following comment on the biblical material dealt with in the last few pages is of special interest, I think.

A scholarly contribution from the Palestinian Arab Christian Naim Ateek to an American book published in 1992, his chapter being entitled 'A Palestinian perspective: Biblical Perspectives on the Land' (and included also three years later in a British book)[52] stressed the importance of 'the Second Exodus' from Babylon. Naim Ateek, a canon of St George's Cathedral in Jerusalem, and currently of the Sabeel Ecumenical Liberation Theology Center, also brings out in what he wrote the special significance of the prophets of the exile, both in their own time and for today:

> 'Most of us are very familiar with the first exodus...' [from Egypt] '...Very few people know about the second exodus. It is more quiet. It is significantly less dramatic than the first. Yet some of the prophets like Jeremiah thought that it would be a greater event than the first exodus... When one compares the two exoduses, it is amazing that the first had all the negative attitudes towards the

---

51. *Ezekiel* 47.21-23 (REB)

52. Orbis 1992 *Faith and the Intifada: Palestinian Christian Voices* and Orbis/SPCK 1995 included in *Voices from the margin*, Ed. R S Sugirtharajah.

indigenous peoples who were already living in the
Promised Land. Every time they are mentioned
the language is very hostile. They are supposed
to be displaced or destroyed. There is no room
for them in the land among the chosen people of
God to whom the land was promised. The second
exodus is totally different. One gets the feeling
that the returning exiles from Babylon reflected
greater realism. They were much more accepting
of the people around them. In fact one of the
greatest passages that comes to us after the exile
is from the prophet Ezekiel who was speaking
the word of the Lord to the people.' [Ateek then
quotes the three verses from *Ezekiel* Chapter 41
just quoted in full above about sharing the land
with 'aliens' after the return to Jerusalem.] 'There
is an amazing switch from the hostile language of
the book of *Joshua*…; now the prophet exhorts
the people… to share the land. It is difficult to
understand why Jews have not emphasised the
pragmatic nature of the second exodus, and why
so much emphasis has been placed on the first
war-like exodus, with its violent and bloody
treatment of the indigenous people. We also see
that in the twentieth century, instead of living up
to the ideal and realism of the second exodus,
many have tried to draw their inspiration from the
first. This is, indeed, a tragedy.' He then goes on to
reaffirm the sadness of the situation in which there
is very little use of the great prophetic material
and its insistence on God's demand for justice,
adding the brief sentence, 'The returning exiles,
in fact, were happy to accept a very small territory
between Bethel and Hebron'.

Much of the rest of what Ateek wrote, in addition,
concentrated on the problem of the land, as something promised to

the chosen people. He writes: 'Chosen-ness, which was intended to be a responsibility for service, was understood as a privilege to hoard.' Although recognising that not all Jews who have a religious understanding of the significance of the land-aspect see no room for the Palestinians in the land, he urges a facing of the challenge to 'study their own Bible to discover that their own tradition has provided answers to... the dilemma by accepting sharing of the land and still maintaining faithfulness to God.' He also fully admits from the side of the Arabs, there must be a full acceptance that 'to fulfil our religious duties here, we do not need an exclusive political control over it all.' But it should be made clear that Ateek's main emphasis, when it comes to his final conclusions, is that for Christians the most important consideration must be found to be what Jesus of Nazareth taught about the Kingdom or Kingship of God, in fulfilment of the spirituality developed during the time of the prophets of the exile.

The *Psalms*

The book of *Psalms*, described in modern times as 'psalms of patience, protest and praise', is obviously a very different genre of writing than the exile and post-exile prophet's genre. But, though with many of the psalms probably appearing in their Jerusalem Temple form about a century later than the writing of much of *Isaiah* Chapters 40-66, they link up closely with those prophetic writings in their passion for justice and mercy and seeing right done. And they used similar poetic symbolism and metaphors, and shared both a strong pastoral touch and a strong concern for what would be decisively liberating, personally and nationally.

After the return from Babylonian exile and the foundation of the Second Temple in Jerusalem, many of the psalms came into their developed forms suitable for festival and royal occasions and for liturgical use generally, for praise, thanksgiving and adoration, and for lament, penitence and intercession. But the *Psalms*, just like the *Isaiah* 40-66 writings in many cases, made a notable and distinctive contribution to what we have called the Jewish perspective in history through the national experience of sufferings and defeats in immediately preceding centuries. They were as a result eminently geared to help people in their dilemmas and bewilderments. Their many metaphors, images and symbols, shared with the *Isaiah* writings, supplied a deep foundation (in a form that the human mind could grasp and in ways that were not complex) for the Hebrew spirituality. As Isaiah encouraged people with 'I, the Lord your God, take you by the right hand', so a person trying to pull out of near-despair could find encouragement and words for expressing feelings, in the psalmist's prayer to God: 'my mind was embittered...; yet I am always with you: you hold my hand'.[53] The honest realism of the *Psalms* is marked, and pastorally of immense use. The expression of protest and resentment against God and against life is not presented in the *Psalms* as incompatible with trust in God. 'Lord, do not hide yourself from my pleading... for my part Lord, I shall put my trust in you.'[54] And just as the big theme of God seeing right done is so prominent in the *Isaiah* chapters, so too in the *Psalms*. The simple posting of a verse from the *Psalms* on the wall of a modern hospital corridor by the entrance to the hospital's chapel brought an immense glimpse of freedom and relief to one critically ill cancer patient being wheeled past the notice board, particularly through its last four words. It has no doubt done the same for many others. The verse was: 'He [the Lord] brought me into untrammelled liberty; he rescued me because he delighted in me.'[55] It should be added that the metaphor of the pathway,

---

53. *Isaiah* 41.13, *Psalm* 73.21, 23 (REB)

54. The first and last verse of *Psalm* 55

55. *Psalm* 18.19 (REB)

the route, the track, along with that of the refuge, is the most commonly used image in the *Psalms*.

The *Psalms'* strong theme of God's purpose of justice and seeing right done is clearly brought out in the metaphor of God as king which appears in many *Psalms*. And that is one of the many foundation elements of the Jewish concept of the kingdom of God. But other dimensions, too, were explored, probably from the Second Temple right down to the century after Jesus' birth. They included the following: the kingly rule or kingship of God the Creator was seen to have ultimate purposes, going far beyond time's 'temporariness': and was seen to transcend without limit beyond the bounds of space, and, like light, to radiate powerfully to all humanity and never to be static: and, above all, the kingly rule was seen to centre on God-centredness, holiness, purity and single-mindedness of basic purpose.[56] All these characteristics are observable throughout in the *Psalms*; though the dimensions are clearly so imaginative and unlimited in scope that, in the view of many, it is fair to say that boundaries and division-lines within the kingdom are apt to be somewhat blurred. Ethical 'means', in the course of any journey in human existence, and 'end-time' destinations, are both the concern of kingly rule.

As a footnote to those comments on the *Psalms*, the name of St Augustine of Hippo in North Africa in the early fifth century CE may be mentioned. He used to give long and popular expositions from the pulpit on the *Psalms*. He also had the depth of mind and heart and spirituality that seemed to be able to range widely over the hugely diverse dimensions of the divine kingly rule as explored and reflected in the writings of the psalmists, reaching out over what, in time, we call past, present and future. He was a busy diocesan bishop involved with desperately fierce divisions within his diocese and church, needing firm ethical, practical

56. See Bruce Chilton. *Pure Kingdom. Jesus' Vision of God.* Chapter 2 on 'Mapping the Kingdom: The book of Psalms'. SPCK 1996

and doctrinal decisions. He brought an outstanding intellect, a passionate heart, and aesthetic sensitivities to bear on these things. That included a love of music: he believed, with a Platonist conviction, that there was a close affinity between music and its rhythms and its depths on one hand and the 'soul' or inmost being of a human being on the other. A mid-twentieth century writer commented that Augustine's preaching 'often turned into music' and verbal beauty.[57] In spite of the many controversies through the centuries about, for example, Augustine's contribution of a defence of what might be called church loyalties and kingdom loyalties, and controversies over human depravity and human sex, we are dealing, in matters concerning the psalms and the kingdom, as said above, with Augustine's depth of personal religion.

One major emphasis in Augustine on the fullness of God's presence and his kingdom in heaven is that it will be the praise of God, 'Amen and Alleluia'. This comes in connection with quotations from many psalms, and a summary given in another writing: 'we shall rest and we shall see; we shall see and we shall love; we shall love and we shall praise'.[58] Links between Augustine's musical sense, and his contemplation on the psalms, on the one hand, and what a British cathedral organist wrote only a generation ago are striking. Alec Robertson, in his *More than Music,*[59] wrote of the inspiration received from 'the whispered alleluia in the last movement of Stravinsky's *Symphony of Psalms* and 'the alleluias I hear in the last movement of Vaughan Williams' *Fifth Symphony*, finding them 'not only aesthetically and emotionally moving' but because 'these few magical chords are to me like an answer to St Augustine's prayer "Hear me, O Lord, as I tremble in this darkness; and stretch forth thy right

---

57. John Burnaby. *Amor Dei* p.249 Hodder & Stoughton. 1938.
58. *De Civitate* XXII end.
59. Alec Robertson *More than Music*. Collins. 1961 p.230

hand to me.'" The Hebrew psalmists' symbolism within the perspectives of Judaism can be seen to have reality in a manner not too far from what has reality for us.

The *Wisdom Books*

The phrase *'Wisdom Books'* is used here for five main books in the *Bible* (*Job*, *Proverbs*, *Ecclesiastes*, *Ecclesiasticus*, and the *Book of Wisdom*) from the slightly larger number of books that were included overall in the Hebrew Bible and the Greek Bible. The last two of the books named above are from the Greek Bible. At the beginning of this 21st century, the following English versions of the *Bible* include the books of the Greek Bible: the New Jerusalem Bible and the New Revised Standard version of the Bible (from the 1980s). These latter books in Greek emerged, within the later Judaism in those centuries, when Judaism spread among Jews who had gone to live in Greek-speaking regions of the Mediterranean world; they were regions which brought Jews extensively, and not only in the Palestinian area, into contact with Hellenistic Greek culture, thought and Greek imperial rulers who succeeded Alexander the Great. The early Christian Church widely recognised these Greek books as being inspired in the same way as the books of the Hebrew bible, though some early 'fathers' were hesitant about or opposed to this recognition, including St Jerome of Italy (and later Bethlehem), who translated the Hebrew Bible into Latin.

The term *'Wisdom Books'* used above of five main books that can be said overall to belong to 'the *Bible*' is in some ways inadequate for giving a clear idea of what this category of books comprises. The Hebrew prophets certainly spoke of three classes of influential leaders of thought and writers: 'priests, sages and prophets' was the listing; and 'sages' or 'wise men' is how the leaders of wisdom-thinking would have been described.

In Judaism they were an influential force dating back probably in origin over five or six centuries, including the first century after Jesus' birth and of the Christian era. They will have had links with the category of thinkers in very many countries neighbouring the Palestinian area who attempted to help people, including dispersed Greek-speaking Jews scattered in countries away from Palestine, to find answers and ways of coping with deep problems of human existence. The focus on human existence and experience has caused the *Wisdom Books* to be called 'humanistic': and so they are. But their approach is that of religious humanism, unlike that type of humanism which members of a modern 'humanist' movement would want to have applied to them. The book of *Proverbs*, as one of the earliest of the *Wisdom Books* in Judaism, makes it quite clear in one of its very first verses that 'reverence for the Lord' or 'the fear of the Lord' is the foundation of knowledge.[60] Undoubtedly, as well as the focus on its humanist approach, it is obvious that the general Greek understanding of ultimate reality in ancient times tended to express itself in mainly rational, intellectual, philosophical, and to some extent mystical terms.

The centuries of Jewish-Greek contacts

The two parties to these contacts and meetings between cultures and traditions of thought clearly came from very different directions. Rooted convictions about the centrality of reverence

---

60. REB v.1.7. In spite of the alternative translation 'reverence' which I have included for the original Hebrew word here, it is almost always in modern translations, in the *Old Testament* books, the translation 'the fear of the Lord' here in *Proverbs* 1.7, that is thought more suitable. But the original Hebrew word carries strong connotations of both fear and reverence. The above mention of humanism owes much to the 'Introduction to the Wisdom Books' given in the New Jerusalem Bible of 1985, and one of its paragraphs.

for God were the position from which Jews started. But rooted convictions about the centrality of truth were the position from which the Greeks started: the author of *Ecclesiasticus*, though a Jew writing perhaps a century and a half later than *Proverbs*, was expressing himself in a very Greek way when he says, 'fight to the death for truth, and the Lord God will war on your side'.[61]

The contacts between Jewish and Greek thinkers here discussed have to do both with views on early history, viz. hopes all round for good historical, political kingdoms to come, and also to do with the realisms of moral values, ideas and thought, and with the rooting of these things in human behaviour and society. The Jews, from their side, had their tradition of kings and kingdoms: some looked forward to the restoration of a stable Jewish kingdom in history, though some, after their national experience of recurring disasters and times of oppression, turned their hopes in other worldly directions. From their side, Greeks in the Hellenic age of Hellenistic rule lasting two centuries, and stretching down into Syria and the Palestinian region, fashioned real and very immediate forms of historical kingdoms. But both Jews and Greeks out of their respective backgrounds and traditions also had strong concerns to do with, not political realms but with the sovereignty and forwarding of moral values, or of philosophical ideals and intellectual search. In all those directions these centuries were centuries when the Jews had major contacts with the Greeks and were influenced by them.

To look ahead for a moment to the *Gospels*, and to the teaching of Jesus recorded in the *New Testament*, we get from Chapters 5, 6 and 7 of the *Gospel of Matthew* some idea of the considerable degree of Hellenistic influence on Palestinian Judaism by the time that Jesus was born in Bethlehem, if we look at the marginal references for those chapters in *Matthew*, as given

---

61. *Ecclesiasticus* 4.28, New Jerusalem Bible.

in a major 'Study-Bible'. In the New Jerusalem Bible's 'Standard Edition' one finds a reference to *Ecclesiasticus* on no less than seven occasions during the course of the three Gospel-chapters. (The references indicate where a phrase or sentence in *Matthew* reflects or echoes a phrase or sentence in *Ecclesiasticus*.)

Route-making through human dilemmas, in the *Wisdom Books*

As outlined above, the *Wisdom Books'* writings, all written by Hellenized-Jews, aimed to provide counsel and advice to people burdened in mind by problems and dilemmas of existence; ranging from problems of some long-standing poison of half-hidden resentment against a fellow human being to problems of despair about life's sufferings in general, and serious illness. In the book of *Job*, the great poetic and literary masterpiece of the *Wisdom Books*, both those types of sufferings were experienced by the figure of Job; he felt that the charge levelled against him by his so-called 'comforters' that his sufferings were due to his past sins was unjustified, especially in view of how everyone around him kept talking to him about God's overall care and love for humanity. Job, as presented, was not at all lacking in appreciation of the good and unexpectedly hopeful sides of life: 'if a tree is cut down, there is hope that it will sprout again… When it scents water it may break into bud'. But at the same time, he adds: 'but when a human being dies all his power vanishes'; and in another passage we find on his lips, in connection with God's overall care and alleged examples of God's judgement on his sin: 'if only there were one to arbitrate between us and impose authority on us both… I should then speak out without fear of him, for I know I am not what I am thought to be'.[62] And in connection with his and his family's suffering, his words are strong words: 'why was

---

62. *Job* 14.7, 9 and 10. Also *Job* 9.33, 35. (REB)

I not stillborn?... Why is life given to those who find it so bitter?'[63]

Ecclesiasticus, probably written almost three centuries later, on matters concerning alleged sin or guilt, often gave much less negative counsel. On the problem of deep-seated resentments, as well as on low 'self-esteem', it has passages such as this: 'Do not be too severe on yourself, do not let shame lead you to ruin... Take circumstances into account and beware of evil, and have no cause to be ashamed of yourself: for there is a shame that leads to sin and a shame that is honourable and gracious... Do not struggle against the current of the river...'.[64] And even the slightly earlier *Ecclesiastes*, though the most sceptical of the *Wisdom Books*, gives time in scholarly meditations to thinking about the sufferings of the world's oppressed people and not only about the author's own difficulties: 'I saw the tears of the oppressed, and there was no one to comfort them.' *Ecclesiastes* also emphasises the importance of moderation: 'Do not be impulsive in speech... Let your words be few.' And in general adds: 'Do not be quick to take offence, for it is fools who nurse resentment.'[65] The final chapter of *Ecclesiastes* (Ch. 12) is a magnificent chapter, giving us a positive completion to our received book's type of Jewish conviction. (The fact that the chapter is widely ascribed as a later addition to the original writing is of importance from a precise analytical point of view, but not from the point of view of Judaism's mingled explorations around that time.) But the book's realism, to put it no more strongly, has repeatedly a negative side to more than match *Job's* earlier realism. 'I came to hate life, since everything that was done here under the sun was trouble to me.'[66]

---

63. *Job* 3.11, 20 (REB)

64. *Ecclesiasticus* 4.22, 20, 26 (NJB)

65. *Ecclesiastes* 4.1 and 5.2 and 7.9 (REB)

66. *Ecclesiastes* 2.17 (REB)

A second problem, puzzle and dilemma expressed in the *Wisdom Books* can be added. It stems from the often bleak *Ecclesiastes'* writer's strong focus on 'time' and the perplexities of time as we experience it. It is not of course unrelated to the *Wisdom Books'* concern with suffering in general, but it deals with a particular area of that suffering. It can be roughly summed up by *Ecclesiastes'* own words about how life is 'overshadowed': by 'gnawing anxiety and great vexation', by recurring uncertainty, 'weariness', depression and an apparent dependence, within God's system of the admitted great 'gift of life', on an apparently unalterable cycle of existence alternating between good times and bad times. That cycle is said to be there in spite of times of 'enjoyment'.[67] That is why the writer of *Ecclesiastes* begins his book with the words 'Temporariness, utter temporariness, says the Speaker, everything is temporary', as one modern translator of the Bible translates it.[68] He follows that early on by writing in the same few verses: 'that everyone should... enjoy himself... is a gift of God'; but also that human beings see, later on, 'God summoning each event back in its turn'.[69]

The *Wisdom Books'* vision of hope

The last of the *Wisdom Books* listed above, *The Book of Wisdom*, probably written about half-a-century before the birth of Jesus, is likely to have come from a devout Greek-speaking Jew in Alexandria, the great centre then of intellectual and scientific learning in the Mediterranean world. Like *Ecclesiasticus* (already

---

67. *Ecclesiastes* 8.15,17 (REB)

68. The sense of the Hebrew word as found in Daniel Fredericks' *Coping with Transience*. Sheffield Academic Press. 1993. See also *Mission and Meaninglessness* by Peter Cotterell, SPCK 1990, in relation to Buddhism and to existentialism.

69. *Ecclesiastes* 3.13-15 (REB)

mentioned above), about 200 years earlier perhaps, much of its material follows on from what we have touched on above about the earlier *Wisdom Books*, and is taken up with instructional passages on how true wisdom is to be applied in everyday life: and on how the fear of the Lord is the beginning of true wisdom. But in both these later *Wisdom Books* the problems, dilemmas, and mysteries of human existence are faced in somewhat more mystical poetic ways, with occasionally the use of terms that could be seen as philosophical.

And more than that, the writers have a message that they clearly wish to present: that there is true hope to be seen beyond the mysteries and dilemmas because of the wonder of the created world and of the divine creative mind which designed it. Creativity, reflected in human creativity, and found, for example, in the work of the potter, is one of the *Wisdom* writers' greatest themes here. '...The potter, sitting at his work,/ turning the wheel with his feet; constantly on the alert over his work,/ each flick of the finger premeditated;/ he pummels the clay with his arm, and with his feet he kneads it;/ he concentrates on applying the glaze right/ and stays up late to clean the kiln'.[70] The author of *Ecclesiasticus* and these lines would not have been unaware of the problems of existence: he seems to have been a Palestinian Jew, and one of the 'Hasidim' of Judaism who a little later were to uphold faith during the ruler Antiochus Epiphanes' persecutions of the Jews. Judaism at the time seems to have such images as that of the creative potter to undergird its faith in the continuing creativity of God.

The Book of Wisdom has its own similar undergirdings. Like *Ecclesiasticus'* 'the glory of the stars is the beauty of heave,'[71] and 'as is his majesty, so too is his mercy' (the stars in heaven symbolising

---

70. *Ecclesiasticus* 38.29-30 (NJB)

71. *Ecclesiasticus* 43.9 (NRSV)

God's majesty).[72] So *The Book of Wisdom* focuses on the world of nature and the cosmos and on light as the great symbol. But none of these outward lights is left unrelated to the power of the divine creative wisdom; 'She is indeed more splendid than the sun.../ for light must yield to night, but against wisdom evil cannot prevail'.[73] And again, the wisdom of God in relation to humanity is seen in the following terms: 'She is a breath of the power of God.../ a reflection of the eternal light.../ ...she renews the world,/ and, generation after generation, passing into holy souls,/ she makes them into God's friends and prophets...'.[74] The *Wisdom Books* use symbolism to assist their age in Judaism, and the Hebrew heritage generally, in its determination to go as far as possible for human minds in tackling the apparent contradictions between opposites and extremes in human experience, and in seeking as rational an explanation as can be made. *Ecclesiasticus* states plainly its attention to the opposites: 'Opposite evil stands good,/ opposite death, life;/ so too opposite the devout stands sinner. Contemplate all the words of the Most High,/ and you will find they go in pairs, by opposites.'[75] And *Ecclesiasticus* itself goes on, in a later chapter, to touch on the wonders of the sun's light. But *The Book of Wisdom's* words above are bold, and make a direct link with renewal in human life. And the *Wisdom Books'* wide use of symbolism seems significant: symbolism famously can often hold together two apparent opposites in a way that words cannot do or express, and that goes into a realm beyond words. As has been said, symbols specialise in dealing with reality in motion, or get things moving, as contrasted with concepts which freeze things.[76]

---

72. *Ecclesiasticus* 2.18 (NJB)

73. *Wisdom* 7.29-30 (NRSV)

74. *Wisdom* 7.24-27 (NJB)

75. *Ecclesiasticus* 33.14,15 (NJB)

76. Paul Tillich. *Systematic Theology*. P.240. John Arapura. *Religion as Anxiety, and Tranquillity.*' P.111.

However, at the end of this present chapter concerning Judaism's perspectives in the centuries before the birth of Jesus, it is interesting to note that recently a noted scientist-theologian in Britain wrote urging trust and hope in 'the continuing creativity of God, and not only in the continuing evolutionary process'.[77] Interesting also that *The Wisdom Books* of Judaism and their theme of the continuing creativity of God should come in those immediately pre-Bethlehem times in history and in Jewish thinking.

---

77. John Polkinghorne in Ch. 5 of *The Work of Love*, edited by him. 2001 SPCK

5

JESUS OF NAZARETH AND
THE CRUCIAL ROUTE-MAKING

About fifty years ago a well known Dutch Christian, Visser T'Hooft, wrote these words which I have never forgotten since reading them: 'When men shout that God is dead, this can only mean that he is not in the place where they are looking for him. He always finds an entrance, generally a very unexpected and unobtrusive entrance. For Christ comes without noise, and the Kingdom of God does not come with signs to be observed.' But I came across those words of Visser T'Hooft's not long before Christmas one year and found myself singing in church that magnificent hymn by Charles Wesley 'Come, thou long-expected Jesus…, Israel's strength and consolation, hope of all the earth thou art; dear desire of every nation, joy of every longing heart.' The two different emphases were striking; the 'unexpected Jesus' in one, 'the expected Jesus' in the other. Both of course true. Those twin-truths, or two-eyed truths (double helixes?), abound in the Gospels, and in the accounts we have received about the historical story and figure of Jesus of Nazareth. The chapters of this present book so far have focused on the story of the Jews and Judaism, including many paradoxes encountered by all their journeyings and 'long expectings'. What follows attempts to carry the story further and is about developments by Jesus both of the Jewish expectations and in his presentation of the not-so expected or unobtrusive surprises and good news.

The Jesus of surprises and the unexpected

Jesus' attendance at, and full involvement in, the life of the synagogues in Nazareth and Capernaum (as Ch.2 has already glimpsed at, covering *Mark* Chs. 3 and 4) comes out clearly in the very first chapter of the *Gospel of Mark*. But the earlier chapters of the Gospels' accounts, as well as the later chapters, are also full of incidents, when Jesus takes issue with the Jewish authorities, mostly 'the scribes' ('the theologians') 'and the Pharisees' (the Jewish leaders of the same type as their successors as leaders after 70CE – the Rabbis), on some major point of disagreement or difference of conviction. These differences arose particularly in connection with rules about what practical activities could be undertaken or not undertaken on the Sabbath;[78] or in connection with Jesus' practice of not only stretching a point, as it were, for the sake of courtesy when he and his disciples shared in meals with outsiders and 'sinners' and tax-collectors, but also of welcoming the move as a sign of the spirit of openness, invitation and warmth which he saw as at the heart of Judaism and of the purposes of God.[79] Jesus' differences, of course, as in the case of discussions about divorce,[80] are sometimes merely commented on by saying that Jesus was preferring the more 'literal' interpretation of Mosaic law of one particular notable Jewish rabbi over that of another Jewish rabbi, whereas here also it is Jesus' conviction about 'openness' and warmth that underlies his stance. One other

---

78. e.g. *Luke* 6.1-11

79. e.g. *Luke* 5.29-32

80. *Mark* 10.2-12

account of Jesus' strong difference of conviction with Pharisees and Scribes is over the fifth Jewish commandment 'Honour your father and your mother.'[81] Here Jesus is seen as pointing out contradictions within Mosaic Law over this. For there was a Jewish regulation which said that what people give to their parents should rather be 'set aside for God' i.e. either for Temple and worship requirements; or apparently widely interpreted as just freeing someone from family obligations but depriving that person of spending the money for his own use. Jesus said that the claim of the fifth commandment's principle, the claim of 'weightier matters of the law' such as 'justice, mercy and good faith', must take priority over particular regulations.

Behind all these differences (of conviction in interpretation and application) lay Jesus' conviction about the Kingdom of God and, although that great theme of his in general is taken up a little later in this chapter, its implication for the undoubted element of challenge in Jesus' ethical teaching needs to be touched on first of all. He saw the sharing of meals with those commonly thought of as outsiders to be a powerful sign of the presence of the Kingdom, alongside healing and the forgiveness of sins. The Qumran community, in the Dead Sea caves, and the Pharisees, linked the Kingdom very strongly to bodily purity and separation from any bodily pollution. They saw holiness as centring particularly round this. Some modern *New Testament* scholars however draw special attention to the words recorded of Jesus that 'nothing that goes into a person from outside can defile him; no, it is the things that come out of a person that defile him', and say that such words are 'completely uncharacteristic of first century Judaism'. More than that, many would say that Jesus not only developed but 'radically changed the concept of the Kingdom of God', and while using expressions related to those used in contemporary Judaism 'used

---

81. *Mark* 7.9-13

them in a sense radically different'.[82] Though obviously such interpretations and conclusions expressed in this way are matters of ongoing discussion and debate, they have proved convincing to many.

So the fact emerges from the Gospels' accounts, in spite of accompanying emphases on how the crowds flocked to him, that Jesus was seen by the religious authorities as out-of-step, not at all what they expected and hoped for, and therefore as a hostile challenging figure. Some might use here the more abstract but stronger word 'otherness' rather than 'unexpectedness,' just as some theologians and contemplatives have talked of 'the otherness of God' in his holiness. But whether or not we talk of 'the otherness of Jesus', the force of his challenge in the accounts remains.

These challenges and tough surprises, however, are matched by surprises consisting of good news, as happens in the so-called 'Beatitudes' – one-line sayings spoken by Jesus in *Matthew* Chapter 5 to the crowds which came to listen to him in Galilee. These eight 'sayings' are couched in terms that often echo or reflect phrases and words taken from more than a dozen instances in the eight verses echoing the *Psalms*, or the *Isaiah*-linked Exile-time prophet, or from *Proverbs* and *Ecclesiasticus*. These sayings spoken to Jesus' hearers, many of whom were oppressed by poverty, the exploitation of farmers and heavy taxes, would have come as great good news.

The Beatitudes are hardly the main focus of attention or enthusiasm of people in western and north-American countries

---

82. *Mark* 7.15 The comments on *Mark* 7.15 and on Jesus' concept of the Kingdom above are drawn from John Riches and Alan Millar's chapter on 'Conceptual Change in the Synoptic Tradition' in *Alternative Approaches to New Testament Study*, edited by Anthony Harvey SPCK 1985. *Jesus and the Transformation of Judaism* by John Riches, London 1980 may also be referred to.

when reading the Gospels at the moment. They tend to be side-lined somewhat, either by those who regard them as 'wimpish,' weak, or 'outrageously idealistic.' or those who recognise that they represent 'the relevance of an impossible ideal' (the latter mostly presenting the Beatitudes as totally impracticable ways of resistance in stopping some forms of evil action in its course, at least in corporate and short-term affairs. Chapter 12 takes this side of the topic up in more detail). We are talking here, of course, about 'Blessed are the gentle; they shall have the earth for their possession' (although 'Blessed are those that hunger and thirst to see right prevail; they shall be satisfied' is clearly a saying with a different thrust alongside the Beatitudes with a gentler emphasis), and about such other phrases in surrounding verses of Jesus' teaching as 'Do not resist those who wrong you: if anyone slaps you on the right cheek, turn and offer him the other also.'[83]

When reading a book such as Gerd Theissen's *In the Shadow of the Galilean*, already briefly mentioned earlier, I saw various angles on the significance of the Beatitudes more clearly. His book, it should be explained, presents the Gospel story in the form of a novel, in an imaginative way, to the extent that the story is told by a fictional character Andreas, an educated Jewish fruit and grain merchant, with some of the other characters also being fictional. However, others of the characters are not fictional and their names will be familiar to those who know the *New Testament*. The book's characters are contemporaries of Jesus who were close enough to catch sight of his shadow, as it were, and to be overshadowed and affected by his activities. I mention the book at this point especially, for the following reason. Theissen as a scholar is known chiefly for his work on the social background and nature of the world into which Jesus was born, though also known for his work on what the early Christian movement's

---

83. *Matthew* 5.5, 6 and 5.39 (REB)

69

position will have been in first-century Galilee and in the cities not far away where Paul of Tarsus' travels and activities were to take place. Naturally his writing on Jesus' teachings, including the Beatitudes, emphasises the social context and setting in the region – one of widespread oppression as mentioned above. The blessedness of the gentle, and the promise that they will have the earth for their possession, is seen, in Theissen's presentation, as not only covering blessings of the end-times foretold by earlier generations, but also especially blessings of life and liberation to be looked ahead to in the present age, by those who bravely and humbly endure present oppression.

For those living under the social conditions described above, including the presence of the Jewish 'Zealot' violent activist movement against the Roman occupation of Palestine, liberation comes across as part of Theissen's presentation of events. Theissen's material has a very modern and topical ring to it. One of his chapters is entitled 'Terror and the Love of One's Enemy', and there is talk of 'terrorism' and religiously-backed resistance fighters. Specifically, when Andreas, who is described as not knowing Jesus himself but just the shadow he cast, is kidnapped by Jewish activists, he wonders whether Jesus himself might be a 'zealot'; and under interrogation he gets a chance to discuss with Barabbas, a figure in the story and heavily involved in the resistance movement, the key-issue of paying taxes to Rome; Barabbas remarks that on the tax-issue, Jesus 'always takes the gentle way'. So for many readers of Theissen's book this is likely to be a main context of references to gentleness in the Beatitudes.

Recently, Dr Dhyanchand Carr, a well-known Christian leader in India, until a short time ago the principal of a large theological college, was invited, on a visit to Britain, to address a seminar in Bristol. He took as his title 'Re-reading the Bible in the Context of the Struggle for Justice', and focussed on the

Beatitudes. He described *Matthew* Ch.5 verses 3-10 as 'the most widely read yet misunderstood scripture'. He urged his audience to look at the Beatitudes with the eyes of India's poor and downtrodden who constitute the majority of her Christian members. He clearly stressed the importance of approaching the Beatitudes as a message for poor and downtrodden people and not as though they present a manual on ethics. For example, 'blessed are those who mourn' should not be seen as though it is an ethical injunction to the mourner. Rather, it was probably highlighted both from the message which Jesus gave and in the light of what is widely taken as background of the *Gospel of Matthew. Matthew* could well have been writing for uprooted Christians of Jewish background now living in Syria about half a century after Jesus' crucifixion, those Christians still then being in fellowship with the local synagogue, though in addition observing the Lord's Day for the breaking of bread. Questions would have arisen for this 'mourning' community, driven out of their homeland after the Jewish uprising against the Romans of 68-70 CE and grievously disappointed at unfulfilled Messianic promises such as 'Then shall they dwell in their own land,' (23.8) in *Jeremiah.*

'Blessed are the poor in spirit' is another example from Dr Dhyanchand Carr's presentation, centring on the poverty of spirit that undoubtedly is marked in the mind of all those suffering from political tyranny, ancient or modern. The Galilean experience of social exclusion from Judaean southerners and Roman heavyhandedness in Jesus' day would have produced the same sort of poverty of spirit from oppression, as that produced prominently, so it is here suggested, in recent times in various parts of the Indian subcontinent (not to mention countless other regions across the world). Experiences in recent decades in Sri Lanka, in Kashmir and the Punjab, and for Dalits in one area where caste-restrictions resulted in especially grave oppression, were all cited, as well as the general undermining of 'spirit' for girls and women in various ways, and the general loss of human dignity for all of non-literate status. To sum up the way in which for first century hearers and for modern hearers and readers the words of the Beatitudes would have come and do come as good news and a liberating force, the presentation spoke of how oppression drains away the spirit, yet the 'de-spirited' are important in God's eyes, as these rejected stones are proclaimed as being God's co-rulers in his Kingdom, which has become theirs.[84]

Along with the Beatitudes and other related sayings of Jesus and their bold, often paradoxical, statement of the unexpected, the Gospels present us of course with the miracles and the miracle-stories recorded about them. It is sometimes pointed out, rightly, that Jesus' healings seem to have been very largely of the disabled and the handicapped, of the blind, the crippled and epileptics, though hernias and haemorrhoids may be part of the picture. The range of those whom he helped was clearly very broad, some types of healing and miracle featured more in one Gospel than in others. We cannot exclude, for example, those with fevers or those traditionally described as having 'leprosy'; nor the stilling of the storm on the lake of Galilee; nor the raising of Jairus' daughter, and then of Lazarus, from the dead. Accounts of these healings and miracles are all there in the Gospels.

Discussion of these stories and of miracles goes back centuries, of course, and makes interesting reading. St Augustine of Hippo in north Africa in the early centuries of the Christian 'era' and dating wrote; 'Miracles are not contrary to nature, but to what is known of nature': a useful reminder to future centuries that on miracles we do well to attempt no complete or instant answer. One cannot help seeing a link between the words of that man of faith and the words of many modern theologians, also

---

84. An article on Dr Dhyanchand's address appeared in *Pilgrim*, the Journal of the Friends of the Church in India, to which acknowledgement is here made.

written in faith. Jürgen Moltmann, writing in 1989, stresses the importance both of what he calls 'the dynamic of the provisional in the experience of Christ's history', and also of what lies beyond the provisional, in that which is promised in the fullness of time, and the fullness of the dimensions of the Kingdom of God.

David Hume, the 18th Century philosopher of the Enlightenment, however, saw a miracle as a violation of the laws of Nature, though sometimes he phrased that by saying just that the ordinary course of Nature does not vary and it is 'improbable' that miracles occurred in Jesus' activities. Bishop Joseph Butler, Bishop of Durham, an older contemporary of Hume and one of the great figures in the history of Christian thought in Britain, put the Christian case strongly. He said, in effect, 'I agree that we are dealing with probabilities and reasonable probability is the foundation of my attitude, but I say that probability is in favour of miracles having happened.' He went on to say, 'I go on to have faith in that probability.' His careful and reasoned approach is very clear. An equally notable Christian figure in British scholarship, though in the field of biblical scholarship, F.J.A. Hort took a similarly careful and reasoned approach in the corresponding prominent national issue among thinkers in his day – Darwin's writings on evolution. Hort wrote to his colleague Bishop Westcott in 1860: 'Have you read Darwin?… In spite of difficulties, I am inclined to think it unanswerable.'

The same issue, seeking the right balance between a reasoned approach and an approach of faith, was taken up in the twentieth century with direct reference to specific miracle-stories in the Gospels. William Barclay, a noted biblical scholar and commentator, while being far from a radical or 'reductionist' in general in his commentaries, described just one or two miracle-stories as not, on any reasoned consideration of them, a true record of what will have happened historically. For example, the story in *Mark* and *Matthew* of the miracle of the withering of the fig-tree, as it is traditionally known. Jesus, feeling hungry on one occasion, and seeing a fig-tree in leaf, hoped to find something on it: though the story tells us that it was out of season for fruiting. Disappointed, Jesus is recorded as saying to the tree 'may no one ever again eat fruit from you!', and 'the fig-tree at once withered away'. In *Luke*, however, there is no such miracle story, but a very similar story, though without any withering at the end, told as a parable by Jesus about a man going to one of his fig-trees and finding nothing on it for three years. William Barclay's commentary on the miracle-story, as in *Mark* and *Matthew*, is: 'This without exception is the most difficult story in the Gospel narrative. To take it as literal and factual history presents difficulties which are well nigh insuperable. To be frank, the whole incident does not seem worthy of Jesus… It is just the kind of story that is told of other wonder-workers, but is never told of Jesus.'[85] Like Barclay, many commentators have regarded the story of the fig-tree as a parable told by Jesus, which had become wrongly turned into a miracle-story in the tradition handed down among certain Christians in the early Christian movement. Perhaps turning the parable story into a miracle was felt to be a heightening and a dramatizing of the story of a sort likely to turn it into a more forceful message. Not all commentators have followed this line of interpretation, but have seen the miracle-story as historical and seen it as Jesus' one miracle of judgement. (My own view is Barclay was right.) In all the above listing of examples of determined attempts to hold together reason and faith, the remark of a noted 20th century contemporary of William Barclay may be mentioned: 'Faith my be more important than reason, but it must not be in contradiction of it.'[86]

---

85. Barclay commentary
86. John S. Whale

We obviously need to use both heart and head if we are to take fully on board the significance of the miracle stories. From the side of the head, the above parables have been analytical about how historically accurate some of the stories are likely to be. But clearly we need to spot also as key factors concerning the stories not so much what precisely happened in the history but the whole drama of the stories themselves and the way in which often heart-rending situations of need within humanity are met by the impact of someone and something newly creative. The key factor in Jesus' healings surely emerges as his forthright courage, determination and dynamism in tackling head-on these barriers of human suffering and experience, and bringing something new into the situation.

The nature of these thrusts of new life may in some instances have lain between 'tackling' and 'breaking through' the barriers. In Nazareth, as the Gospel of *Mark* has it, 'He was unable to do any miracle there, except that he put his hands on a few sick people and healed them; and he was astonished at their lack of faith'. The probably later Gospel-writer *Matthew* has: 'he did not do any miracles there, such was their lack of faith.'[87] Both Jesus' praying beforehand and the sick person's faith are spoken of as factors. In accounts of several miracles Jesus is said to have been earnestly praying beforehand. Before healing 'the man who was deaf and had an impediment in his speech', it is said of Jesus that 'looking' up to heaven, he sighed, and said to him 'Ephphatha' which means 'Be opened.'[88] Along with Jesus' sighings, perhaps there was in his mind, as an accompaniment, the vision and assurance of the blessings of the 'fullness of the Kingdom' in the end-times in the eternal dimension.

---

87. *Mark* 6.5, Mark 13.58 (REB)
88. *Mark* 7.32-34 (REB)

But always there were the unexpected factor and the surprises of this thrust of new creative and re-creative life. Jesus kept on decisively pushing forward the boundaries and breaking into the barriers facing humanity. Decisively, along with the sighing, he had, against the barriers, the faith that rebels (to borrow the title of a 20th century book about Jesus).[89] Jürgen Moltmann was quoted earlier as writing about 'the dynamic of the provisional', and the importance and power to be found in Jesus' historical life that was provisional to what came later. 'Dynamic' seems the word to hang on to, in trying to describe the miracles.

The sensitiveness of Jesus

Along with the more challenging aspects of Jesus' activities in Galilee and Judaea, one cannot forget his acute sensitiveness to people's needs and to what life was meaning for them at the moment. In the Gospels' profiles of his encounters with people, we read constantly throughout not least about handicapped people, the unrecognised, and those who have either been battered by life or experienced it as turning into a tangle of bad actions and bad things. (I use the word 'sensitiveness' in the heading above rather than the more dictionary-correct word 'sensitivity', because the latter can, obviously, easily slide over into suggesting touchiness, or being easily offended, or wounded, by criticism, which is one of its dictionary-meanings.)

A phrase often used of Jesus in the Gospels is 'his heart went out to them…' The original Greek word used in the Gospels really means something like 'his gut-feelings were touched': a phrase hardly suitable for most general use, but clearly able to communicate with circles of modern parlance. On one occasion when Jesus had been in a boat on the lake of Galilee, we read; 'when he came ashore and saw a large crowd, his heart went out

---

89. D.S. Cairns. *The Faith that Rebels* (SCM 1948)

to them, because they were like sheep without a shepherd…' And on another occasion when he was in the town of Nain, just south of Nazareth, we get the phrase again: he met a funeral procession at the gate of the town, the dead man's widowed mother being among the mourners, and he her only son. 'His heart went out to her' are the words. In telling his parables, too, Jesus is found highlighting people in his stories who are either deeply moved by someone's distress or showing themselves downright insensitive. This is so in the picture of the Prodigal Son's father when welcoming back home his half-starved, ill-clothed, broken son. And then again in his telling of the story of the Good Samaritan, in response to someone who had asked a question: he highlighted, among others, the priest travelling down the same road where the man at the centre of the story had been 'left half-dead' by robbers: the priest 'passed by on the other side', and a Levite, coming later, did the same.[90]

Jesus' own sensitive awareness of injustices and corruption in contemporary society and culture in his day, and his reaction to those responsible, emerges strongly and strikingly in the Gospel narratives: it is noticeable especially in *Luke*, the Gospel written by someone who many centuries ago was called 'the scribe of the gentleness of Jesus'. The story of Zacchaeus is an example. He was a tax-collector in Jericho, probably a superintendent, and maybe the most hated and lonely man in the town, with a rake-off grip for himself, as he collected tax-money to go to the local Herodian puppet-rakers who acted for the Roman imperial occupation of the region. As Jesus made his way through the city he noticed Zacchaeus up a sycamore tree where he had climbed, to get a view on a day when there was much excitement and large crowds. The account says that he was 'a little man'. Jesus looked up and said 'Zacchaeus, be quick and come down, I must stay at your

---

90. *Mark* 6.34 (REB), *Luke* 7.13 (REB), *Luke* 15.20, *Luke* 10.31,32

house today', although this would clearly meet with widespread disapproval. Zacchaeus would have no doubt been astonished, but in his loneliness, hugely appreciative. He came clambering down. When questioned subsequently over his friendly approach to Zacchaeus, Jesus said, 'This man too is a son of Abraham.' For many readers this is one of the most striking of the many Gospel stories about Jesus making contact with individuals. (For modern readers, too, the phrase 'a son of Abraham' used here may have implications and significance in relation to political and religious discussions in modern times about who has a claim as a 'homeland' to the region that can roughly be described in ancient terms as Galilee and Judaea. The phrase on Jesus' lips may send us, if we see the interpretation of the *Bible* as important, back to the book of *Genesis* from its tenth chapter onwards, about Abraham's descendants.)

So far in these chapters I have said nothing about the reliability of the Gospel-accounts from which biblical passages and verses have been quoted in this present book. What about detailed academic study into the biblical text and historical and analytical assessments on possible original, orally-transmitted memories in the early Christian movement having been an earlier stage through which the earliest authentic record passed to the Gospel-writer? And what about the Gospel-writer's text having perhaps been subsequently edited a little later by someone else in the Church? Such matters in general will receive somewhat fuller comment in Chapter 8. But I mention the point here, because in the case of a story that in the Gospel's text is written so well and so strikingly as the *Luke* story about Zacchaeus in the manuscript form on which our modern *Bibles* depend, the suggestion is able to be made in our day that, say, the author of *Luke* as written down originally, was clearly someone with a literary gift and a poetic touch in places, and that he could well have 'made the most' of early oral accounts as received: in other words, that Jesus' caring and sensitive attention to Zacchaeus in this particular passage, could well have owed much to *Luke's* presentation, as a poet. That may be a false supposition, and for the moment any discussion here on such matters is delayed.

For our most obvious general record and pointers in the Gospels, for a main outline of Jesus' first-century historical life and activities, twentieth-century scholarly researchers have often largely kept to the first three Gospels, *Mark, Matthew* and *Luke.* The *Gospel of John* has been taken as clearly more meditative and poetic in its profile and presentation. However, *John* apart from anything else, is recognised as supplying certain detailed, small but remembered historical touches: nowhere else is the stream and ravine 'Kedron' identified as the route followed by Jesus and his disciples from the supper in the upper-room on the final journey to the garden of Gethsemane. And *John* is receiving positive commentary in many recent commentaries.

In connection with the sensitiveness of Jesus, one commentary in the middle of the twentieth century can be seen as having passages of very particular significance. Rudolf Bultmann's *The Gospel of John* in 1941[91] was extremely radical and experimental in its views about some of the *John* chapters and material, as we have them; he said that they had become wrongly located chronologically in the Gospel. He also developed his own views on the origin of the early Church's precise tradition on Jesus' true identity, and in general used strongly existentialist language. But Bultmann, a foremost international and German scholar of the time, came from a European generation that had lived through the horrors and massacres of the First World War, and his presentation and commentary on *John*, and his profile of Jesus, reflected this. Some words of John Riches[92] help us

---

91. Rudolf Baltmann. Göttingen 1941 English translation 1971

92. John Riches *A Century of New Testament Study* Lutterworth 1993 p. 58

to get in English the thrust of Bultmann's interpretation of Jesus' teaching and life in this commentary and connection. Of Bultmann's commentary, Riches writes: 'He invites his readers to hear Jesus addressing those questions of human existence, of its transitoriness, of its questionableness and its fragility, in short, its hopes and fears, which concern them and Jesus' original hearers.' Riches also adds this remark, on the 1941 commentary, that 'it remains…. the greatest single work of *New Testament* exegesis of the century.'[93] Many parts of *John's* text clearly link up with the thrust mentioned above. The context of Jesus feeding a crowd on the hillside near Passover time is a case in point. Jesus is described as saying to the people that what he is giving to them signifies his gift of himself and his presence: 'my flesh is real food: my blood is real drink'.[94] The original Gospel word from which the English 'real' (or 'true') is translated is a keyword in *John*: and the themes of 'reality, ultimate reality', 'eternal life', and 'truth' are of course recurring ones. Bultmann provides two reminders for us. He calls the Gospel of *John* 'the Gospel of decision', between 'what is real' and 'unreal'. He brings in Jesus' frank and sensitive recognition both of the fears and fragilities of much human existence as well as its hopes and expectations.

The main quotation from Bultmann given above is amplified usefully by something which Bultmann also wrote about Paul of Tarsus' understanding and forging of a Christian language about human existence.[95] John Riches says that Bultmann shows this as a language:-

> 'in which to express an understanding of human
> existence that is open to its restlessness and
> creativity, its possibilities and failure. To be

---

93. Riches *A Century…*' p82

94. *John* 6.54 (REB)

95. Riches. *A Century…*' p72

human is not to possess some predetermined essence; it is rather to be faced with responsibility and choice, with the possibility of finding and losing oneself.'

A brief quotation, from further back and from English literature, may be added, on Jesus' challenging and sensitive teaching in the Gospels about human nature. Matthew Arnold, the nineteenth century poet and educationalist, believed in Christian morality but said in effect that he did not believe in those matters of Christian credal belief which crossed over into doctrinal matters and the supernatural realm: of course he lived in an age when such things as Darwinian scientific development lay behind this, and anything like dialogue between scientists and theologians had nothing of the quality comparable to what we have today. That makes it all the more distinctive that Matthew Arnold should have written these forthright words:-

> 'Jesus Christ and his precepts are found to hit the moral experience of mankind, to hit it in the critical points, to hit it lastingly – I believe that Christianity will survive because of its natural truth.'[96]

If the above suggestion of a sensitive adjustment by Jesus to meet the ins and outs, predicaments and sufferings of humanity is accepted, it can hardly fail to suggest a link in our minds with the very early Hebrews' experience already noticed in an earlier chapter concerning desert days; that is, their experiencing of a recurring sense of their being provided with help at critical moments, the experience of Provision and Providence.

An emphasis on the latter is found prominently in Jesus' teachings; for example, in one passage in the presentation of the teaching in the Gospel of *Luke* – Chapter 12, verses 22-32.

---

96. Matthew Arnold *Last Essays on Truth and Religion* 1877

(The New Jerusalem Bible actually gives this passage the sub-heading 'Trust in Providence'.) The thread running through the passage spoken by Jesus 'to his disciples' is, 'I tell you not to worry', and 'Do not be anxious', 'Your Father knows what you need' concerning food and drink and human need, above all 'set your minds on his kingdom', and 'have no fear, little flock: for your Father has chosen to give you the Kingdom'. (REB) One of the earliest modern versions of the Bible, James Moffatt's, combined literary flair and accuracy, with 'it is your Father's delight to give you the Kingdom'.

Jesus' closeness of understanding of, and concern for, ordinary human feelings clearly underlies the above: he knows that people want to be prudent in planning ahead and to have the future ahead in life, as far as possible, known well in advance: no one wants to be caught out. But he says in effect: 'Be prepared to go more slowly, for life is complex.' He draws a parallel with our own length of life or physical height. (There is something of a detailed difficulty over the precise meanings here of two words in this sentence in the Greek original: the sentence is usually taken to mean 'Can anxious thought add a day to your life?', with a note in the margin of the possible alternative meaning of 'add a cubit to your stature?' But the parallel is effective whichever way it is taken.) Jesus urges the same realism, patience and slowness of pace where necessary in his disciples' approaches to life's succession of complexities and turnings on the way. We meet this call to realism, patience and to acceptance of the need of slowness also in the Gospel of *Mark*, of course, and in a more extended form, in Jesus' parable of the sower passage in Chapter 4 of the Gospel. The teaching there is about the obstacles to the coming of the Kingdom (the problems of many of the soils encountered) and the negative character of such human response to what he himself was teaching.

In the middle of the twentieth century, from his prison-cell under the Nazi regime in Germany in the early 1940s, Dietrich

Bonhoeffer delivered a powerful message which ties up closely with the above whole sensitive aspect of Jesus' teaching and words about human existence. Bonhoeffer's writings and phrases that have come down from that time were spoken out of the resistance movement to the persecution of the Jews, in which he had been very active, until his imprisonment which led to his death. He saw himself as protesting from within his own Lutheran Church, and also on behalf of all the human victims outside the Churches. His historic and traumatic experience of fighting for justice seems to have moved him to see new depths in Jesus' involvement in human existence, and new depths in his teaching. Among his phrases were these:- 'Jesus is there only for others: … faith is participation in this being of Jesus': also 'it is only by living completely in this world that one learns to have faith… By "this-worldliness" I mean living completely in this world unreservedly in life's duties, problems, successes and failures, experiences and perplexities'.[97] Bonhoeffer has as thorough-going a belief in the significance of Jesus' route-making as that. This was to be followed of course in the decades following by thinkers and writers of many sorts (some of whom would call themselves 'Christian humanist' and others of whom have belonged to traditions unaccustomed to such phrases) putting emphasis on 'being human'. One of them writing that 'exploring the roots of the Christian heritage may well provide us with a route through to a new way of being human'.[98]

The secret of the Kingdom of God

'The Kingdom of God' lay at the very centre of all Jesus' teaching and of his message. Of Jesus travelling through Galilee early on, it is said that 'he proclaimed the good news of the Kingdom'.[99]

---

97. *Letters and Papers from Prison* SCM London 1971 pp201,193
98. Robert Warren *Living Well*. Fount. Harper Collins. 1998 p.xiv
99. *Matthew* 4.23 (REB)

So what is this about the Kingdom being a secret? Jesus said to the twelve disciples:- 'to you the secret of the Kingdom of God has been given.' ['The secret of the Kingdom of God' (*Mark* REB NRSV), 'the secrets of the Kingdom of Heaven' (*Matthew* REB RRSV), 'the mystery of the Kingdom of God' (King James' Bible[100]).] Some well-known writers have been apt to emphasise that 'the Kingdom' could only be described as having an elusive background, and as being best defined as in origin 'an Eastern idea'. And when a first-time reader of the *Bible* comes across the phrase as something secret or mysterious in the biblical text, he may be inclined to get the impression of the concept as surely vague, and basically just clouded in mysterious ideas. Or not so much that, as just extremely complex. And it is complex, like many things that go deep. For example, in speaking about God and the 'Kingdom of God', human beings cannot avoid including the thought of awe and wonder, 'mystery' in that sense. But that takes no account of the accompanying truth also, about a secret that can be great news as a moment of revealing arrives. A modern wife and mother may say to her family, 'Shall I tell you a secret? I'm going to have a baby.' And in ancient times (and in the various meanings of the original word used in our verse about the 'mystery of the Kingdom of God') the word 'mystery' was used a great deal in religious circles in the very positive sense of an open secret, a mystery now revealed to believers in a religion.

More than that, of course, and rather more straightforwardly, we know that the word 'kingdom' in English can have the connotation of 'realm' in it, not only in the traditional sense of old terms such as 'a peer of the realm', but in more abstract usage as when someone says 'Yes, that's within the realm of possibility'. Similarly, kingdom-type words used when talking of God's Kingdom can clearly carry various nuances of 'kingdom',

---

100. *Mark* 4.11 (REB)

'kingship', 'sovereignty', 'realm'. And in Jesus' time, historically and in our time now, the phrase 'the Kingdom of God' could and can be used by some people especially in the sense of a hoped for, divinely given institutional time of the fullness of an earthly Kingdom to come at some future dateable moment in history; and be used by other people especially in the sense of some spiritual, divinely-creative and dynamic realm and movement of values, standards, relationships in history. This type of a realm of values emerges clearly when Jesus speaks of 'the weightier matters of the law – justice, mercy, and good faith,'[101] and in the writings of *Paul*, as in 'the harvest of the Spirit is love, joy, peace, patience, kindness, goodness, fidelity, gentleness and self-control.' [102](REB) In the presentation in the Gospel of *Mark* of Jesus' teaching of the Kingdom of God, with the phrase 'the secret of the Kingdom of God', and *Mark's* emphasis following, in the parable of the Sower, on poor soils for the seed as well as good soils, stress is laid on hiddenness, secrecy and the Kingdom as a divine spiritual movement and dynamism meeting with many setbacks in history. In the often meditative Gospel of *John*, one notices that Jesus is recorded as saying at his trial before Pilate 'My Kingdom does not belong to this world.'[103] As we read the Gospels, we are led into a richness and depth of meanings about the Kingdom of God that can certainly be viewed as complex, but in a complexity holding together, in the twin-truths of paradox, both the awe and mystery of the Kingdom of God, and its good news of open secrets. Some simple brief descriptions of what is meant in Jesus' teaching and in the Gospels by 'the Kingdom of God', descriptions coming from those who are or have been prominent church leaders or biblical scholars, need, of course, to be mentioned.

---

101. *Matthew* 23.23 (REB)

102. *Galatians* 5.22,23

103. *John* 18.36 REB

David Sheppard, formerly Bishop of Liverpool, in his moving autobiography, along with its many warm-hearted and profound personal and pastoral touches, gave three general summaries of the message of the Kingdom in the Gospels:-

> 'It was God's reign, in his world, that was "at
> hand" and was just around the corner. It was also
> going to be coming in power when all things
> were to be put under God's feet. It was not least
> a kingdom that was a kingdom of utterly free
> grace.'[104]

James Dunn, Emeritus Professor of Divinity, Durham University, was described by a reviewer of a recent book of his as writing of the 'Kingdom' as 'Evidently something sublime, only imperfectly apprehensible, something both imminent and actual...'[105]

Edward Sanders, sometime professor of Exegesis in Oxford, later Professor of Religion in Duke University California,[106] sees some of Jesus' sayings as possibly implying that 'the Kingdom' refers to 'a special realm on earth; one that consists of people living according to God's will and that exists both in and side by side with normal human society'. But in many of Jesus' sayings, he says, 'the Kingdom is future, but not otherwise defined'. His main conclusion is that Jesus expected a divine transforming miracle', in which God would restore the 12 tribes of Israel in a kingdom in a transformed, 'ideal' world.

Steve Chalke, Baptist leader, preacher and evangelist, says that we get the best insight into Jesus' meaning of 'the Kingdom' if we turn to the Hebrew word 'shalom' and hear Jesus saying...

104. *Steps Along Hope Street*

105. Dunn *Jesus Remembered* Eerdmans 2003

106. E.P. Sanders *Jesus and Judaism* and *The Historical Figure of Jesus*, Allen Lane, Penguin, 1993

'...the Kingdom, the in-breaking "shalom" of
God, is available now to everyone through me'....
Chalke sees an important part of the 'kingdom'
language as being to do with awareness of, and
social concern for, community with others.

It may be added that Alan Richardson's writings on 'shalom',
from the middle of the twentieth century, underlie many later
explorings of the meanings of 'shalom' and 'kingdom'. "Shalom",
though translated usually as "peace," he said, 'does not carry so
much a negative sense e.g. "absence of wars"; but it is:-

'a comprehensive word, covering the manifold
relationships of daily life and expressing the
ideal state of life in Israel's day-to-day overall
well-being – both an ideal, but also viewed as
achievable." So fundamentally 'shalom' was
seen as meaning 'totality', 'wholeness', 'well-
being', 'peace', 'harmony', in the context of that
Richardson quotation, and this sheds light on
'kingdom language.'[107]

Those brief statements are of course based in particular
on a number of Gospel verses. For example, Steve Chalke's
sentence on the inbreaking 'shalom' of God is in line not only
with *Mark* 1.15's recorded words of Jesus, 'the kingdom of God
is upon you,' as in the Revised English Bible's translation (what
William Barclay translated as 'the Kingdom of God is almost
here'), but is also in line with the generally similar *Luke* 11.20 and
Matthew 12.28; in both of which the original verb in the Greek
text is different from the Greek original verb in *Mark* 1.15, *Luke*
11.20 and *Matthew* 12.28, and the translation is 'the kingdom of
God has already come upon you' in REB and 'the Kingdom of
God has reached you here and now' in Barclay. And in both those

---

107. Alan Richardson in *A Theological word book of the Bible* SCM
1950

Luke and *Matthew* verses the New Jerusalem Bible brings out the Greek verb's first root-meaning, and possible meaning of the original verb in these verses, with its NJB 'the Kingdom of God has indeed caught you unawares'.

In any discussion about hiddenness and openness in connection with the phrase 'the Kingdom of God', and about complexity and beauty in describing a God who is both far and near (descriptions which inevitably use paradoxical, poetic and meditative language), it is useful to remember one thing; that behind the Gospels' 'kingdom-language' lies all Judaism's tradition of spirituality in earlier centuries, especially as found in the *Psalms* (and already touched on) and all its language about God as king and God's kingdom and kingship.[108] Here are a few, out of many possible examples about the latter, to be found in the *Psalms*. They give us a reminder that first-century Palestinian Jewish language about the Kingdom of God would be likely to be complex, but not vague. Chilton is keen to stress that in any final analysis it is a dynamic connotation that the word 'kingdom' had in Jewish understanding. It is 'a force' and movement for change 'that pushes along the dimensions of time and space, which demands better and purer behaviour', and 'a dynamism that is restless until it completes its course'.

---

108. See Bruce Chilton *Pure Kingdom* Eerdmans & SPCK 1996 p.31-44, for his account of *The Dimensions of the Kingdom* in the *Book of Psalms*.

1. *Psalm* 8, verses 1, 3, 4 & 5 (REB):

'Lord our sovereign…/When I look up at your
heavens, the work of your fingers, / at the moon
and the stars you have set in place, / what is a frail
mortal, that you should be mindful of him, / a
human being, that you should take notice of him?
/ Yet you have made him little less than a god,
crowning his head with glory and honour/ You
make him master over all that you have made…'

God is seen as king, in transcendent, creative, dynamic
kingship. He transcends our predicaments about coping with
two thoughts, by his 'farness' and nearness: the thought of
the vast natural creation and universe, and also the thought
of our immediate, practical, personal and social world. His
transcendence compasses both the creativity in the natural
creation and his creative bestowal of the potential for courage,
love and imaginativeness in the human spirit, as seen in countless
heroes, known and unknown.

2. *Psalm* 15.1-4 (REB):

'Lord, who may lodge in your tent?/Who may
dwell on your holy mountain?/ One of blameless
life, who does what is right/and speaks the truth
from his heart;/who has no malice on his tongue,
who never wrongs his fellow, and tells no tales
against his neighbour;/…who holds to his oath
even to his own hurt…'

God is seen as the king of justice and of mercy and mutual
trust within the community, local and national. The king of the
rule of values, standards and right relationships, with the way most
obviously and immediately open to those who already sincerely
subscribe to these ideals.

3. *Psalm* 130.1,2,4,7,8 (REB):

> 'Lord, out of the depths I have called to you;/
> hear my cry, Lord;/ with you is forgiveness... let
> Israel look for the Lord,/ for in the Lord is love
> unfailing,/ and great is his power to deliver.'

God is seen as the king of love and forgiveness and of the second chance and of a continuing power to deliver. Miles Coverdale in 1611, for his translation of the Latin version which was the version available to him at the time, translated the last sentences quoted above as... 'with the Lord there is mercy, and with him is plenteous redemption'. Peter Levi in 1976, in a Penguin volume translation, rendered them as 'mercy is with God/, and continued rescue'. '*The (USA) Jewish Publication Society of America*' in its 1980 edition had "with the Lord is steadfast love/ and great power to redeem".[109]

4. *Psalm* 96.10,12,13 (REB):

> 'Declare among the nations, "The Lord is
> King;/... let all the trees of the forest shout for
> joy/before the Lord when he comes,/ when he
> comes to judge the earth./ He will judge the world
> with justice/ and peoples by his faithfulness".'

God is seen as a judge who will see right done, who will be seen as such when he comes in decisive judgement. In Bruce Chilton's book already mentioned, he writes that judgement-times at the end of history or in the future are not more emphasised in the *Psalms* than are important present times of ethical decision and activity. Both are brought out.[110]

---

109. Peter Levi. Penguin Classics 1976. Jewish Publication Society *The Book of Psalms*, Philadelphia. 1980.

110. Chilton. Op. cit.

5. *Psalm* 119.105,108 (REB):

> 'Your word is a lamp to my feet,/ a light on my
> path;/... Accept, Lord, the willing tribute of my
> lips,/ and teach me your decrees...'

Although in most English translations, the translation 'offerings' or 'freewill-offerings' is given (rather than 'tribute' with its possible meaning of payment to a state or king), yet God is seen again here as king and sovereign who directs and guides.

6. *Psalm* 30.4, 11-12 (REB):

> 'Sing a psalm to the Lord, all you his loyal
> servants.../ ...You have turned my laments into
> dancing;/ you have stripped off my sackcloth and
> clothed me with joy/, that I may sing psalms to
> you without ceasing./ Lord my God, I shall praise
> you for ever.'

God is seen as king of glory and majesty, light, joy and celebration, in the meditative context of worship of God in his heavenly realm. Needless to say, the above quotation is just a single quotation of countless quotations in the *Psalms* along these lines.

The above paragraphs make clear that the kingdom is seen as a realm with a broad compass of ethical, visionary and worshipful dimensions. Among further sayings of Jesus several emphasise or clearly imply this breadth. When a 'scribe' (theologian) asked him which commandment was the first of all and in the subsequent conversation said that he himself believed in what the Jewish prophets had said about 'love of neighbour' as well as 'love of God', Jesus replied: 'You are not far from the Kingdom of God.'[111] This makes clear that the Kingdom, while being concerned with

---

111. *Mark* 12.34 (REB)

dimensions far from vague, equally cannot be spoken of as having edges of any cut-and-dried sort. This point has already been touched on earlier, but perhaps deserves some further comment.

Although to speak of the Church is not the same as to speak of the kingdom, the church being the sign of the kingdom rather than identical with it, yet some words spoken by George Carey when Archbishop of Canterbury, about a broad Church, are bound to apply also to the kingdom as a broad kingdom with broad concerns and dimensions. The words were these:

> 'I believe with all my heart that the Church of
> Jesus Christ should be a Church of blurred edges,
> where people can ask their hardest questions
> without condemnation, and share their deepest
> fears without reproach... I raise the question; will
> the Gospel ever be public truth if our preachers
> are not grappling with the challenge of scientism
> from their pulpits, or drawing on literature, art,
> science and theology to show that the Christian
> world view is relevant today.'[112]

These words will recall for many F.D. Maurice's call in the 19th century within the Church of England for a Church that was willing to embrace within itself a diversity of views and approaches. He said that he wanted a 'broad' Church, 'as broad as the love of God', and seems to have preferred that to the adjective 'liberal'. (Certainly in modern times and parlance, 'liberal' is a blanket-term in this context, that can have the meaning, confusingly, of anything from 'generous' to 'permissive'.) In the present climate of the tendency of a polarisation of views, as between 'traditionalist' and so-called 'liberal' viewpoints, there is obviously much talk of 'extremist' viewpoints. Any talk of 'a broad Church', one might think, is bound to be regarded by

---

112. Words spoken at a Swanwick Conference on 'Gospel and Culture', as reported in the *Church Times* of July 24th, 1992.

some as dangerous, and inevitably impeding a clear voice going out from the Church on what it believes. But it is encouraging to find that people of many different church backgrounds believe in the idea of a 'broad Church' as an idea that in no way destroys conviction.

I once worshipped in Cambridge for two years, as a student, in the church where the great Charles Simeon, the evangelical church leader, was vicar for very many years in the 19th century. And I have been remembering that he said interesting things about extremism. He said in effect that just as he found himself at one moment in one situation taking a strict Calvinist position and then soon after in a quite new situation, taking a broader, so called 'Arminian' position, so he felt that St Paul, whom he was keen to follow, found himself in similar complex pastoral situations. In other words, he felt that Paul is found to move from one extreme or polarised position to another extreme or polarised position, as the Holy Spirit guided him, a situation in which he was holding them together, as it were. Charles Simeon's actual words were: 'The truth is not in the middle, and not in one extreme, but in both extremes.'[113] Among various particular situations that Simeon will doubtless have been referring to would have been Paul's tough warning in *Galatians* 5.21 about selfish and sensual indulgence: 'no one who behaves like that will ever inherit the kingdom of God' (REB). That illustrates one extreme: a strictly traditionalist position is taken about unfettered indulgence not in tune with Christian faith. But Paul adopted a broader and more adjusting position in another situation described in the letter to the *Galatians*, and particularly in *Galatians* 2.11 and 12, where Paul says that 'he had opposed to his face' a representative from the Jerusalem Church to the Church in Antioch, when he had visited Antioch earlier, where there were many non-Jewish Christians

---

113. H.C.G. Moule. *Charles Simeon*

as well as Jewish Christians. They were in Antioch, contrary to rules in the original Jewish Church in Jerusalem, in the habit of all eating together and sharing fellowship on a regular basis. This was objected to by Jerusalem as breaking a tradition which had established their separate identities; Paul disagreed, believing that God had been equally present with Jewish Christians and non-Jewish Christians when each had become Christians. The inwardness and breadth of Paul's position is well expressed in two other passages. One in *1 Corinthians* 9.22, again in the context of the Jewish Christians and non-Jewish Christians in the Church. Paul writes: 'to them all I have become everything in turn, so that in some way or another I may save some' (REB). Then a further, less broad passage in *Galatians*: 'it is by the Spirit and through faith that we hope to attain that righteousness which we eagerly await…, the only thing that counts is faith expressing itself through love.' (*Galatians* 5.5 & 6 REB). It is certainly interesting to find Charles Simeon, in effect, discussing this complex piece of Christian route-making emerging in these early days of the Christian movement.

The down-to-Earth parables of Jesus

It seems clear that when Jesus wanted to explain the meaning of the phrase 'the kingdom of God', he had two main lines of explanation. First, to tell a story, i.e. a parable, and said the kingdom of God was all about what the stories were all about. He told a story about a wounded man lying by the roadside, a priest going past and doing nothing about it, and then a man going past, who belonged to a group usually regarded with contempt, immediately turning aside to render every possible help and taking the wounded person on to where he would be well looked after. And Jesus told another story about a wedding and ten bridesmaids, five of them somewhat scatterbrained and five of them sensible: the bridegroom was hours late in arriving and it was dark: the scatterbrained bridesmaids had found they had not put enough oil in their lamps and had gone off to find some when the bridegroom arrived: they never got to join in the wedding or wedding-feast. Jesus told these sorts of stories in order to emphasise that the kingdom of God was all about in the one case, love and compassion, and in the other, all about decisions and choices, and not just muddling through.

And, secondly, Jesus' other line of helping forward the understanding of the kingdom's meaning was by getting his hearers, through these 'parables', based on an old Jewish type of parable, to do some hard thinking for themselves on what some sudden turns of events in life, or crises, might signify for them, in terms of either opportunity or warning. A parable as used by the Hebrew prophets of earlier days had in origin been not only a saying or story of an allegory sort, but something intended to be puzzling and challenging for the reader about some sudden turn of events in human life – more like a riddle than anything, to get the hearer, as already said, to wrestle out some hidden meaning in it or truth of reality. In the first Gospel parable-story cited above (the Good Samaritan story), Jesus' first-century Jewish hearers would have been startled to learn that it was a Samaritan, that is someone belonging to a group ostracised and dismissed as unorthodox by most Jews, who could have been the one to be loving and compassionate. So the first parable story had some hidden messages in it about unexpected sources of love and compassion. In the second parable cited (styled by the King James Bible as that of 'The Wise and Foolish Virgins') the hearers could well have been upset to hear the apparently totally joyful wedding story turn out as a sad decisive moment of judgement and crisis for five of the girls, because they had failed to face prior need for some choice and decision, or to do some planning ahead over the oil, and not let things slide. So the second parable too, had a hidden message in it, about the need to take necessary decisions without delay.

To use the term 'teaching-method' about Jesus' inspired parable-method sounds somewhat odd and jargon-like; but good teaching-method was what in fact it was, and good communication of the truths which he was teaching. The parable-method challenged and led on his hearers to respond to the parable with their own ideas, insights and chosen preferences as to their own right behaviour and path in any problem area of life. Those who in modern times conduct seminars, or teach classes beyond elementary levels, testify as we know to the great dangers that lie in any domination by a teacher, by means of forceful presentation of his or her own convictions and ideas. Sometimes, so some who have been through teacher-training courses have said, training colleges seem to have gone so far as to work on the principle 'don't teach your students anything, or it may harm their creativity'. Jesus' parable-method certainly seems to have worked on the principle of presenting a story that was aimed to startle or provoke a response, but, above all, of stimulating creativity, and so result in a real communication of some depth between presenter and hearer. It is noticeable, of course, that along with stimulating creativity and choice, Jesus in his teaching stimulated his hearers not to forget the value of inherited teaching from the past and of the example of classic heroes and figures found in traditional narratives. In the Gospels, he noticeably alluded to Moses and the message of the burning bush, to David and the story of the sacred bread in 'the house of God', to Noah, and to Jonah, and others. He appears to have wanted his hearers to combine their own creative choices with what was received from others, past and present, in deciding on ways ahead.

The realism of Jesus' parables and their diverse depictions of familiar everyday life were not only imaginative but able to catch the attention of Palestinian hearers. A book of Church of Scotland prayers caught the realism well:

'If I met you, Jesus Christ,
I might not think that you were on a mission.
Your talks would be of common and curious things:
Salt, dough, lost lambs, lost coins, paying taxes,
hosting a meal, wise virgins and foolish house builders.

I would not know you were on a mission,
I would think you were making sense of life,
lighting up the ordinary, identifying the truth.
When you look with compassion on the world
and need mission done in your way,
Lord, send me.'[114]

The realism of the parables is brought out in a different way by an American writer and scholar who makes the point that Jesus' parables deal with hints concerning human life-situations rather than over-emphasising any orderliness in those situations (cf Emily Dickinson's poetic words '...tell the truth but tell it slant...'?) Sally McFague describes his parables as:

'...the kind of story which does not assume an ordered world but perceives order only indirectly, intermittently, and beneath the complexities of personal and social chaos...',

adding the comment that this makes them the kind of story pertinent to our modern times.[115]

This is of course borne out by the beginning of so many of the parables told, and the realism with which in them some slow process of waiting or searching is described before some joyful surprise comes suddenly later in the story: '...a woman had ten silver coins and loses one of them: does she not light the lamp, sweep out the house, and look in every corner until she finds it?' And the realism is far greater still in the account of Jesus' parable

---

114. *Pray Now.* St Andrew Press 1994

115. Sally McFague *Speaking in Parables* Fortress Press 1975 p.141

of the sower sowing the seed as told in *Mark*, where Mark seems to want to make this 'slow' bit of the parable particularly significant in his narrative: 'some of the seed fell along the footpath; and the birds came and ate it up. Some fell on rocky ground, where it had little soil, and it sprouted quickly because it had no depth of earth; but when the sun rose it was scorched and as it had no root it withered away. Some fell among thistles; and the thistles grew up and choked the corn and it produced no crop. And some of the seed fell into good soil... and the yield was thirty-fold, sixty-fold, even a hundred-fold.'[116]

Taking the parables in the Gospel not just in what is often their 'slow-ness' but also in the climax of joyful surprise in which most end, Sally McFague adds this splendid description of the parable in general: 'the hidden way of locating the graciousness of the universe within the ordinary and the humane'.[117] So the parables are bound to be a signal example of Jesus' guidelines on route-makings in among human dilemmas and different courses of action. It is, however, important to notice that McFague also sees Jesus himself as 'the parable of God' and as living out the truths he taught. (The same thing being true of the radical biblical scholar of fifty years ago, Rudolf Bultmann, as is not always realised: in his commentary on *John* 14.6, 'Jesus replied, "I am the way, the truth, and the life",' he wrote, 'one does not come to him to ask about truth, one comes to him as the truth'.[118])

The bridge-maker symbols of Jesus

In Jesus' rigorous route-making through human existence, the use of symbols featured prominently, alongside their 'cousins'

---

116. *Luke* 15.8 (REB), *Mark* 4.4-8 (REB)

117. Op. cit. p.95

118. R. Bultmann. *The Gospel of John*. Blackwell. The 1971 English edition. P.606

the parables and metaphors. Symbols are of course a little like 'logos' in modern life, as, for example in the area of religious faith we have the Iona community's' 'Wild Goose' logo printed on their publications, symbolic of their thinking and conviction about the Holy Spirit. So symbols, whether figures, objects, pictures, icons, or other artistic and musical designs can be powerful and effective communicators, making impact often at deeper levels of people's receptiveness than words do. Jesus said in the course of his teaching at one point, as already quoted, 'think of the lilies,' to help drive home his message about God's providence and overall ordering of the world, in providing for clothing and in supplying human needs, just as he said everyone can see how thoughtfully and beautifully God has 'clothed' the lilies with their outward appearance.

Most of the many other symbols found in all the Gospels are drawn from the huge stock of symbols to be found in the *Old Testament* and in the *Septuagint*, which was the translation into Greek of the *Hebrew Old Testament*, and some other writings, which emerged in the few centuries before Jesus was born, in considerable areas in the middle-Eastern Mediterranean world where the Greek rulers had come in. For example, the symbolic figure of the Shepherd, so frequently in the *Old Testament* used as a symbol by the prophetic writers and in the *Psalms*, is used in parables and teaching in *Luke*, *Matthew* and *John*, and also in *Mark* in Jesus' words at the Last Supper, where *Old Testament* language about shepherds who get struck down and the sheep scattered is applied by Jesus to dangers for his followers after he is killed. Other great Hebrew symbols such as rocks, shields and bright-shining lamps are to be found underlying the language of the Gospels. And the Gospel of *John* is especially notable for its symbols for Jesus himself with him describing himself in vivid symbolic terms six or seven times. For example, as 'the living water', in language using the symbol of wells and fresh running streams: as 'the light of the world': and as 'the true vine'. This deep aspect of Jesus' teaching in *John* is looked at further, briefly, a little later.

In a moment, we come to listing some of the definitions and descriptions that biblical scholars, and poets, and all sorts of people have given to us of what a symbol and symbolising really is. But first we need to consider the sorts of questions which are often asked, such as 'Is not religion in the end just fantasy, and its scriptural stories often compounded of subjective fantasy?', and consider whether the symbolism shares in fantasy. Above all, the definitions and descriptions about symbols prove helpful to many of us by reminding us of the usefulness of symbols on our journeys and experiences in life.

It has been noticeable that for many decades now scholarly writers in Britain in the forefront of writings on the Gospels have focussed on the significance of symbolism in the Gospels. In 1971 C.H. Dodd wrote: 'In the whole story' (of *the Fourth Gospel*) 'and in each item of it, the discerning reader will perceive a traffic between two worlds'... 'Symbols and images... cluster thickly in the scenes of the "Christmas Story"... in *Matthew* and *Luke*...' '...That there is a basis of fact somewhere behind it all need not be doubted, but he would be a bold man who would presume to draw a firm line between fact and symbol...' '...This use of symbolism is fundamentally poetical. It is not a flight into fantasy. It means that the facts are being viewed in depth not superficially...' '...In this Gospel' (of *John*) 'the symbolism is integrated into a massive theology'.[119] Twenty years later, Mark Stibbe wrote: 'The truth value of *John's Gospel* is...related to the poetic value of its redescription of Jesus...' '...Aristotle wrote of poetry that it was more valuable than history because history is concerned with the contingent while poetry is concerned with the universal...'

---

119. C.H. Dodd. *The founder of Christianity* Collins. 1971 pp. 29-33

'...what is remarkable about John's story is its fusion of poetry and history, of the universal and the particular...' '...It is also and above all a narrative in which the author, inspired by the Spirit of truth, evokes the transcendent significance of Jesus from the traditions concerning his earthly words and works. It is a work of poetic history.'[120]

Those who refuse to attach almost any historical value at all to the Gospel of *John* have to contend with its notable inclusion of details of the timing of events: 'it was near the time of the Passover' comes three times, and come in an early, middle and late chapter, giving us the three-year range of Jesus' ministry and activity clearly, something not found in other Gospels. Precise place-names are not ignored about John the Baptist's activity, in 'Bethany beyond Jordan' and 'Aenon near Salim'. Nor precise distances: 'Bethany just under two miles from Jerusalem', disciples rowing 'about three or four miles'. The names of the individuals encountered and talked to by Jesus are not ignored as though that would be over-minute detail, but personally recorded: 'Nathaniel', 'Thomas', 'Philip', 'Nicodemus...' All these things receive special attention in the Gospel of *John*.

Then again attempts have often been made in comments on *John* to dismiss as no more than 'airy-fairy' any types of mysticism, aesthetics or symbolism. And book-reviews of studies in the theology or interpretation of *John's* text may get written off as 'merely impressionist'. Although the dangers of 'woolliness', and the ignoring or softening of tough and hard biblical statements about the realities of sin, have indeed to be warned against and taken seriously, all this does not help in ensuring that symbolism in *John*, in its turn, is taken seriously. But things are changing.

---

120. Mark Stibbe. *John*, Sheffield Academic Press 1993 p.19. For a modern statement of a more definitely negative view of how much history there is in *John*, see Anthony Hanson's 1991 book *The Prophetic Gospel* T & T Clark. p.2 and 3, 293 ff.

Not many years ago a responsible churchman, himself well-placed to make such a comment, wrote in his autobiography that Christian evangelical tradition has in the past 'not been interested in aesthetics or history'. However, this often does not apply at all these days, when eminent evangelical preachers and theologians are giving broadcast talks on Radio 3 on faith and music, and, in preaching, make considerable use of Shakespearian passages as a parallel illustrating of tragic or moral realities about human life.

Descriptions of what religious symbols are have of course come from many directions. The theologian Paul Tillich thought of the symbol as a kind of bridge, and wrote, 'Religious symbols... force the infinite down to finitude and the finite to infinity.'[121] Others have said that they act as bridges between imagery and intuition (with some of course wanting to add that, in the leap across the bridge, intellect and reason may indeed need to act as reminders to us, from their own private function, where there is anything untrue in our conclusions). And one philosopher and theologian, whose background is Eastern (Syrian) Orthodox has observed that religious symbols act as bridges not only between the finite and the infinite, in the sense of participation in the divine, but through symbols of the Person of Christ which lead us across to accepted mediation by him and redemptive rescue: he finds this summed up in the words of Paul of Tarsus, 'I live, yet not I but Christ liveth in me'.[122] John Arapura goes on to say that 'symbol is always in motion', and that only symbol can deal with reality in motion. That surely gives us the truth that symbol is of enormous help in dealing with all the moving and changing stages, the turns in the road, and the borderland areas between

---

121. *Systematic Theology* Vol. 1 p.240

122. John G. Arapura *Rediscovering The Meaning of the Symbol*. From *Indian voices* in *Today's Theological Debate* ed. Burkle and Roth. Stuttgart. 1966. Quoting *Galatians* 2.20 on p.110, as in the 1611 Authorized Version.

divine grace and human effort, encountered in the journey of human existence.

As for any further listing of how symbols have been described, here are a few descriptions. As fords, thresholds, crossroads: as stepping-stones or footprints on the way: as signposts, pocket-compasses, and maps, providing us with perspective on foreground, short term and distant long-term features ahead: as antechambers to an area of presence and mystery, waiting to be entered. In other words, many of them descriptions touching on the business and tools of route-making.

6

THE COSTLINESS OF WHAT JESUS DID

I use the word 'costliness' for this Golgotha part of the Galilee-Golgotha route, the Calvary and Crucifixion part, because 'costliness' certainly seems to be a 'hallmark' word for the central significance of what Jesus was doing on the cross, in ancient and modern understandings of that event. The months and days leading up to it were full of what was costly for Jesus, including his long last journey from Galilee to Jerusalem, so full of diversions and interruptions. Gethsemane was costly for Jesus. The events of the Calvary story itself were obviously costly.

Also, in mentioning the costliness for Jesus of those parts of the story in the Gospels, we cannot fail to mention the constant theme in the rest of the *New Testament* of the sacrificial self-giving of God which the writers see behind the events of Calvary and indeed the whole of what followed Jesus' birth at Bethlehem: it is hard for us not to talk here also of a painful costliness to God. 'Christ dies for us while we were yet sinners, and that is God's proof of his love towards us.'[123] 'God was in Christ reconciling the world to himself, no longer holding people's misdeeds against them.'[124] 'God so loved

---

123. *Romans* 5.8 (REB)

124. *2 Corinthians* 5.19

the world that he gave his only Son…'[125] Did this giving by God not involve pain for God the Father? A modern British theologian, Paul Fiddes, answers in the affirmative: in the sense that the cross stood not only for Jesus' saying 'yes' to his father in his accepting of the cross, but also stood for humanity's long perversity and rejection and indifference towards God which had to be pain-giving for God. Fiddes writes of humanity's 'pain-giving "No"' to God.[126] (However, the Christian Church has traditionally held, ever since the Councils of the Early Church, that God the Father cannot be spoken of as suffering: this view was partly then held because they had in mind the doctrinal views of certain other leaders which they wished to exclude at the time, and it was partly held for philosophical reasons, such as a belief that God, as Source of all, and distinct from God as Redeemer, had to be seen as transcendent Reality above pain and suffering.) This issue will be looked at again in the next chapter, as, in the field of theology, many modern thinkers take a line similar to that of Paul Fiddes, and the whole issue remains under discussion.

The word 'costly', of course, has remained a hallmark word in key events such as the South African 'Truth and Reconciliation' proceedings and Commission from 1994-1999 after the end of 'apartheid'. Leadership was given by Archbishop Desmond Tutu; the theme of 'reconciliation', mentioned in one of the *New Testament* verses quoted above, was to the fore. But in what he wrote at the end about it all,[127] that though the trials had been 'a costly privilege' for those involved in perpetrating the cruelty, they were truly 'costly', he says, for the victims also, to take part in. For example, black individuals who had been victims of terrible violence done to them were asked to meet with the perpetrators

125. *John* 3.16

126. Paul Fiddes. *Participating in God* Darton, Longman and Todd. 2000 p.184

127. *No Future without Forgiveness* Rider. 1999. Chapter 5.

of the violence done to them. Some of the victims had nervous breakdowns, and he himself had suffered great nervous strain, and had sometimes himself broken down in tears publicly during the hearings, of which he was chairman, when listening to someone, often themselves in tears, describing what sort of violence had actually happened. It was in these sorts of circumstances that the giving of amnesty and the giving of forgiveness took place. It is in these types of ways that costliness is built into the fabric of human life, into the history of humanity in modern times, and seen deep down to be built into the fabric of all of God's creation, and of ultimate reality. It is supremely central, of course, in relation to our understanding of the significance of the events of Calvary. Central to what was happening on the Cross were the demands of justice. But, as such things in Britain as the Church of England 'Rethinking Sentencing' report about prison reform (2004) says – the demands not only of 'retributive' justice but also of 'restorative' justice are both important.

Some Christian thinkers among the scientists, certainly, speak and write of how costliness is built into the physical world. For example, when Arthur Peacocke writes of this in relation to biology and evolution, one of his chapters is headed 'The Creative Suffering of God'.[128] He there writes (with a brief note that not all scientists agree with his approach to evolution here):-

> 'The processes of creation are immensely costly
> to God in a way dimly shadowed by and reflected
> in the ordinary experience of the costliness
> of creativity in multiple aspects of human
> existence'... 'we are seen not to be the mere
> playthings of God, but as sharing, as co-creating
> creatures, in the suffering of the creating God
> engaged in the self-offering, costly process of
> bringing forth the new.'

---

128. *Paths from Science towards God* Oneworld. 2001

Elsewhere, he writes that God suffers 'in, with and under the creative processes of the world with their costly, open-ended unfolding in time'. (*Theology for a Scientific Age*. SCM 1993.)

Gethsemane and its night-pressures

'Pressures' in the above heading may sound too mild a word to describe what Jesus went through in Gethsemane. The Gospel of *Mark* uses, in the original Greek, very strong words indeed: 'horror and anguish overwhelmed him, and he said to them' (his disciples): 'My heart is ready to break with grief.'[129]

But I use it in the heading because 'Gethsemane', the garden or olive-tree orchard on the side of the Mount of Olives (just outside the Jerusalem city walls, to which Jesus and his disciples went after the Supper in the upper-room on the night before the Crucifixion) means literally just that: it means the place where there was what was called an 'oil-press' for pressing out or squeezing out olive-oil from the olives: 'geth' means 'press', and '-semane' means 'olive-tree' or 'oil-tree' in Hebrew. It was a place known to have some oil-presses, oil vats and other apparatus for the job. And this Palestinian industry was not just restricted to Jerusalem. There is today in India, in Mumbai (Bombay), a 5000-strong Jewish community who are descended from what they describe as 'oil-pressers' who sailed from the Palestinian coast, in 'Galilee province', around 150 BC (members of this community long ago intermarried and forgot their Hebrew and speak Marathi: but they maintain the Sabbath tradition strongly). There was, in those centuries, and the early centuries AD, a shipping industry both in the direction of India, bringing a return cargo of spices and so on, and in other Mediterranean areas. And the olive and oil-trade featured much in all this, it seems. So the place 'Gethsemane' and its 'presses' truly symbolise the fact and reality of Jesus' coming into his time of horrific pressure.

---

129. *Mark* 14.33-34 (REB)

The olive features centrally in the symbolism also that lies behind many central phrases and passages in Christian liturgy and scripture, such as the Greek phrase 'kyrie, eleison', 'Lord, have mercy'. The Eastern Orthodox Church leader, Archbishop Anthony Bloom, has reminded us that 'eleison' in Greek is of the same root as 'elaion' which means 'olive tree' or 'olive-oil'; that 'kyrie eleison' literally means 'let the olive-oil of your love and peace flow over us', and that 'have mercy' is an inadequate translation in English.[130] The olive-tree and olive-oil are of course symbols of healing, wholeness and peace.

Into this place of an underlying atmosphere, at least potentially, of healing, wholeness and compassion, Jesus has come with his situation of facing opposition, enmity, division, and the prospect of looming death. In other words, it was for him a place, this time (for he had been accustomed to come here for quiet prayer, we are told), of huge dilemma. The dilemma being between what he longed to be able to do, not to have to face death, and, on the other hand, what he knew he was probably being called to by God, for the sake of divine purposes affecting humanity in the deepest of ways. His prayer to his father in heaven was this, an acceptance of God's will: 'Abba, Father, all things are possible to you; take this cup from me. Yet not my will but yours.'[131] So Gethsemane stands second only to Calvary as the place where Jesus experienced and endured dilemma at its most profound level in relation to human existence. It points us ahead to Calvary where, within the divine purposes, the differing claims both of justice and the claims of compassion, in relation to humanity's sin and suffering, present a stark dilemma of the utmost depth. This issue, the issue between the divine justice and the divine

---

130. Anthony Bloom. *Living Prayer*. Darton, Longman and Todd 1966 p.86

131. *Mark* 14.36 (REB)

love, has been and is seen as tackled vigorously and powerfully, though paradoxically, by Jesus in what he was 'doing' on Calvary. (The great Christian leader Anselm many centuries ago famously called the issue 'a problem worthy of a God'.)

Briefly, if one mentions Gethsemane as a key moment leading on to Calvary, one cannot help recalling two other events in the days just before the Crucifixion. These are the scene of Jesus travelling into Jerusalem in the week before Passover, accompanied by his followers, and the moment when Jesus and his disciples joined together in what was to be a farewell meal: the two events known to us as the 'Palm Sunday' event and the 'Last Supper' event. The travelling into Jerusalem was a magnificent paradox, with those accompanying Jesus shouting triumphal Hosannas and waving palm-branches on the one hand, and, on the other, the figure of Jesus riding in on a donkey, in seemingly non-kingly simplicity and gentleness. Like the paradox inherent in Jesus' baptism by John the Baptizer long before, here was Jesus' combination of authoritativeness and vulnerability shining through. The vulnerability here was only too real. Any sort of emergence of what could look like popular acclaim for a potential new claimer to leadership could only arouse the hostility of the establishment, personified by the Herod family which ruled the area under the Romans, and which had allies and supporters among the Jerusalem Temple authorities as well as politically. Previously, Jesus' popular following had aroused religious and political hostility.

The last Supper, too, was a magnificent paradox, a paradox of 'broken-ness' on the one hand and 'sharing (communion)' on the other. Within the pattern of Passover meal there was a solemn moment of the 'breaking' and distributing of bread, and a solemn moment when a cup of wine was shared around: 'they all drank from it' is what the Gospel of *Mark* records.[132] The 'breaking' and distributing of bread was declared by Jesus to have the very special significance on this occasion, because of his coming death. 'During supper he took bread, and having said the blessing he broke it and gave it to them, with the words: "Take this; this is my body". Similarly, with the wine "this is my blood, the blood of the covenant, shed for many".'[133] (Commentators have pointed out that in the words 'for many', it is likely that original Hebrew and Aramaic meanings of the phrase would include something like 'for the many', i.e. not just for the few, and not just for you my disciples.) Anyway, the special significance that Jesus declared to be present for all his words here is couched throughout in very strong phrases, not least in his words when giving the cup of wine, as recorded in the Gospel of *Luke*. 'This cup that is poured out for you is the new covenant in my blood.'[134] The impression throughout is nothing less than that of Jesus' total giving and pouring out of his life to the point of death, and that he was sharing out God's whole movement of love, in a movement to be ongoing, for the disciples themselves and, through them, to be spread. When the disciple Judas, with an armed mob encouraged by the religious authorities, came to arrest him, and a sympathetic bystander struck out at them with a sword (in the account of one Gospel), Jesus just said: 'Put up your sword. All who take the sword, die by

---

132. *Mark* 14.23 (REB)

133. *Mark* 14. 22-24 (REB)

134. *Luke* 22.20 (NRSV) Readers of the *Bible* and its marginal notes will notice that very different phrasings appear in the different English translations we have today, at this point in the Gospels. This is natural, as the ancient written evidence for the biblical text here is very diverse, reflecting different forms of what was said precisely, as remembered by different figures and groups in the early Christian Church.

the sword.'[135] As already touched on, we look ahead, from these pre-Calvary events, to the further spelling out of the significance of the broken-ness and the sharing.

One year, not long ago, on the day before Good Friday, thinking that the Gethsemane night may have included for Jesus huge feelings of depression, I jotted down the following lines about that night. Not poetry, just lined-out reflection on 'Gethsemane':

> '"If I'd spent longer talking to Pharisees"
> (Did Jesus ask himself under the olive trees?)
> "I might have softened their formal bearing,
> But there was Judas needing caring.
> If I'd allowed myself more hours
> To meet Romans with wide powers,
> I might have given a world lead,
> But there was Bethany and their need.
> If I hadn't had to meet Zachaeus
> Or help folk like Bartimaeus,
> I might have been an instant saviour,
> Changing at once human behaviour."
>
> But, Lord, wasn't that basic to our salvation,
> Your path through "ifs" and long frustration:
> Through endless ambiguities
> And all our proud iniquities?
> Each choice triumphant love revealing,
> Part of your victory for our healing?
> You come to us as Truth, Life, Way,
> In the dilemmas of each day.'

The Golgotha self-giving and Crucifixion

The hill just outside Jerusalem's city-walls on which the Crucifixion took place, though what the precise site of this hill was remains

---

135. *Matthew* 26.52 (REB)

unidentified, had the Aramaic name 'Golgotha' (Aramaic was the first century colloquial language of that part of the Middle East) because the whole valley or ravine area in which the site must have been had traditionally been a well-known place of burial and many tombs; and 'Golgotha' means 'The Place of the Skull', a name given for that burial-linked reason, or because the hill had the appearance of a skull. Some interpreters will want to say no more than that. But those of us who find that the writers and presenters of the Gospel stories often seem to have a strong sense of the importance of symbolism, in their presentation, will like to see the 'skull' name as also symbolic. Skulls are empty things, emptied of what was formerly there, and Golgotha may well be seen as the place of Jesus' self-emptying and self-giving in his crucifixion.

The phrase 'he emptied himself' about Jesus is not absent from the *New Testament*, though it comes, in Paul's letter to the church in *Philippi* Chapter 2 verse 7, when the discussion is on all the theological implications of saying that Jesus in his whole life in Galilee and Judaea was emptying himself. Paul's phrase literally translated is 'he emptied himself, taking the form of a servant', and Paul goes on in his very next verse to refer to Jesus 'death on a cross'. NRSV – the New Revised Standard Version – translates *Philippians* 2.7 literally, 'he emptied himself'. Other translations of that same phrase, including the Revised English Bible's 'he made himself nothing' and King James' Bible of 1611 with its 'he made himself of no reputation', have been profound translations, weighing up, as I said, the theological implications of what Paul was saying. But my point here is simply that the idea of Jesus emptying himself is not absent from the *New Testament*. A little later the point is made again in this chapter that the 'skull' name stands as a symbol of the paradox lying at the heart of the Cross. 'Emptiness' and 'Fulfilment', 'Nothingness and Fullness' paradoxically join hands in the 'mystery' or 'open-secret' of the Calvary truth about God's love and also his power.

Apparently the pathetic pockmarks of countless wooden crosses on the Palestinian hilltops during the Roman imperial occupation of the region were a notorious feature of those Roman times. There were many 'resistance fighters', 'dissidents' and 'violent rebels' in those days who suffered such deaths. But our Gospels have not that broad picture, of course, but many details of one death, Jesus' crucifixion. Among quite a number of Jesus' sayings from the Cross is 'My God, my God, why have you forsaken me?', Jesus' use of those words, from *Psalm* 22 in his pouring out of what he was going through. The loneliness of Jesus on the Cross, a sense of abandonment even by his father in heaven, though also of course by his disciples like Peter, is what stands out almost more clearly than anything in the Gospel accounts. Then, there is the saying 'Father, forgive them, they do not know what they are doing.' No part of the accounts brings out more starkly than this the sheer tragedy, sorrow and humiliation of what was happening on the Cross, when the mocking heaped on him called out from him not rage but a plea for forgiveness for the mockers. George Herbert, the 17th century poet, wrote a poem entitled *The Cross*, in which he saw all his own dilemmas and what he called 'the contrarieties' of his own experience of life reflected supremely and savingly in the sufferings of Christ on the Cross: such contradictions as the shameful cruelty of much in life and yet the abundant goodness too. 'Ah, my dear Father, ease my smart!/ These contrarieties crush me: these cross actions/ Do wind a rope about, and cut my heart:/ And yet... these thy contradictions/ Are properly a cross felt by thy Son/...'; and in the light of those last words George Herbert felt he himself could say 'Thy will be done.' To those two features of what stands out from the Gospel accounts – the loneliness and the humiliation inflicted on Jesus on the Cross – we must of course add the physical pain.

His scourging and the details of the crucifying indeed stand out, but they are not given so much space or highlighting as the other points (though the film on *The Passion of the Christ* could hardly be said to reflect that, since the film deals so centrally with displaying the pain). However, whatever may be our own main impression of all the aspects of Jesus' suffering in the above paragraph, Jesus the Route-Maker, and the Crucified, experienced and went down into these most stark of all realities and tortuous turnings of human existence, plumbed in the Crucifixion.

When we try to define what was deep down happening on the Cross and being done there, we naturally turn to the Bible. Two, out of all the verses that might be quoted, have always stood out prominently: *St Paul's Second Letter to the Christians in Corinth* Chapter 5, verse 19, 'God was in Christ reconciling the world to himself, no longer holding people's sins against them...' (REB), and the *Gospel of John* Chapter 3, verse 16: 'God so loved the world that he gave his only Son...' (REB). The word 'reconciling' and the word 'love', together with the mention of the word 'sins', seem to take us to the heart of what was happening. Though somehow it is less frequently quoted, *John* 12.24, recorded as spoken by Jesus when speaking about his coming death: 'Unless a grain of wheat fall into the ground and dies, it remains that and nothing more; but if it dies, it bears a rich harvest.' (REB) can hardly fail to be mentioned, also. And the verse in *John* finds companion-passages in *Mark* on the wonder of seeds, growing secretly and having unexpected fruit, growth, harvest. (Did the wistful words of *Job* in *Job* 14.7 'If a tree is cut down, there is hope that it will sprout again and fresh shoots will not fail' somehow lie behind the words in *John* 12.24? Perhaps.) And who can fail to add to that list of two or three key biblical verses about the Cross, *Romans* 8.38 and 39: 'I am convinced that there is nothing in death or life, ...nothing in all creation that can separate us from the love of God in Christ Jesus our Lord'?

In later centuries of the Christian era, Christians in the Church were always looking for types of language and for metaphors that they could use to communicate to people, in ways easily understood, what Jesus was doing on the Cross. So in the different centuries, in line with a century's particular culture and type of society, variously worded descriptions of the Cross emerged and were regarded as the Church's traditional guides to different aspects of the Cross's significance.

One description, from the theologian Peter Abelard in the eleventh century, saw the message of the Cross to be forgiveness, and used the language of personal relationships, of disputes, alienation, love and reconciliation. The alienation which Jesus tackled on the Cross was seen as being between humanity and God, because of all humanity's sin against God and its perversity. The Cross, it said, was a revealing of the depth of God's love and an appeal for human repentance and love in response. This approach to the Cross as an invitation to reconciliation was, one could say, emphasised especially early in the twentieth century by those classified at the time as 'liberals' in theology. And indeed it may be said to have quite a lot of things in common with the modern styled 'religious-humanist' approach. But it reflects deeply the subjective aspect of humanity's experience of the Cross.

In contrast to that was a description prominent as early as the sixth century, which saw the Cross as a battle against evil, and used the language of victory and defeat; an act of power actually changing things, and of justice and right being done. This language and approach finds an echo in the late twentieth century description already referred to of what was happening on the Cross as reflected in the struggle of a mountaineer or his/her rock-climbing team finding or making a pioneer route up a huge mountain barrier and making a vital hole in the barrier as a way to the summit, in spite of the fact that much of the barrier remains as before. The Cross's victory was its crucial 'hole' of access through to reconciliation, even though that does not mean all human sinning and indifference and cruelty, and that whole mountain barrier, as it were, will cease to exist for the moment, until the fullness of the kingdom comes. Paul's *Letter to the Christians in Rome* tackled radically the depths of alienation between divine justice and divine will for what is right on the one hand and the perverse realities in human existence on the other: but it is that letter that can also use the language of victory before it ends: 'throughout it all, overwhelming victory is ours through him who loved us' and there is 'nothing in all creation that can separate us from the love of God in Christ Jesus our Lord' (*Romans* 8.37 REB). Words written in the conviction that 'the divine love has a promise, potential and power against which nothing can prevail.' The early Church hymn: 'Sing, my tongue, the glorious battle,/ Sing the ending of the fray;…/ Tell how Christ, the world's redeemer,/ As a victim won the day'/ was written by Venantius Fortunatus, an Italian teacher and poet who became a bishop in northern Europe, and it sums up this type of message seen in the Cross. Much later the Reformation leader, Martin Luther, developed this, presenting the Cross as a victory of God's love and justice reconciling the world to himself.

A third description came to its most articulate form after the end of the first millennium, and used the language of the law-courts. This was the beginning of an era when there was a great focus on order and on hierarchies, such as barons and serfs. The requirements of justice had to be satisfied; that is, God's honour, outraged by humanity's sin and disobedience, had to be satisfied by some act of restoration, retribution or the paying of a price. The Cross was seen as the great act. This approach to the Cross is associated particularly with the name of St Anselm, the great (French) Archbishop of Canterbury in the 11th century. He was not keen on any emphasis on the Cross as the paying of a price of any sort that could not go together with love being seen as part of God's attitude; but he felt that Jesus' offering of his life, from within humanity, for the satisfaction of both the claims of justice and the claims of love, was so great a wonder that that fully satisfied the rightful honour of God. He challenged Christian thinkers with his remark 'you have not yet considered the weight of sin,' lying at the root of the issue.

A fourth description uses the language of sacrifice. Most of 'the languages' already looked at have had behind them a large number of biblical passages mostly not touched on in these pages. But this type of language has behind it a particularly thorough examination (in *A Letter to Hebrews*, especially Chapters 6 to 10) of the Cross, as the fulfilment of the Jewish system of priestly and sacrificial explanation of sin. The writer of the *Letter* declares his conviction of how Jesus in his death had provided himself, under the Father, as being the ultimate, personal, loving expiation who was able to be that because he had actually 'experienced death' for all humanity and from inside human existence. The *Letter* was probably written about three-quarters of the way through the first century. Centuries later in the nineteenth century, some theologians suggested that we need to take seriously the inevitable reaction of some modern people to those *Hebrews'* central chapters (focussing on a background language of 'the blood of goats and bulls') since such language seemed to such people a crude and primeval way of describing the Cross's sacrificial significance. So the theologians in question suggested that *Hebrews* spurs us on to seeing the Cross deep down as a profound penitential sacrifice on behalf of all humanity, before God, by Jesus. For many this type of sacrificial language has proved to have a true and ultimate decisiveness of action about it and to be deeply convincing. One theologian wrote:- 'Christ's perfect confession of our sins…must have been a perfect Amen in humanity to the judgement of God on the sin of man.'

I myself strongly believe, as I wrote above, that if one had to pick on one type of language, I would go for the language and description of the Cross in terms of a dead looking seed going into the ground and having the splendid potential for new growth. One eminent Church-leader in Scotland in the middle twentieth century said he saw the Cross not in terms of a punishment being undergone, but as a 'winter ploughing for a future harvest'.[136] This clearly reflects, and tunes in with, the words of Jesus presented in the *Gospel of John* ch. 12 verse 24: 'unless a grain of wheat falls into the ground and dies, it remains that and nothing more; but if it dies, it bears a rich harvest.' It may seem an old-fashioned 'language' to use, becoming stale: cities, not rural areas, are taking an increasingly central place, and so on, across the world. But that language may not grow stale. 'Costly growth' language, as we have clearly touched on, applies to evolutionary science and to the realms of spirituality. The 'anti-evolution-theories' protesters have a point, because belief in natural evolution becomes dangerous if it denies the realities of a more-than-natural dimension at work. And the anti-religion protesters have a point, because we know the dangers of extremism in religion, in personal, or faith-community, matters. Those are salutary warnings, but seem to be unconvincing if they advance into negativism all round on many of life's realms, and if they have no time for some of the deepest realities, data and issues that, for example, in their turn science and religion centre on.

However, all these languages have much in common in some of their characteristics. Each of them makes a complementary contribution to the truth. The secret of the divine sacrificial love, and of self-giving as the dynamic core of ultimate reality, may be said to underlie all the above 'languages'.

---

136. *God's February*, a biography of Archie Craig. Elizabeth Templeton. BCC/CCBI 1991 p.121.

Golgotha's paradoxes and open secrets

John Bell of the Iona community in Scotland is often to be found approaching the Cross and describing the Cross in an imaginative way, using the language of paradox. On Good Friday 2003 I listened to an hour's devotion by him on the theme of 'Man of Contradictions' which he had led in Ely Cathedral earlier that day and which was broadcast on BBC Radio 2 later. I jot down here what I wrote down later of some of the sentences which I remember were used, and what I recall of the general thrust. They seemed to complement finely the profound but measured and textbook-selection of approaches which I touched on above. John Bell, as both a musician-composer and a Church of Scotland minister, touches on theological issues profoundly, but in a different way. He has provided us with a powerful picture of Jesus on Calvary, as tackling in effect the contradictions and paradoxes of human existence seen there, the very real 'opposites' between good and evil, right and wrong, response and indifference, and the subtleties of paradox portrayed starkly and at the deepest level:-

- Jesus made people hate him, because he made all people the object of his love.
- Jesus died because he was too much for us to live with, and had to die.
- One of the two men being crucified alongside Jesus said to the other 'This man has done nothing wrong, unlike us: he's done nothing wrong, except doing good.'
- Jesus, whose voice had spoken to so many people words of encouragement and empowering, and whose life had been so abundantly eloquent until now, was now reduced to a whispered cry of desolation from *Psalm* 22. He had kept silent before the authorities at his trial, instead of giving a performance for them.

- Jesus, whose hands and feet had been so active in going on journeys and stretching out his hands to people, was now pierced and nailed fast to the Cross.

- The carpenter who knew all about wood, and how to work it, was now on the Cross to be close to more wood, and know it well.

- On the way to the Cross he was the stumbling man who had taught others to walk.

These and other words and thoughts of John Bell were combined with much music and many songs.

The language of paradox as centrally taking us to the heart of the Cross can hardly be said to have gone unused in many other types of modern Christian 'cross-shaped' writings, not least in poetic, artistic and theological writings. In them too there has been a wrestling with the pathos and poignancy of the 'nothingness' of Jesus on the Cross, and yet the magnetic appeal also of that Calvary scene. Just as in Chapter 1 above the words the 'authoritativeness' of Jesus and the 'vulnerability' of Jesus were used to describe the perceived calling of Jesus when he was baptized by John the Baptist in the river Jordan, so those words return with full significance in relation to the Cross, and in a full fruiting of the seed-sowing which Jesus had used as a metaphor to describe his dying in words to the disciples.[137] Any examples of modern Cross-shaped thinking are bound to be selective, but I give here a few examples of strongly paradox-centred writing or thinking that focuses on human nothingness and proceeds from there.

In his autobiography, entitled *Neb* in Welsh (*No-one* in English) published in 1997 in an English translation three years before R.S. Thomas' death (by J.M. Dent under the title *Autobiographies*, translated from the Welsh by Jason Walford Davies), R.S. Thomas

---

137. *John* 12.24.

wrote how, as he gazed on the ancient pre-Cambrian rocks on the North Wales coastline, and mused on the question 'who am I?', he got the emphatic answer: 'No-one. But a no-one with a crown of light about his head.' Although he wrote that the idea of 'a crown of light' had several very different associations for him, it is hard not to notice a close connection with the wording of two verses in *Psalm* 8: 'what is a frail mortal that you should be mindful of him, Lord, or a human being that you should notice him? Yet you have made him little less than a god, crowning his head with glory and honour.' (For he was a priest in the Church of Wales, with a quite-often-mentioned practice of the saying of daily morning and evening prayer.) And it is hard indeed not to see some connection with that big moment very near the beginning of the Bible (*Genesis* Chapter 1 verse 27) where it is written that 'God created human beings in his own image'. (REB)

Gordon Wakefield, in a notable article (in the *Expository Times*, October 1994) on Thomas' poetry, wrote that the Cross is inescapable in Thomas' poems, and that trees, which are focussed on often in his verse, invariably remind him of the Cross. For Thomas, 'The tree, with its roots in the mind's dark, was divinely planted, the original fork in existence.'[138] He hears God saying to the hard of heart, who have no time for spiritual 'dimensions': 'I/ will come to you in the simplest/ things, in the body/ of a man hung on a tall/ tree you have converted to/ timber and you shall not know me.'[139] But he writes of God having made provision for those whose prayer has become bleak: yet find this following sort of prayer forming in them: 'Deliver me [Lord] from the long drought/ of the mind. Let leaves/ from the deciduous Cross/ fall on us, washing/ us clean, turning our autumn/ to gold by

---

138. *Collected Poems* 1945-1990. p.267. J.M. Dent 1993. The poem 'Amen'.

139. ditto. p.275. The poem 'Meditations'.

the affluence of their fountain.'[140] Thomas writes of the world's problems, and how he 'shivers' at the thought of them; but as he closes his eyes, he says, the darkness implies God's presence. And he leads on immediately and typically to 'it is not your light that/can blind us; it is the splendour of your darkness.' Although 'doctrines' may be found to want to protect us from wrestling too much with such deep thoughts, he finds 'a warmth' in 'the shadow of the bent cross', and adds 'I see how the sinners/ of history run in and out/ at its dark doors and are not confounded.'[141] I have found those last 19 words of his to be perhaps the most moving and the greatest that I have come across in his poetry.

Five years before he died, a late collection of poems was published including a poem called *At the End*: 'Few possessions: a chair/ a table, a bed/ to say my prayers by,/ and, gathered from the shore,/ the bone-like and crossed sticks/ proving that nature/ acknowledges the Crucifixion./... I who/ have been made free/ by the tide's pendulum truth/ that the heart that is low now/ will be at the full tomorrow.'[142]

R.S. Thomas admitted that many in the Church of Wales found his poetry 'depressing'. But he also says that his own experience as a poet had been that it is often 'tension from which creative work arises.'[143] And his poetry, full of paradox, has been described as really discussions with himself about two sides of an issue.[144] In Thomas' writings it becomes clear that he saw human imaginativeness, and the imagination, as the channel through which the Holy Spirit often moves in humanity: a thought

---

140. *R.S. Thomas Collected Poems* p.270. The poem 'The Prayer'.

141. ditto. p.343 The poem 'Shadows'.

142. *No Truce with the Furies*. Bloodaxe. 1995.

143. *R.S. Thomas Autobiographies*: J.M. Dent.

144. Sir Andrew Motion at the RST memorial occasion in Westminster Abbey in 2000.

which may be seen as linked to his 'crown of light' phrase noted above.

All the talk of nothingness may be said to get capped and brought to a head when, at the end of the poem 'Counterpoint', the major later work, he gives a direct quote of the words from Paul of Tarsus (as already mentioned) : 'When we are weak, we are/ strong. When our eyes close/ on the world, then somewhere/ within us the bush/ burns. When we are poor/ and aware of the inadequacy/ of our table, it is to that/ uninvited the guest comes.'[145]

Edwin Muir also naturally stands out, from somewhat earlier in the 20th century, as a poet rich in cross-shaped writing. His great poem, 'One Foot in Eden', in a 1956 collection of poems,[146] takes its place in a centuries-long line of past religious and poetic meditation on the Cross, including the Latin liturgical phrase in a Good Friday and Easter versicle and response beginning 'O felix culpa...': 'O blessed human perversity, that gained for us so great a salvation'. Edwin Muir's poem just mentioned, and phrases in one or two other of his poems, centres on what he calls the 'strange blessings' of charity, love and compassion received from Calvary, blessings that grew out of the seed of Jesus' dying, dug deep into the soil of humanity's life and all its desperate sin, tragedy and sorrow. Starting with Eden and the Creation, Muir writes of 'these fields that we have planted/ So long with crops of love and hate.' But he focuses then on what he terms those 'strange blessings' that, in a splendid and paradoxical way, came from the Cross for humanity. 'Famished field and blackened tree/ Bear flowers in Eden never known. Blossoms of grief and charity/ Bloom in these darkened fields alone. What had Eden ever to say/ Of hope and faith and pity and love/ Until was buried all its day/ And memory found its

---

145. *Counterpoint* Bloodaxe. 1990 p.62.

146. *Edwin Muir. Collected Poems*. Faber and Faber, 1960.

treasure trove? Strange blessings never in Paradise/ Fall from these beclouded skies.'

In emphasising the importance of poets among those to whom we look for interpreting the meaning of the Cross to us, it is obviously necessary to recall very briefly several of the further biblical passages that lie behind this language of 'nothingness', 'failure', and the getting-beyond 'ego-self'. That is, in addition to the few passages already referred to. I am thinking especially of the words of Jesus as given in the *Gospel of Mark*: 'Anyone who wants to be a follower of mine must renounce self' (R.E.B.) (or as traditionally in English, and in very literal translations, 'let him deny himself'). And also I think of further sentences in what St Paul wrote and what is in the letters by those in the tradition of Paul: Paul wrote (as the King James Bible translates it): 'As workers together with God, we beseech you that ye receive not the grace of God in vain... As having nothing, and yet possessing all things.' Or again, in a letter written to another group 'you died; and now your life lies hidden with Christ in God.'[147]

It is true that for some interpreters, and among theologians and philosophers, a focus on the paradoxes and 'opposites' encountered in scripture and in the Christian story includes seeing them sometimes as messengers of challenge and sometimes as messengers of twin-truths held together, in depth and mystery. (This was touched on in Chapter 3.) The message may be 'Choose either the one or the other...' e.g. right and wrong. Or the message in a particular case may be 'See both as to be held together', e.g. toughness and sensitivity. In other words, paradoxes may signal real contradictions, or they may signal apparent contradictions. Kierkegaard, for example, the creative and highly

---

147. *Mark* 8.34, 2 *Corinthians* 6.1,10, *Colossians* 3.3. As in REB unless otherwise stated. In *Mark* 8.34 The New English Bible's 1970 translation; 'a follower of mine must leave self behind' surely best catches the text's meaning in English.

124

influential Danish Christian thinker lying behind existentialist philosophy, spoke and wrote much about paradox in matters of Christian faith. He stressed the importance of the individual's personal, human part and responsibility, through decisiveness and choice: that is, the importance of individuals knowing about and accepting the given way of access through faith to God, but in face also of God's Otherness. The title of one of his best known works was 'Either-Or', and of another 'Fear and Trembling'. God could indeed be approached by human beings in all their smallness, but only with fear and trembling. This conviction of Kierkegaard grew in the aftermath of what he saw as sentimental and woolly understandings of faith in the Church of his day. His conviction was a reaction against, and a challenge to prevalent philosophical lines of approach to religious belief, which sometimes tended to stress only the importance of making good, objective statements of the truth in relation to human beings in very general terms, rather than also of dealing at the individual and personal level.

Following on those last words above, it seems important to make absolutely clear that Kierkegaard, in addition to his challenges, was a devout Christian and a man of prayer, and what he wrote about the way of access to God through faith was a strong side of his belief. (R.S. Thomas acknowledged his debt to Kierkegaard and wrote a poem with his name as the title. He would have felt a resonance, no doubt, with what I called above 'the two sides.') Bishop Kenneth Cragg has stated this aspect of Kierkegaard in very definite terms: of Kierkegaard he writes: '...his meditations on "Holy Communion" represent his most intense message to posterity in their discovery of grace.'[148] And Kierkegaard says that in a true sense paradoxes can be resolved in prayer: 'God in heaven,/ Let me feel my nothingness,/ Not in

---

148. Kenneth Cragg. *Alive to God*. OUP 1970 p.167

order to despair over it/, But in order to feel the more powerfully/ The greatness of thy goodness.'[149]

In mentioning a further striking contemporary response to Calvary, I quote not from biblical passages, or poetic and theological thinkers, but from a well-known British broadsheet newspaper. On the day before Good Friday in 2001, the *Guardian* had a leader headed 'Passion Play'. (By 'Easter', throughout, the leader-writer really means 'Easter-time' or 'the Easter-weekend', as he makes clear, and concentrates on the Crucifixion.) The leader contained a hard-hitting challenge to what it called the neglect by British society as a whole of the religious significance of the weekend:

> 'Easter's neglect owes much to the way an
> increasingly secular society finds the Christian
> beliefs it celebrates simply fantastical. More and
> more of us do not believe in the resurrection or
> that by this event Christ, as the only son of God,
> conquered death and sin and promised eternal
> life to the saved. Strip out these huge theological
> claims and what you are left with is the torture
> and brutal death of a gentle Galilean carpenter.
> That is not something many people want to
> spend a bank holiday weekend thinking about,
> because it challenges two of our most powerful
> contemporary taboos, death and suffering. In
> a competitive, capitalist culture, success is the
> preoccupation and happiness the great dream.
> Death and suffering have no place in either… Our
> culture sees little meaning or purpose in suffering
> when Easter is above all else a celebration of the
> redemptive power of suffering…'

The leader goes on to say that the Crucifixion confronts us

---

149. *Kierkegaard's Journals*, English translations by A. Dru. 1938 p.78

overall with 'some of the most painful questions of the human conditions: even the innocent and the virtuous are brutally killed. Christianity's dilemma is close to that of Amnesty, as it struggles to publicise the abuse of human rights among good and innocent people.' That leads on to the unhesitating statement that the story of the Crucifixion 'encompasses in one narrative thread so much of human experience.' And the leader ends as follows: 'Underpinning Easter is a set of beliefs about power, evil, suffering, forgiveness and justice: we may no longer believe in all of them, but they can still give us insight into some of human nature's most persistent dilemmas.'

Although that leader, as it stated, did not wish to touch on what it called 'theological claims' concerning the Crucifixion and the Resurrection of Jesus, yet its prophetic challenge written out of its own line of strong conviction is a contribution to comment on the Cross which cannot be left unvoiced, and unnoticed, and one which is badly needed in any attempt at noting 'cross-shaped' comment.

Modern or post-modern attitudes can, of course, produce fierce, 'jokey' comments on the Crucifixion. In a display of 'images' by the artist Sarah Lucas in Tate Liverpool recently, one image was entitled 'We do it with love'. It showed a section of a pregnant body with a miniature cross pinned on its garment, the upright arm of the cross being a cigarette-stub. The image seemed strangely and sadly somehow to be dismissive of any significance in the Crucifixion. Strange in an artist who no doubt had no time for anything authoritarian of an old-fashioned sort, yet surely might have still recognised the Good Friday authority respected by the newspaper leader above, or might have still been on a wavelength to recognise the authority of what R.S. Thomas wrote about in 'When I am weak, then I am strong', in *Counterpoint*.

7

THE RAISING OF JESUS, AND GOD'S UNENDING LIFE-GIVING

In commentaries on the Gospels concerning the Resurrection it has been customary to give a great deal of time to discussing and analysing fully the details of the sometimes very diverse accounts in the different Gospels of the events surrounding the empty tomb and the appearance of Jesus after his death to a number of his followers and disciples. This is good and necessary to some extent, insofar as it takes seriously the need to get as close as possible to what really happened historically; as long as we do not get too worried and confused if we find, with regard to the accounts in the four Gospels, four very different accounts in many ways (as indeed we generally find in ordinary life when we hear several people who have all been present at some event presenting later very different pictures of what they saw or experienced) and find that no very neat single and precise picture emerges.

There seems a lot to be said basically for starting off by taking a single story, such as that about Jesus' recorded appearance to two of his followers and disciples on the road to Emmaus from Jerusalem, as written about fairly fully in Chapter 24 of the *Gospel of Luke*. That story seems to cover much of the total situation originally surrounding the Crucifixion and Resurrection, including the despair, confusion and questioning about Jesus by his followers after his death; and yet it does also present how, gradually, some disciples and followers came to a realisation that Jesus was present among them. And that is a message about the Resurrection found in all the Gospels.

On the road to Emmaus, a destination seven miles from Jerusalem, Cleopas and his companion, not recognising Jesus when he came up with them on the road as a fellow traveller on the road, said to him about events in Jerusalem and the Crucifixion, 'we had been hoping that Jesus of Nazareth was to be the liberator of Israel.' Their expectation had been of Jesus coming to power among Jews in the future and in 'the fullness of the kingdom'. To have him die now was a huge bombshell. But, as happened later, after a meal with them when they invited him in after reaching their destination, and they saw him breaking bread in front of them and giving it to them, their eyes were opened and they recognized him. Gradually, the impact of the Crucifixion on them was joined by the impact of the Resurrection on them: the latter was a strong sense of the abiding presence of Jesus with them. The story as a whole seems to sum up, for all its homely details, in a way told more fully than in the case of other recorded 'appearances', this revolutionary moment for the early Christian movement in and around Jerusalem, and within Judaism.

This particular approach to glimpsing and so exploring the significance of the Resurrection, provided for us by the *Gospel of Luke*, has happily been found increasingly within our modern Christian Churches, and indeed came to the fore noticeably as far back as three or four decades ago. A relatively small book, *Interpreting the Resurrection*, by the Baptist theologian Neville Clark, was published in 1967.[150] One of its chapters was entitled

---

150. SCM Press

'Tomorrow is now'; it put the approach to the Resurrection which I have attempted to label above as a concentration on the abiding presence of Jesus risen. His book was written in a readable and uncomplicated way, but goes deep. The phrase 'Tomorrow is Now' also concentrated on another key point. Explaining that the Jews of Jesus' day already had the belief that there would be a general 'resurrection of the dead' for all humanity by God, spoken of by them in such phrases as 'in the fullness of the kingdom', in the future, Clark wrote that, for Jesus' disciples and his followers, the resurrection was no longer simply the great future event but 'had become a present reality:... the general resurrection has moved forward from the End to take present shape in the one case of Jesus the Messiah,... raised by the sovereign act of the Living God.' Clark calls this 'the staggering assertion which the Church was driven to make.'[151] So that the significance of Jesus' Resurrection is seen as the coming of a new age for humanity, or rather 'the new age'; with God's abiding presence, 'today' and 'now', newly and decisively dwelling with humanity, in a joining of earth and heaven, time and eternity, for always.

Thirdly and lastly, Clark used the phrase that Jesus was 'raised by the sovereign act of the Living God'. We rightly like to use also, as the Church has always used also, the other phrase 'Jesus rose from the dead' ('Jesus is risen'). But many of us like to see particular significance in the phrase 'God raised Jesus from the dead'. That was in fact the form of phrasing found in what is almost certainly the earliest reference to Jesus' resurrection in the *New Testament* to have been written (*St Paul's* passage in his *first letter to Christians in Corinth* – ch. 15 verse 4). 'I handed on to you as of first importance what I in turn had received, that Christ died for our sins,... he was buried,... he was raised to life on the third day'(NRSV). Also the phrase 'God raised Jesus from

---

151. Clark. P.51

the dead' is used about two dozen times in the *Acts of the Apostles* in the accounts of talks given by Christian speakers to various gatherings. And more than that, Paul, in the passage just quoted, goes on in the following verses, as one commentary says in effect at this point, to declare his own conviction that Jesus' being raised to new life gave us a full and deep assurance that that giving of new life by God would continue for us: new life in the present, new life when we die, new life to everyone who belongs to Christ when Christ comes again at the end of the world. Christ's resurrection was to bring a newness, an altering, a continued creative life-giving into all situations in which human beings feel defined by their past, perhaps punishingly; for into past, present and future the raising of Christ has brought newness and an altering, and ways of access and invitation in between the things of time and of eternity.

No one will want to speak too airily, and certainly not glibly, about all this, or without a sense that to our earthly minds it must be in the realm of mysteries beyond our present understanding. It is in this realm, of course, that we turn to poets and other creative artists, who, as mentioned earlier, give us language that comes closest to expressing the inexpressible. Comments on, and understandings of, Jesus' resurrection have come from a very wide variety of writers in recent decades. Before turning to poetic writings, a few further brief quotations from writers on theology or spirituality seem important to add here.

Harry Williams in *True Resurrection* wrote about Jesus' resurrection using the language of human experience of being raised out of some deep loneliness, alienation or emptiness in life. That does not mean that the book lacked a deep theological foundation, for it was a book with firm theological base to it. But it had the gift of relating theological truth to life. Its tackling of the question of the Resurrection of Jesus as miracle came in the following passage:

131

'The miracle of our being given life beyond
the grave is no greater than the miracle of our
continually being given life here. Creativity is
ever one and the same. It is always the calling
into being of what is non-existent; and to those
who are created it means for ever receiving what
for ever is being given. If in this life we know
that we are poor, that we are nothing and have
nothing which we are not receiving from the
unknown, then it will not seem uniquely strange
that life should continue to be given beyond the
boundaries of physical death...'[152]

In the same book it was made clear that what was meant
by a human being's receiving of life's creative power was, at its
deepest level, the gift of the discovering by a human being of his
or her full self as created in God's image, beyond the self which
we have learnt in modern times to call our 'ego-self'.

A more recent statement on the significance of Jesus'
resurrection came from Rowan Williams, the present Archbishop
of Canterbury, in 1994, in an Easter sermon at that time:

'The resurrection is not a resuscitation: it is the
gift of a new <u>kind</u> of life, the life that exists on
the far side of death and hell, of destruction and
disintegration... He is no longer the prisoner of
the past: from now on he belongs to all people and
all times, he is available to all...

In every extremity, every horror and pain, Jesus
is accessible as the one who continued to make
God's loving presence wholly present in the depth
of his own anguish and abandonment. There is
place for God now in all suffering, at the heart
of suffering and even of death, because we have

---

152. H.A. Williams. Mitchell Beazley 1972 p.177

seen the glory of God abiding in the squalor
and humiliation of Jesus' execution. Jesus has
"authority" in that he has the right to be there and
to be called on in suffering and death...

Jesus is Lord. Jesus of Nazareth is the face of
God turned towards us in history, decisively and
definitively. All this is God's act.'[153]

Bishop Stephen Verney, in 1985, took up, strikingly, what he saw as a piece of characteristic symbolism recurring in the *Gospel of John*.[154] At the beginning of the Gospel prominence is given to some precise dating ('on the third day') concerning a wedding in Cana of Galilee.[155] Verney saw this as a highly significant symbolic phrase near the beginning of the Gospel, which had near its end and at its climax 'another third day': the day of the resurrection of Jesus, which was widely referred to as 'the third day' after the crucifixion. (According to three of the Gospel accounts, a remembered saying of Jesus had been that, when the Son of Man came in the fullness of the messianic kingdom, after suffering, 'on the third day he would rise again'.) Verney saw *John's* 'third day' phrase for the Cana marriage as 'a pointing forward' to the Resurrection, 'another third day' and another marriage; that is, he saw the Resurrection as 'the marriage of heaven and earth'. Rather than understanding the Resurrection as telling us that Jesus was alive again 'in the same human sense as he had been' before his death, or understanding it as Jesus 'coming alive again only in the memory of his friends', he wrote that for him it was a marriage that happened 'in eternity', and meant the beginning of a 'new age of eternal life',... 'about 6 am on a Sunday morning' and 'it continues', he wrote, 'in our experience'. He added further: '"Eternity" does

---

153. Rowan Williams. *Open to Judgement* DLT 1994.

154. Verney. *Water into wine* Collins. Fount 1985. pp.193,194,197

155. *John* 2.1 (NRSV)

not mean out of time and space, it means NOW, in the depths of each present moment, and in every place where the eyes of men and women are opened to see.' All of this seems to spell out for us what must be some of the Resurrection's deepest dimensions – of the eternal 'now', and the 'always', of God's presence.

In discussion about the Cross and Resurrection in the preceding and much earlier pages in this book, the paradoxical couplings of the words 'authority' and 'abandonment', 'glory' and 'suffering' will have emerged as central communicators of meanings and significance. But we are also fortunate to have, beyond only words, some more visual communicators in sculpture and the shape of stone-crosses, and other symbolic objects, still visible in and around old monastic Christian settlements and sites in this country, a legacy from past centuries: they, too, communicate the same splendid paradoxes. Many of them are to be found in Christian Celtic settlements in Cornwall, Wales, Ireland and Scotland, though not only here in Britain. The Christian civilisation of the Celts in Europe during the 6th, 7th and 8th centuries AD was well-known for and gave a firm base to the legacy. The tenth-century St Martin's Cross, a high standing cross, stands by the west door of the Abbey on Iona, and has marked Iona as a place of pilgrimage for over a thousand years. On Iona they will remind you that it is typical of Celtic spirituality, and of that abbey and its worship, as 'it suggests that worship often occurred out in the midst of the wide worship of earth, sea and sky', through the years, and that 'the Celtic "everlasting" pattern of the weaving vine on the cross points to the intertwining of heaven and earth'. The cross is described as typical of the Irish-Celtic tradition of standing crosses and Irish monastic skills in artistic sculpture, carving and decoration. On the west face of St Martin's cross is carving with scenes from the *Bible*, and on the east face examples of 10th century contemporary artistry with intertwining lines, signifying the intertwining of life now and hereafter, of time and eternity, of earth and heaven. The characteristic of Irish crosses, usually called 'the ring of glory', the circle encircling and binding together the intersection of the two arms of the cross, proclaims the truth of God's surrounding and encircling Presence (though it has been traditionally thought to be due specifically to the desire of St Martin – a fourth-century Roman soldier, originally – to mark the cross as a cross of victory, not of defeat, and to have something circular recalling the laurel crown placed on the victor's head in the Roman games). The wealth of imagery seen in all the above is a reminder of the different cultural ways in which the message of the Cross and Resurrection have been and are communicated.[156]

Cross-imagery and circle-imagery among Celtic Christians in Scotland were to be found, and still can be seen in many cases, in less immediately accessible places such as in caves in isolated monastic spots. On the island Eileann Mor, a small island in the Sound of Jura and two miles out to sea from Kilmory, there is a small cave a short distance from the island chapel. The cave is known as St Cormac's Cave, from the saintly figure who lived here in about the seventh century AD. Beside the cave is a stone wall from a ruined building that used to be here. A historian describing the scene wrote that 'on the stone wall are incised a circle, emblem of eternity, and a small cross delicately carved'.[157] In the same coastal area east of Jura, at a place called Cove on Loch Caolisport, there is a ruined chapel and a cave where St Columba may have lived for some time. The cave is called St Columba's Cave. The old altar on the site is still there. Seton Gordon's description is this: 'On the wall of the cave above the

156. See Ron Ferguson *Chasing the Wild Goose (the Iona Community)* Harper Collins 1988, and *Iona Community*, and *Worship Book* Wild Goose Publications 1991, from which many details and phrases have been taken.

157. Seton Gordon *Highways and Byways in the West Highlands* Macmillan 1935 reissued 1979. p.341

altar is carved a small cross, thick, sturdy and shapely – the work of master hands. High on the opposite face of the cave is incised a cross within a circle.' One imagines the latter cross to have been in something like the ⊕ symbol, but I have never been there. Whatever the precise detail, it seems clear that, spread in many directions, these isolated crosses and circles were strong symbolic witnesses: strong both as challenging reminders of the sacrificial side of the Cross and Resurrection, and assuring-reminders of the constant eternal encirclement of God's presence and love.

Having used quite a few words about Celtic 'intertwinings' and 'interweavings', in their rhythms of spirituality between the twin-poles of the earthly and the eternal, and about the things of nature and the things beyond nature, it is time to look (or look again) at one or two twenty-first century poets, musicians or artists in poetic prayer who give us, or have given us, their rhythms of spirituality, as we live among the poles and paradoxes of our human existence. In David Adam's focus on simple rhythms of tides and seasons in the natural creation, of ebb-tide and incoming-tide, of mountain ridges and looking over the edge to the other side, and so on, many have found that in his mostly small poetic prayers in Celtic style, there are to be found good vehicles and pointers for realising God's presence in and surrounding our lives, where divine grace can interweave with human experience and effort.

David Adam's 'new life-giving' underlying theme (as I see it) never seems to depart far from a 'home-base' in the message of the Cross and the Resurrection and its paradoxes:

> 'He was crucified, dead and buried. His life could
> seem a complete breakdown, a total failure. But
> the Cross is empty. Breakdown is not the end. It
> is only part of the process of this earth. Without
> the Cross there is no resurrection; without death,

136

no newness of life. Without breakdown, there is no breakthrough… Too often I keep things that should be scrapped. I have an old petrol-driven lawn mower… I need to admit it has broken down… So it is with life. We must say something is broken down, only then can it be repaired or renewed. So often… we are hesitating on the very edge of a new world for us…; death is a gateway to glory.'

Very often it is the poetic writers and the song-writers who have driven such points home. John Bell's song 'Here I am' has the following last verse: 'Wherever you go I will meet you,/ Till you draw your last breath/ In the birthplace known as death;/ Yes, wherever you go, I will meet you/ Saying "Here I am".'[158]

David Adam applies Cross-and-Resurrection truths to human lives as a whole, seeing the intertwining lines between earth and the eternal as enabling God's grace to interweave with human existence and human effort. He writes of the St Patrick's Breastplate prayer: 'Here we have weaving of the Presence around our lives like the Celtic patterns on stones and in the illuminated Gospels: Christ moves in and out, over and under. We are encircled by him; encompassed by his presence and love.' (This seems close to *St Paul's words to the Christians in Philippi*: 'Work out your own salvation in fear and trembling; for it is God who works in you, inspiring both the will and the deed, for his own chosen purpose.')[159]

Images of rivers and estuaries, tides and seasons, are never far away from David Adam's mind. 'We meet you, Lord of sea and land./ Ebb-tide, full tide/ Let life's rhythms flow/ Full tide, ebb-tide/ How life's beat must go.' And the more personal:

---

158. John Bell and Graham Maule. *Wild Goose Songs Vol 1* 1987 p.119

159. *Philippians* 2.12,13 (REB)

'It is your tide that pulls me, Lord,
Draw me to yourself.
When one tide ebbs another flows.
Nothing is lost, only it suffers a tide change.
Lord of life, when the tides wane,
Grant me a hand till I rise again.
When the strand is becoming wide,
Keep me safe at the ebb tide.'

Another strong image that appears in Adam's writings is that of the mountain ridge (or 'edge'), where one reaches the ridge and can look over on to the other side. With this image in mind, he writes of God's presence as 'a reality to become aware of, a glory that is ours but we so often miss. We are on the very edge of glory, but we seem to choose the wrong side'; and he adds: 'the prayers of this book are written out of a desire to walk on the edge of glory and see for oneself the ever abiding presence, that never leaves us or forsakes us.'

In the following quotation, the precise Celtic words of long ago about 'the ring of glory' binding together, as it were, the two intersecting arms of the cross on Calvary, the latter signifying the Cross's tragic dilemma and cruel destructiveness, are not used, but the same thought is memorably and simply emphasised in David Adam's prayer:

'Circle me O God
Keep hope within
Despair without.

Circle me O God
Keep peace within
Keep turmoil out.

Circle me O God
Keep calm within
Keep storms without.

Circle me O God
Keep strength within
Keep weakness out.'[160]

Before ending mention of those for whom poetry, spirituality, music, art is their medium of expression, I cannot leave out Elizabeth Jennings' poem 'Mozart's Horn Concertos'. Taking the French horn as a symbol of the paradox, and the 'apparent opposites', of the horn's martial side and also its ability to communicate a sense of deep poignancy and tenderness (a dictionary of music mentions one of the special features of the instrument being 'its wide range of intensity in producing both the loudest and the softest effects'), Jennings seems to hear in this music of Mozart not just a simple contrast between a clarion call and a soft call, but profound moments where, in her words, 'God is proved in every note'. If that is a true reading of the poem's horn paradox, then the poem surely takes us very close to the power-and-love twin-truth, and paradox, of the Cross and Resurrection. Near also to Celtic spirituality's intertwining lines between things of earth and things of eternity, as symbolising and making real God's abiding presence bridging heaven and earth. And to the modern horn-paradox as doing the same in our times. Deep down the power and the love, the clarion call and the tenderness are seen as belonging together. Or rather that is how I read Elizabeth Jennings' poem:

'Not for war or hunting cry.
Is this; it gentles down the heart,
So there's no question asking "Why

---

160. Details of this, and five other quotations from David Adam in recent paragraphs have been in serial order: *The Cry of the Deer* SPCK 1987 p.39/ *The Edge of Glory* SPCK 1985, 12th impression 2003 p.2/ ditto p.106/ *Tides and Seasons* SPCK 1989 p.131/ *The Edge of Glory* p.2,3/ The Cry of the Deer p.12.

Does man exist?" God gave him art,
And God is proved in every note
And every sound takes its own part

In what a young composer wrote
Who ended in a pauper's grave.
The disc is on, the patterns float

And I feel back at some strange start
And marvel at what Mozart gave.'[161]

The traffic between time and eternity

The truth of the Raising of Christ has sometimes been stated by theologians not only via language about a marriage between earth and heaven, but also by language about time and eternity. Herbert Farmer fifty years ago said 'God is the master of time:... he is in the time-process as its master.' This was expressed, too, in those years in the same terms in a small, classic book entitled *The Master of Time* by Max Warren.[162] Starting from a philosopher's phrase that 'incompleteness at any moment is of the essence of time', he goes on to say that eternity completes time; and to give great weight to Jesus' recorded words to his disciples before his imminent death: 'Now the Son of Man is glorified, and in him God is glorified,' stating the message. Warren says that in 'the Now of every moment'... 'the reflection of eternity' is to be found, a 'supreme moment of junction' and 'mutuality', which in turn is reflected in the invitation to the disciples to find in the breaking of the bread a personal mutuality between them and Christ. Great weight is also given by Warren to some words written by Paul to Christians in Corinth: 'Everything belongs to you... and you

---

161. Elizabeth Jennings, in a 1975 collection of poems of hers (*Carcanet*).

162. M.A.C. Warren. *The Master of Time*.

belong to Christ, and Christ to God.'[163] From those words, and from their presentation in Warren's book, the reader could not escape the message that human beings are not helplessly under the control of people or things, not even death, but, finally and accessibly, belong under the presence and eternity of God.

Nearly half a century later, in another classic book of spirituality, Gerard Hughes' *God of Surprises*, in its own distinctive way, the same theme, of the things of eternity being accessible in the present and 'The Now', rings out. Hughes writes: 'God is in all things. God is within my own being, constantly creating it. The object of all prayer methods is to help us meet God "closer to me than I am to myself".'[164] It is of interest to note that the author says that the book was written 'In gratitude to all with whom I have walked the inner journey', and that splendid inscription shows that we keep returning to the language of routes and inner routes.

Max Warren combined his writing on spirituality, theology and the Bible with reminders of the contributions of poetry and verse, such as these two verses on the Cross and Resurrection. The author of them has always remained untraced, apparently, though the suggestion that they may have come from the age of A.E. (George) Russell or G.K. Chesterton has been made:

> 'The stars wailed when the seed was born
> And heaven wept at the birth of the thorn;
> Joy was pluckt like a flower and torn,
> For Time foreshadowed Good Friday morn.
>
> But the stars laughed like children free
> And heaven was hung with the rainbow's glee
> When at Easter Sunday, so fair to see,
> Time bowed before Eternity.'

---

163. The references are *John* 13.31 and 1 *Corinthians* 3.21-23 (REB)

164. Gerard W. Hughes *God of Surprises*. Darton, Longman and Todd. 1985 (with a 28th reprinting in 1994) p.46

Many of us would delight at that combining of good analysis or searching out of the accurate meanings of words and concepts, such as biblical study and theology involve, on the one hand with, on the other hand, a listening to the poets or other artists who may be able, as it were, to help us peep round the corners of words and concepts and pick out some key nuances and symbolism and half-hidden thrusts lying there. And on time and eternity, such chances of listening may seem to be often badly needed, and welcomed.

The poet Patrick Cavanagh died in 1967, but his poem 'Beyond the Headlines' is perhaps brought to mind for many people by the prominence which the Iona Community has given to the symbol of the wild goose. It has, in many cultures, been a symbol of that which lives in two worlds, between eternity and time. Ron Ferguson has written: 'A Celtic symbol for the Holy Spirit is the Wild Goose, a turbulent sign which is more appropriate to living the faith in our day than is the gentle dove.' Cavanagh's poem is:

'Then I saw the wild geese flying
In fair formation to their bases in Inchicore
And I knew that these wings would outwear the wings of
    war
And a man's simple thoughts outlive the day's loud lying.
Don't fear, don't fear, I said to my soul.
The Bedlam of Time is an empty bucket rattled,
'Tis you who will say in the end who best battles.
Only they who fly home to God have flown at all.'[165]

Stevie Smith's poem 'The Airy Christ' (sub-titled 'After reading Dr Rieu's translation of St Mark's Gospel') comes from the same era.[166] It provides a fine balance to some of her more astringent

---

165. Copyright. Katharine B. Cavanagh c/o Peter Fallon, 19 Oakdown Road, Dublin.

166. Reprinted by permission of James MacGibbon Executor, and New Directions, New York.

references elsewhere to Christianity, certainly Christianity's institutionalised form:

> 'Who is this that comes in splendour, coming from the
>   blazing East?
> This is he we had not thought of, this is he the airy Christ.
>
> Airy, in an airy manner in an airy parkland walking,
> Others take him by the hand, lead him, do the talking.
>
> But the form, the airy One, frowns an airy frown,
> What they say he knows must be, but he looks aloofly
>   down,
>
> Looks aloofly at his feet, looks aloofly at his hands,
> Knows they must, as prophets say, nailèd be to wooden
>   bands.
>
> As he knows the words he sings, that he sings so happily
> Must be changed to working laws, yet sings he ceaselessly.
>
> Those who truly hear the voice, the words, the happy song,
> Never shall need working laws to keep from doing wrong.
>
> Deaf men will pretend sometimes they hear the song,
>   the words,
> And make excuse to sin extremely; this will be absurd.
>
> Heed it not. Whatever foolish men may do the song is
>   cried
> For those who hear, and the sweet singer does not care that
>   he was crucified.
>
> For he does not wish that men should love him more than
>   anything
> Because he died; he only wishes they would hear him
>   sing.'

It would be wrong, obviously, just to see Stevie Smith's poem above, and its title, in terms of what we might call an 'airy-fairy' sort of description of Jesus. E.V. Rieu was a literary figure; and the contents of the poem of Stevie Smith suggest that she saw Rieu bringing out imaginatively and liberatingly the picture of an airy Christ in the sense of a singing Christ and a Christ of wonder and mystery. Many commentators have seen the *Gospel of Mark* as presenting us with a figure of mystery and miracle very strongly, as well as a figure of humanity. Some have put this very markedly, one commentator speaking of the Gospel as one of 'mind-blowing mystery and tremendous revelation which impresses and disorientates its readers', adding that it may perhaps be seen as a picture of an 'undomesticated' Christ for a church community and situation of crisis and persecution, and contrasting it with the *Gospel of Luke* and its more 'domesticated' and 'humanised' picture written for a more immediately settled situation.[167] It has often been said that the *Gospel of Mark* mirrors the faith of an early Christian community that was full of expectation rather than backward reminiscence. A community, that is, looking in faith at the Christ that is yet to be, not only to the Christ already known.

Late in his life, R.S. Thomas put these closing lines at the end of his 1990 book of poems called *Counterpoint*, as already referred to twice:

> 'When we are weak, we are
> strong. When our eyes close
> on the world, then somewhere
> within us the bush
> burns.'[168]

The pioneer Jesus: two followers' descriptions

After the Gospels, and in the earliest days of the Church, the *Bible's* emphasis on Jesus' route-making in Galilee and Judaea never lets

---

167. John Drury in *Luke* Collins Fontana 1973 pp.12-13

168. *Counterpoint*. Bloodaxe. 1990 3rd impression. 2000

up. One passage in *Acts of the Apostles* notably highlights it, as do two chapters in *A Letter to Hebrews*. It is true that in one or two verses of the writings of *St Paul*, he seems to declare no interest in the historical events of Jesus' life before his crucifixion and to discount the importance of the Jesus of history in the Galilee and earlier years and months: 'though we once knew Christ from a human point of view, we know him no longer in that way', he wrote to the Christians in Corinth about a quarter of a century after Jesus' death.[169] But these words come in a passage where Paul is stressing vigorously the supreme importance of 'being in Christ now', with no doubt a quiet recognition that he himself was unlike Jesus' original twelve disciples in not having known Jesus in the flesh.

In contrast, Stephen, a member of the church in Jerusalem in its earliest days and one of the 'seven men of good repute' appointed to look after the need for practical care and help for a particular group of widows in the Church, became in due course very active in preaching and pastoral care and is recorded, in the seventh chapter of *Acts*, as giving a long address before the Supreme Jewish Council in Jerusalem about the movement around Jesus and its significant place within the long line of Jewish history past and present. He presented Jesus as the historical climax of a long line of Jewish heroes who had pioneered their way through one crisis after another. The address, as it appears in *Acts*, includes five verses on Moses and the paradox of the burning bush, and seven verses on how God was providentially present with the leading figure of Joseph in all his experiences. At the end of the long address, and challenging the Jewish Council over their forbears' constant killing of prophets throughout past history, Stephen said about Jesus: 'was there ever a prophet your fathers did not persecute? They killed those who foretold the

---

169. *2 Corinthians* 5.16 (NRSV)

coming of the righteous one, and now you have betrayed him and murdered him.'

In addition to those later verses mentioned, it is true that in the last half-century many comments on *Acts* have reminded us that the figure of Jesus is presented there in the context of various factors that had particular prominence for the Church in the first century. Some of the comments have been that Luke the physician had made a point at the beginning of the Gospel attributed to him that he was especially concerned to provide what was historically accurate in what he wrote. Other comments have obviously seen in *Acts* (probably written about three quarters of the way through the first century) a presentation that brings out the figure of Jesus in relation to the spread of the Gospel in new places in the Roman Empire, rather than only in relation to the Jewish base and focus on teachings about the 'end-times' and the end of history in senses to do with the hereafter. Further comments have naturally paid special attention to how far Luke himself, with his undoubtedly creative mind, gave shape to received data of early Christian rememberings of Jesus and of the earliest days of the Church. One 'study-edition' of the *Bible*[170] has this comment, for example, concerning *Acts'* presentation of the speeches given by figures such as Peter, Paul and Stephen: 'It is reasonable to suppose that Luke did not receive these speeches just as they are, but composed them freely, using the pattern of the first apostolic preaching, with its basic proclamation and its arguments drawn from the scriptures.'

But, beyond such important considerations, the fact remains that, as the Moses-verses and the Joseph-verses mentioned or referred to above show, *Acts* basically presents Jesus as the historical climax in a long line of Jewish heroes in the past, and presents him in his route-finding and route-making identity.

---

170. *The New Jerusalem Bible*. Darton, Longman and Todd. 1985

Precise details about the author of *A Letter to Hebrews* are not given, but he may well have been Apollos, the Alexandrian Jewish Christian mentioned by Luke in *Acts*, and the date of writing looks like the years just before 70 of the Christian era. In *'Acts'*, Apollos is described as 'full of spiritual fervour' and 'eloquent', with the additional detail that 'in his discourses he taught accurately the facts about Jesus' and was 'powerful in his use of the scriptures'. So it seems likely that the *Letter* was written by a second-generation Greek-speaking Jewish Christian who was a learned theologian, and that the *Letter* was written to Jewish Christians, and may be taken as vital evidence for early Christian understandings of Jesus as current in an important Mediterranean area outside Jerusalem.

But, here again, beyond those important points, there is the fact that out of five titles for Jesus given in the *Letter* '(including 'Forerunner', 'Mediator' and 'Guarantor' of God's covenanted forgiveness, and 'High Priest') the title 'Pioneer' appears prominently both in the opening chapters and in the closing chapters that form the climax. The word 'pioneer' is the English translation given both in the Revised English Bible and the New Revised Standard Version for the key original word in the Greek. He is seen as the one who pioneers the way, and breaks through the barriers, from the side of humanity into the presence of God, so that humanity may follow. In one passage he is called 'the pioneer of salvation' who 'experienced death for all mankind' and who has 'himself passed through the test of suffering'. And in the later passage he is 'the pioneer and perfecter of faith'.[171] These passages and this title about Jesus come notably in a letter which is agreed to be both a deep human picture of Jesus and a deep theological understanding of him. They certainly provide a culminating point in the *Bible* for the use of route-making imagery, and for

---

171. *Hebrews* 2.10, 2.18, 12 (REB)

the underlying continuance in the *Bible* of the ancient Hebraic heritage of pioneering experience from desert days, on which we have focussed earlier.

8

PRESENT-DAY UNDERSTANDINGS AND QUESTIONINGS OF THE GOSPELS' PICTURE OF JESUS

The chapters of this present book have so far not touched on a variety of questions. How far and how straightforwardly do the Gospels relate to what actually and historically happened? How intelligibly and without coded language do the Gospels' contents get across to the general reader? How is the *Bible* to be interpreted? How valid are the objections of those, for example, who say that the *Bible* and a biblical-based faith are mainly just for people who want a message of comfort for present life and beyond it? The chapters so far have also largely kept off much reference to a discussion of whether our new global world of wide communication has brought new light on Jesus and the Gospels from, say, third-world countries to those of us living in 'Western' and Mediterranean parts of the world; for undoubtedly many of our established expressions of the meaning of Christianity, and understandings of the figure of Jesus, were formulated centuries ago.

This chapter and the next two chapters focus on one or two of the above topics directly, and also on the contribution of poets, visual artists and musicians to an awareness of many of the perspectives of the Gospels' message.

The Gospels: Jesus a historical figure?

Do we have impartial evidence from people not Christian followers of Jesus on this? The answer is Yes, some. It is not the sort of evidence that could be called proof. But where it is not proof, it has the weight of the evidence of witness. Many Christians would agree with the remark of the 20th century Jewish mystic and philosopher Martin Buber about religious faith, that faith does not provide proofs but does provide witnesses. So such evidence as we have is important, for faith and rational analysis. Modern understandings of Jesus can look back to some statements from historians who lived in the century after Jesus' death, for evidence other than that provided by writers from inside the Christian Church.

Historians in Roman Empire days

Suetonius was a Roman historian writing up to about the year 20 of the Christian Era, and he wrote about the reign of the emperor Claudius, about 20 years after the crucifixion of Jesus. Among points mentioned by him was that in the time of Claudius there were riots among the Jews living in Rome, at the instigation of one Chrestus. He also refers to some conflict between Jews and Christians living in Rome at that time, but no more is said about Chrestus. Then in Suetonius' book on the Emperor Nero, a little later than Claudius, he wrote that the Christians in Rome were punished by Nero for conspiracy and incendiarism inspired by a 'new and evil-doing superstition'.[172] So we seem to learn tantalisingly little about Jesus from Suetonius.

---

172. Suetonius *Nero* 16.2

Rather more comes from another Roman historian, Tacitus, who also lived and wrote about eighty years after Jesus' crucifixion. He wrote that Christians derived their name from 'Christ, who was executed at the hands of the procurator Pontius Pilate in the reign of Tiberius'.[173] Tacitus also wrote a phrase about those who were 'hated by the human race', though apparently referring there to the Jews in general. Clearly, Tacitus' statement about Jesus' death is an important piece of evidence on the historicity of the figure of Jesus.

A third historian of that age from outside the Christian Church is Josephus, who became the Roman governor of the region of Galilee thirty years after the crucifixion. He was a Jew and a Jewish historian who had previously been a leader in the Jewish resistance movement against Rome in Palestine, but was captured and later became a Roman citizen. He gives us important evidence in such sentences about Jesus as that 'Pilate condemned him to the cross' and that in his life and death 'he won over many Jews'.[174] It has to be added that in modern times it is widely considered that the whole of the Josephus material about Christ and the Christian community can hardly be regarded as authentic and trustworthy (probably having been edited at some stage by a Christian hand).

For Josephus sometimes sounds like a convinced Christian which he was not: his original material may have been edited. However, Josephus does corroborate key points in the Christian story e.g. that point emphasised by Tacitus about the fact of the crucifixion. Josephus also mentions Jesus' 'surprising deeds' and his 'teaching', and so on.

The interpreting of the statements of the above historians is obviously not entirely a straightforward matter, in common with

---

173. Tacitus in his *Histories*. 5.5.1.

174. Josephus *Antiquities*. xviii, 63.

the interpreting of any material from centuries long past. But there is witness, too, in those historians' books.

The questioning of the Gospels' reliability

Even if the historical existence of a man called Jesus of Nazareth is hard to refute, charges continue to be made that the account in the Gospels is unreliable and romanticised. The original figure perhaps, some say, has been more than ordinarily touched up, or, more than that, has been blown up into a profile of Jesus that has been developed and embroidered by the fantasising of devoted followers.

The whole subject of current Christian conclusions in general on the reliability of the Gospel accounts themselves is not of course unconnected with more general questionings and difficulties expressed in our age both within the Christian Church and by those having no particular church commitment or no particular Christian commitment. Those questionings cover general matters of Christian belief, whether matters based on particular recorded sayings of Jesus or wider topics of belief.

In 1988 John Bowden, an Anglican priest and noted writer, publisher and translator of religious books, wrote a book called *Jesus: The Unanswered Questions.* [175] In it he picked out the poet Stevie Smith as someone who had articulated strikingly some widespread modern questions. He quoted her poem 'Was He Married?':[176]

> 'Was he married, did he try
> To support as he grew less fond of them
> Wife and family?

---

175. SCM Press

176. (2) *Stevie Smith The Collected Poems.* Allen Lane, The Penguin Press and New Directions, New York. 1975 p.389

Did he feel pointless, feeble and distrait,
Unwanted by everyone and in the way?
Did he love people very much
Yet find them die one day?
Did he ask how long it would go on,
Wonder if death could be counted on for an end?
Did he never feel strong
Pain for being in the wrong?
He knew then that power corrupts but some must
govern?
Did he lack friends? Worse,
Think it was his fault, not theirs?'

John Bowden called this her 'heartfelt puzzlement', and added a couplet from another poem of hers:

'Oh Christianity, Christianity,
why do you not answer our difficulties?'[177]

Bowden, in his book as a whole, tackles among other things questionings of many sorts related to the above poems. Some of them he calls 'problems – which go with the claim that Jesus is the supreme representative of human kind', or problems over 'the view expressed in such terms as "whatever you may be suffering, Jesus suffered too, because he took the whole of humanity upon himself."' Questioning is also and similarly levelled at 'the common tendency to "modernize" Jesus, to treat him as though he belonged to our age. How can a man from first century Palestine possibly speak to our age and at the same time remain in his own, as he must, if we are to begin to understand him as a historical figure?' The book's questions, he makes clear, 'are all my questions, and those of a large number of people with whom I have talked over the years.'[178]

---

177. *Stevie Smith. The Collected Poems*. p.416

178. John Bowden. *Jesus: The Unanswered Questions*. SCM 1988. pp.10, 11, xiii

Among biblical scholars and biblical historians, naturally, some assessments of the reliability of the Gospels' contents have been very radical or negative. Not that the modern scene has been all negative. The researchers have come up with a diversity of pictures of Jesus, some of the researchers certainly seeing their own particular suggested picture of Jesus as complementary to and mingled with other scholars' particular suggestions, and not seeing them in an exclusive way but as one strong colour in a spectrum. One list of such suggestions and understandings of Jesus could be as follows:

> Jesus the foreteller of an apocalyptic future,
> leading to the 'fullness of the times'; and a
> restored Jewish Kingdom;

> Jesus the Jewish messianic figure, and the
> presenter and fulfiller of what Jewish national
> symbols (temple, torah-law) stood for;

> Jesus the compassionate and personal counsellor,
> sage, or healer;

> Jesus the activist for social change in a society
> where much poverty existed.

> The list of course could be extended.

But the event called 'The Jesus Seminar' in 1993 in the United States showed the existence of some very radical scrutiny of what was described as the 1500 sayings of Jesus recorded in the Gospels. Its findings had an extremely negative ring to them. This was a seminar under the auspices of the Society of Biblical Literature in America and the American Academy of Religion. It consisted almost exclusively of North American scholars, and was described by some as founded and dominated by a few of the more radical 'Jesus scholars' in the United States. It declared its topic as the sayings of Jesus, and on 'What did Jesus really say?', so it may be said to have had a declared and confined focus on the 'sayings' aspect of Jesus' significance.

The criterion by which the seminar judged whether a saying, and neighbouring words, was authentically a saying owing its origin to Jesus was this. Only a saying that would not have been invented by the early Church because the saying went against an early Church belief, or a saying that could not have derived from contemporary Judaism, could be counted authentic. Sayings that were not counted as authentic would have been what either a Gospel-writer had written or received from his sources or a later editor had been responsible for putting in. Non-authentic Gospel-sayings of Jesus were graded as just paraphrases of what Jesus said or words said in the spirit of Jesus but not from him, and very many verses were listed, including almost all of the Gospel of John, as not able to be accepted as having a Jesus-link. The seminar wanted an additional Gospel to be accepted, alongside the four Gospels: that was the Gospel of Thomas, first excavated (by accident) at Nag Hammadi in Egypt in 1945, which has sayings parallel to those in Matthew and Luke but which also is written from the sort of humanist approach that was non-supernaturalist and presented Jesus as mainly one who propagated a Gospel of self-knowledge. Although the Gospel of Thomas has proved attractive to some in an age of post-modernism, researchers may probably be described as having mostly found the Gospel as likely to have come from a very late date. Those sayings of Jesus in the four Gospels counted as authentic by the seminar (and its system of majority voting), together with verses immediately neighbouring them, and linked to the sayings' message were listed at the time by one British biblical scholar as amounting to 41 verses only. They include 'Render to Caesar the things that are Caesar's...', 'Blessed are the poor...', and 'Our Father...'.[179] The significance of the seminar is not only seen of course in the fact that 7000

---

179. Meg Davies, reviewing *The Five Gospels, the Search for the Authentic Words of Jesus*. Seminar Report. Macmillan New York. 1993; a review in *The Expository Times*.

scholars attended: it showed trends of thinking in one part of the world of biblical scholarship.

A founder and leader of 'The Jesus Seminar' enterprise has been John Crossan, a long-term noted Catholic scholar and now Emeritus Professor in Chicago, a biblical historian and authority on Palestinian archaeology. In summarizing the Seminar development as a whole and emphasising negative aspects, it may be no bad thing to personalise matters slightly by mentioning his as one leading personality in the Seminar. In a later part of his book The Historical Jesus,[180] he has a section called 'Brokerless Kingdom', or egalitarian Kingdom, where human beings are invited to come in under the kingship of God, without need of mediators, and in this section Crossan lays great stress on the importance of Luke 7. 28 and its final clause: '...among all who have been born no-one has been greater than John; yet the least in the kingdom of God is greater than he is' (REB). The verse contrasts John the Baptist's important movement; and then, Jesus' supremely important movement. Crossan sets Jesus historically particularly in the context of Herod Antipas' puppet-kingdom or client-kingdom of Roman rule, and focuses on the significance of the two Messianic movements within his territory, in the early decades of the 1st century; that is, John the Baptist's apocalyptic call to repentance before a rapidly approaching Day of Judgement and Jesus' call to a Kingdom movement. And Crossan concludes that though Jesus might be seen as in the apocalyptic-call sense, yet, even deeper, he was basically to be seen as an ethical, practical guide for present-day life in an egalitarian, sharing community. So in Luke 7.28, in Jesus' recorded words, John the Baptist is to be honoured beyond measure, yet it is the Kingdom-future that

---

180. July 1994. Details in this paragraph above also include some points from an article in the *Church Times* by Angela Tilby in December 1993.

is to be final in God's purposes. In general, Crossan is far from being confident about the reliability of the Gospel accounts (and E.P. Sanders, in the United States, another noted biblical scholar, could be said to be confident). Yet along with negative assessments of the Jesus Seminar, one should of course not fail to point out how Crossan takes Luke 7.28 as an anchor-verse, and how basic that is, in his writing of the book mentioned.

However, before leaving mention of Crossan, one cannot leave out his views on accounts in the New Testament of developments in the early Christian movement (what Crossan prefers to call 'Christian Judaism') and the Jerusalem church beginnings. These views are highly controversial. Crossan believes that in its picture of Jesus, the early church should have stuck to that of the original Jerusalem Christians – i.e. the Jewish-peasant-Jesus, in Crossan's terms – and believes that the 'so-called' development of that, when Paul and the Church in Antioch were placed in a situation with Gentile-Christian members and not only Jewish-Christian members, was a distortion by Paul. In other words, he believed that most of our New Testament material, deriving from Paul's Letters and from Paul's time, distorts the authentic Jerusalem picture of Jesus by bringing in theological ideas formed in Greek ways and Hellenistic terms and not in the Hebrew-based original terms. This has been Crossan at his most radical.

Responses to the questionings

For a short response to the Jesus Seminar's collective report, one can look at Meg Davies' review, written six months later, that rather bluntly gathered up what seems to have been the very heavy negative criticism with which biblical scholars in Britain at that time reacted to the seminar. The review ends with the sentence: 'This seminar's Jesus can be safely ignored.'[181] One main reason

---

181. Meg Davies in *The Expository Times*, July 1994

for this rejection was said to be the lack in the seminar, judging by its report, of any thorough textual work on the Gospel material, to give foundation to the seminar's negative conclusions. The reviewer also criticised the seminar's concentration only on the sayings of Jesus, stripped of their settings in main Gospel passages, and presented without any discussion of nuances or probabilities and the absence of discussion about the criteria on which sometimes crucial conclusions were reached. The latter topic was still being discussed nearly ten years later in British biblical reviews. [182] Noting the seminar's brief reference to criteria used, and to the exclusion of anything that might have originated with the early Church or been derived from contemporary Judaism, it was argued by one reviewer that Jesus 'may have taught in ways that were continuous with Jewish or later Christian teaching'; and that a single criterion could not help one to discover about that. It was also said that what is 'unique' to Jesus (the seminar's focus) 'may not also be what is most characteristic of him.' On more general matters concerning the Gospels' reliability in recording what Jesus said and did, in the years after the seminar, books have come from biblical scholars stating that there has been a shift in Jesus research from severe scepticism to cautious confidence. [183] In relation to Crossan's assertion that Paul distorted the original Jerusalem church belief, it is interesting that the modern study of Palestinian Judaism has been shown to help understandings on early Church developments. While it is shown that from the second century of the Christian era Judaism did make itself free from intermingling with Hellenistic and Greek thinking and contribution, yet before that (and so in the first century, the century

---

182. John Barton in *The Church Times* of February 2003, reviewing Gerd Theissen and Dagmar Winter's *The Quest for the Plausible Jesus*.

183. Michael McGlymond *Familiar Stranger: an Introduction to Jesus of Nazareth*. Eerdmans. 2004.

of the Christian Church's development, where the roots of later Christian doctrinal development are to be found), first century Jewish belief would have some intermingling with Christian developments. As mentioned in a previous chapter Judaism had mingled with Hellenistic culture for some centuries before Jesus' birth. So some of Jesus' most Jewish sayings and teaching would never at that time be completely walled off from some Hellenistic thinking. [184]

Objections and questionings raised in what was touched on in earlier paragraphs above about John Bowden's book are of course related to the spirit of the Jesus Seminar. But the questions Bowden raised are clearly of a more general nature about Christian belief, and responses to them from theologians and biblical scholars take up issues of a more general nature raised, such as what sort of documents the Gospels are. A review of Bowden's book at the time by a biblical scholar, David Edwards, values the fact that Bowden fully admits that a believer in God must be willing 'to live with questions', but finds Bowden's attitude on the historical reliability of the Gospels' accounts of Jesus to be frequently 'in the end we cannot really know' and no more. Edwards considers that the New Testament evidence is not really assessed by Bowden with sufficient scholarly balance: also that Paul's Letters are said by Bowden to show a striking absence of material relating to the earthly life of Jesus, whereas in fact, and most importantly, Paul's Letters and prayers 'give quite a strong impression of the character of Jesus'. Edwards' main comment may be found in the following paragraph: 'The Bible does not contain a biography of Jesus or a legislative code to control ethics. But it does witness to a historical Jesus of more substance than is allowed by Dr Bowden or by the scholars whom he cites. And this is the Lord with whom all Christians must, so to speak, wrestle.

---

184. See Rupert Shortt in a review article in *The Church Times* in February 2003, entitled 'A Question of Faith.'

[185] The word 'witness' stands out from that paragraph, and once again Martin Buber's dictum that faith does not provide proofs, but does provide witnesses, may be found relevant.

Particularly useful on the Gospels in general have been recent books written in dialogue form such as the book The Meaning of Jesus: Two Visions by Marcus Borg and N.T. Wright (Bishop Tom Wright). [186] Written as it is by two people who are biblical scholars or biblical historians or both, and who are able to share both their convictions and their thorough textual scrutinies in interpreting the Gospels' message. It seems to be written on the good principle of 'two eyes are better than one', transcending our tendency to concentrate only on an adversarial presentation. Many may find the section on the Resurrection of Jesus particularly interesting. Wright as a historian concentrates particularly on Jesus as a first century prophet who announced God's Kingdom, and as 'Israel's Messiah'; and says that Jesus believed himself to be Israel's Messiah, with the Jewish prophecies of old fulfilled in his life. And Wright adds that what is written in Paul's writings and in the Gospels backs up belief in a resurrection that happened historically: and also adds, importantly, that New Testament language about a new creation brings out for us most profoundly the significance of the Resurrection. Borg, too, finds Easter 'utterly central to Christianity'; and asserts that, for him, 'the historical ground of Easter' is to be found in the fact that the followers of Jesus 'both then and now, continued to experience Jesus as a living reality after his death'. But Borg prefers the phrase for Jesus 'Jewish mystic and the Christian Messiah.' He questions whether the narratives in the Gospels about the Crucifixion and Resurrection tell us of events that all historically happened, seeing

---

185. Review of John Bowden's book, in *The Church Times*, June 1988.

186. SPCK/Harper Collins 1999. *The Expository Times* for Dec. 1999 gave a full review-article by C.S. Rodd on the book.

them frequently as Old Testament prophecies the fulfilment of which is put in the Gospels in historical terms, without them having been fulfilled in that way. But Borg emphasises that he agrees with Wright in affirming the Resurrection of Jesus.

Perhaps, however, one of the most critical points to be noted among what many theologians and biblical scholars are currently writing about or talking about is the Gospels' material, and Christian teaching, about the providence of God. Luke Chapter 12 verses 22-34 is one clear block of teaching on this ('do not set your minds on what you are to eat and drink; do not be anxious; your Father knows that you need these things… Have no fear, little flock, for your Father has chosen to give you the Kingdom'). Teaching on this today by Christian thinkers is perhaps the great challenge facing the world of theology, according to many comments. And Professor Keith Ward urges us, in the pages of a newspaper, to face the following question: 'What is the relevance of Jesus' sayings and the significance of Jesus for today, in a world seen by many as ruled by chance, violence and triviality, with their view reinforced for all ages by television and electronics?' This is not a new question of course. It leads into the sort of things that Paul of Tarsus in the New Testament was writing about in a letter to church congregations in Corinth, at a difficult time for him (a passage of treasures of pastoral encouragement, all about providence): 'we are hard pressed, but never cornered; bewildered, but never at our wits' end; hunted, but never abandoned to our fate…'. [187]

In the twentieth century they were the sort of things that Henri Nouwen in his writings and personal encounters was passing on to people; things to do with people's questionings. As someone wrote after his death: 'by sharing his own struggles he mentored us all, helping us to pray while not knowing how to

---

187. *2 Corinthians* 4.8-9a (REB)

pray, to rest while feeling restless, … to be surrounded by a cloud of light while still in darkness, and to love while still in doubt.'[188] Clearly, both the scriptural and the modern quotation there are describing God's providence at work, and his interweaving of grace with human effort. But, through a known modern question mentioned already, Keith Ward reminds us that it is a question for us now to face who do not live in Corinth and who may not have met the particular challenge mentioned by Keith Ward. (Nouwen is touched on again a little later in these pages.)

Questioning the Gospels' emphasis on comfort

Most of us will be familiar with the view, or will know those who hold the view, that, for themselves, they prefer to stick to a morality and a spirituality that does not go on to focus on trust in a religious figure who seems above all to be spoken of as promising comfort.

I was encouraged to find recently, in the newspaper that I read, a discussion of this issue between someone who is education officer for the British Humanist Association, Marilyn Mason, and someone who is the Canon Theologian of Manchester Cathedral, Andrew Shanks.[189]

The discussion does not mention the name of Jesus directly, though there is one reference to 'faith in God incarnate'. But since 'Christians' and 'The Church' are referred to, the figure of Jesus and his constant bringing, according to the Gospels, of the encouragement of the words 'Fear not' to individuals whom he encountered, together with the words 'anyone who comes to me I will never turn away', [190] will never be far away from any

---

188. Ronald Rolheiser in *The Holy Longing*, Doubleday, New York 1999

189. An article entitled 'Never on Sunday' in *The Guardian*. October 2004

190. *Mark* 14, 27, *John* 6, 37 (REB)

general discussion of this nature, about religion and comfort, and the pastoral caring for people with terminal illness or despair and anxiety.

Marilyn Mason states her case clearly: 'I know there are people who find support and comfort in religion, but I don't, and I doubt whether society has much need of it either.' Her points are put in a very reasoned way. That she certainly believes in commitment to moral values and in the need for individuals and societies to have hopes and values. That she does not find it difficult to live with a few 'don't knows'. That being committed to truth and moral values causes her misery and disquiet in the face of suffering and tragedy. But, she says, on issues where we encounter 'don't knows', she does not find religious answers helpful or convincing. As for hopes and values, for many people these may not be religious, since 'there is no going back to the piety and conformity of the past.' She admits that people are committed to religion for other reasons than comfort and the need of supernatural support, but these latter are the things 'that will get people into churches.'

As for herself, she says, in spite of the difficulties of commitment to moral values, the basic focus must be on 'goodness and moderation', even though these may not catch the media headlines.

Andrew Shanks is also reasoned in his remarks. He says that he does not want to suggest that purely secular affirmations are any less sincere than religious ones. And stresses that his 'faith in' humanity has never been in doubt, though 'as a Christian priest I identify it with faith in God incarnate.' His main contention, as I understood it, was that he didn't go to church for comfort, or to escape life's stresses and propaganda. 'I don't want,' he says, 'to escape the prevailing propaganda culture – I want to resist it.' And the same goes for 'the cult of mammon' which 'thrives on the ever-increasing… individualism of our society.' This is linked to his other main point; that if we are no longer to think that social cement depends so much on religion, that means 'that now, as never before, religion is set free to do its real job; of vindicating truthfulness precisely, as an infinite demand': or again, 'I just want to help keep alive a certain quite seriously endangered intensity of resistant hope.' 'Much more could be said, of course, on secular humanism and religious humanism, and on humanism and faith; and I can never forget a sentence that Bertrand Russell wrote:- "My intellect goes with the humanists, though my emotions violently rebel." [191] But the emphasis on "resistant hope", central above, is a powerful focus.' So, interestingly, instead, in his reply of adopting the role of defender of Christianity as 'comforting', Andrew Shanks finds it more relevant in response to put his emphasis on saying in effect 'since society is seen as not needing comfort from religion all that much, that leaves many of us free to try and do, as Christians, some "resisting", on behalf of truth and hope, of those things in our culture and society that are wrong.'

I find all of that dialogue helpful, particularly in stimulating thoughts of the importance both of comfort and of challenge in the Christian message as found in the Gospels. One hears echoes of the theme of what has been called 'holy restlessness' in some of the Wild Goose songs of John Bell and the Iona Community: such as the opening and closing lines of 'Heaven shall not wait' – 'Heaven shall not wait/For the poor to lose their patience/;... Jesus is Lord/ In our present imperfection/; his power and love are for now and then for evermore.' [192]

---

191. Bertrand Russell in 'a Free Man's Worship', in his *Mysticism and Logic*. Allen and Unwin. 1976.

192. *Wild Goose Songs* Vol. 1. John Bell and Graham Maule. Wild Goose Publications 1987. See also *Wrestling and Resting (Exploring Stories of Spirituality from Britain and Ireland)*. Churches Together in Britain and Ireland, 1999.

After describing the above dialogue, however, I cannot help adding yet another comment: that is of how integral to the picture of Jesus given in the Gospels the emphasis on compassion and comfort is. As already mentioned, the original Greek word in Mark Chapter 8, verse 2 lying behind the traditional English translation of what Jesus said to his disciples, 'I have compassion on the multitude', is a verb derived from the Greek word for human guts or entrails which were seen as the seat of the emotions in a way corresponding to modern usage of 'heart' to describe that. So that modern translations which give the phrase as something like 'My heart goes out to these people' (as the Revised English Bible) rightly try to bring out the full force of the phrase.

Questions about what Jesus said, or the rest of the *New Testament*, on natural disasters

The journalist and column-writer Martin Kettle wrote immediately after the horrific Indonesian earthquake and disaster at the end of 2004: 'How can religious people explain something like this?'; saying that the event poses no problem for the scientific belief system which sees it as 'a mindless natural event', which destroyed Muslim and Hindu alike.[193] 'What comfort does a Christian give in this particular situation, and what explanation?' he asked. And others ask if there is anything in the Gospels about Jesus speaking of natural disasters, or in other New Testament writings, interpreting the message of Jesus as they do. On this last point, we do find one occasion in the Gospels when Jesus is asked about 'the eighteen people who were killed when the tower fell on them at Siloam'.[194] This would probably have been one of the towers that guarded the aqueduct bringing water to the pool of Siloam

---

193. *The Guardian*. 28.12.04

194. *Luke* 13.4-5 (REB)

in the area above the Kidron Valley on the edge of Jerusalem. It seems that it was believed by many people that the people killed were being punished for some sins of theirs, and it is this that is the point of Jesus' reply about the event; he says that their death was not a punishment for any sins of theirs, though adding some words about the urgency of repentance in general. Further details for the interpretation of the passage are not easy to arrive at; the destruction of the tower may have been connected with the activities of Jewish Zealots – that is activists – who had attacked Pilate's aqueduct, which was constructed out of Jerusalem Temple funds. Much insurgency was evidently going on at the time against the authorities.

It is to Paul's Letters, and the Letter to Christians in Rome, that one has to go to find New Testament verses that touch on the whole huge issue that Martin Kettle raised.

In 22 verses, from Romans ch.8 verses 18-39, Paul gives first a highly realistic account of the present state of the universe: 'the whole created universe in all its parts groans as if in the pangs of childbirth'; and though 'we do not even know how we ought to pray, but through our inarticulate groans the Spirit himself is pleading for us...' – verses 22 and 26. And this leads on towards his conviction that, in spite of the depth of tragic pain in the created world, 'nothing in all creation... can separate us from the love of God in Christ Jesus our Lord', 'nothing in death or life,... or in the forces of the universe, in heights or depths...' – verses 38 and 39.

Responding to Martin Kettle's article in the same newspaper, we were fortunate to get a succinct and immediate short letter from Bishop John Saxbee, Bishop of Lincoln. He was not in favour of religious attempts to 'explain' the tsunami disaster. 'Belief in God enables us to respond to disasters such as this, but not to trump scientific explanations with moral ones. People of faith look to a horizon beyond the limitations of scientific enquiry and secular morality. It is a horizon at the limits of time and space beyond which eternity provides a perspective which might yet make sense of what science can only explain.' That highlighting of perspective and perspectives seems to point us usefully towards some good 'alternative commentary' on the spirituality of Jesus' message as found in the Gospels: commentary, that is, from artists, musicians, poets, and others, who are often purveyors of 'wide-angle' perspectives, and who can communicate to us truths of human experience, and truths and glimpses of dimensions of reality, which verbal communication can find difficult to express.

The discussion about the interpretation of the Bible and of Biblical passages about same-gender sex and homosexuality

To attempt a fairly brief taking up here of so hugely wide a topic may not be easy, but it cannot be omitted, and we can be thankful that in recent decades adequate attention is being given to what has previously been a sadly neglected subject. Undoubtedly it is inevitable that a subject concerning the understanding of meanings in biblical passages has to give attention to many diverse and complex factors, e.g. 'study' factors about the original content of a passage and the original context and situation in which it was probably written; 'social and economic' factors, where readers of a passage may be living in situations where many are being oppressed or victimised, or where there is prosperity and wealth but no just distribution of it; and 'cultural' factors of different global and international understandings of biblical meanings, and related to different gifts and insights into meanings and relevance. (Chapter 10 follows up the latter point.)

However, in spite of the complexity, there is at least an opportunity now for the topic of biblical interpretation to get attention. The Lambeth Conference in 1998 had a preparatory edition and a subsequent edition of a volume on the whole subject, and on the clash of convictions in the Anglican Communion on it. It was entitled The Way Forward? [195]

It cannot be said to be 'an easy read' throughout, as it needed to cater for both academic and non-academic readers. But its many contributed chapters can be said to represent fairly the many sides in the debate, coming variously as they do from the viewpoint of two conservative-evangelical theological colleges, Jeffrey John (now a Cathedral Dean), Tom Brown, a consultant psychiatrist, Elizabeth Stuart, a Professor of Theology, Gerald Bray, Simon Vibert a vicar in London, and many others. [196] Much the longest chapter comes from Anthony Thiselton.[197] In his thorough study of biblical interpretation, and as emeritus professor of Christian Theology in Nottingham University, he provides a close study of the main biblical passages quoted on the topic, and also a wide survey of traditional interpretations and those which are sometimes described as 'revisionist'.

Again, the fairness and balance is maintained in the discussion of complex textual and linguistic points. The complexity will be obvious to anyone reading two modern translations of *1 Corinthians* Chapter 6, verse 9. The Revised English Bible has, for Paul's words to Christians in Corinth, 'make no mistake: no adulterer or sexual pervert... will possess the Kingdom of God,' ('sexual pervert' covering two distinct words in the original Greek). The New Revised Standard version has, not 'no adulterer or sexual pervert,' but 'no adulterers, male prostitutes, sodomites...'

---

195. Ed. Timothy Bradshaw, SCM Press. 1997 and 2003 editions

196. See, for example, Jeffrey John *Permanent, Faithful, Stable (a Study of Same-Sex Relationships)* DLT 2000; Elizabeth Stuart *Just Good Friends: Towards a Lesbian and Gay Theology of Relationships* Mowbray 1995: Dave Leal *Debating Homosexuality* Grove Books, 2001.

197. AC Thiselton. *New Horizons in Hermeneutics*. Paternoster. 1995.

In other words those are two possible ways of spelling out the meanings: and they reflect ongoing debates continuing among interpreters. In instances over which there is a clear difference of interpretation between traditional and some gay understandings, Anthony Thiselton is found strongly upholding the traditionalists and describing that gay view as untenable. But on the other hand in his theory of interpretation developed over many years (as seen in his use of the word 'horizons' in the titles of his books) he writes in *The Way Forward?*: 'a valid hermeneutical approach should take more account than we have so far achieved of the horizons of experience today which all sides bring to the text. Clinical accounts of homosexual orientations remain relevant; but we need to note that no clear consensus about these issues yet exists among professional researchers.'[198]

The editor of the book just quoted, Timothy Bradshaw, a theologian on the staff of Regent's Park College in Oxford University, displays the same balance and fairness of presentation. Though far from dismissing the traditionalist approach, he suggests that, with discernment, we may all well come to see something 'prophetic' in the gay community's reminder to others that there are limitations in any view of the communal life of the Church that focuses only on the heterosexual family type of unit. Bradshaw writes that what we may need to be discerning is 'that single people also need community, warmth, depth of honesty and support in their relationships in the body of Christ...', and adds: 'Such a challenge carries with it struggle for all the Church, a radical review of openness and honesty and mutual care'.[199]

On the question of same-gender sex, the passage in *Paul's Letter to the Romans* Chapter 1, verses 26 and 27, seems to have an explicitness that may be held to end the whole discussion

---

198. *The Way Forward?* p.184
199. *The Way Forward?* p.204

immediately and to discount any talk of two sides talking to each other. They can seem to apply directly and decisively to present discussions, when they say that 'God has given up' humanity, as a retribution for sin, to practices in which 'women have exchanged natural intercourse for unnatural' and that 'men too, giving up natural relations with women, burn with lust for one another', and that 'males behave indecently with males'. (REB) However, this is where one of the factors in biblical interpretation, mentioned earlier, needs to be given attention; viz the 'study' factor concerning a passage's context, and also the situation in surrounding verses, which may be of help in our understanding of the writer's meaning. We may find ourselves finally concluding that the context does not alter our initial view that the two verses, verses 26 and 27, are themselves decisive in ending discussions; but may well see it a duty to be open, and to listen to 'the other side'.

There are biblical commentators who give special and primary importance to certain wider issues than only same-sex gender, sex issues which a study of *Romans* Chapter 1 and the beginning of Chapter 2, as the context of 1.26, 27, reveal.[200] In Chapter 1. 14 and 15 Paul writes 'I have an obligation to Greek and non-Greek, to learned and simple... and to you in Rome as well.'

He was writing, in a situation common also in many areas where Christianity was taking root, about the mixed background in Christian congregations and communities where there were both converts with a background of Jewish culture and converts with a background of Gentile and Greek culture. In this line of interpretation, the teaching of Chapter 1 is focussed on how all humanity has been 'given over by God' to idolatry, in that 'knowing God, they refused to honour' and reverence 'him as God, or to

---

200. William Countryman *Interpreting the Truth* Continuum. Trinity Press International 2003. pp. 172, 173

render him thanks', in spite of the fact that 'God's... everlasting power and deity have been visible to the eye of reason, in the things he has made.'[201] In Chapter 1 Paul is seen to be issuing a stern warning to converts from Greek and Gentile culture about the dangers of getting involved in same-sex relationships which they would know were very common in their culture. At the same time, from the beginning of Chapter 2 Paul can be seen issuing a stern warning to Christians of Jewish background-culture about the danger of their taking up an attitude of superiority as compared with Gentile Christians, for all humanity has been 'given over' to the sin of idolatry and the refusal of reverence. The opening words of Chapter 2 underline the challenge that is a challenge to the Jews and to others, 'You have no defence..., whoever you may be, when you sit in judgement... on the guilty, while committing the same crimes yourself.'[202] (It is of interest to note that Anthony Thiselton, in *The Way Forward?* mentions the words just quoted as 'legitimately pressed' by writers and commentators who follow newer and non-traditional ways of biblical interpretation, including those who see Paul's condemnation of same-sex relationships as applying only to 'call-boys' and pederasts and those who use such people.[203] So the beginning of the *Letter to the Romans* becomes a complex study of the importance (or otherwise) of contexts.

What are we to make of the above complexities of reasoning? Nothing, I think, except that sorting out the implications of faith sometimes makes us do some hard thinking, including thinking concerning biblical interpretation. The latter can often be simple: note the splendid words written in the *Letter to the Colossians*: 'Pray that I may make the secret plain', *Colossians.* 4. 2 (REB).

---

201. *Romans* 1. 20, 21 (REB)
202. *Romans* 2. 1-3 (REB)
203. *The Way Forward?* p.175

Sometimes not simple. It should never be simplistic. It is often claimed that we just need to follow literally what the Bible says. But the phrase 'a literal interpretation' obviously needs careful use, and not only concerning homosexuality. A literal reading of *1 Samuel* 1.2 looks clear enough at first sight: 'Elkanah' (father of the prophet Samuel) 'had two wives,' and Samuel was born to Hannah, one of them. Abraham and Jacob also had more than one wife, the situation in all these instances containing a childless first wife, resulting in the marrying of a 'maid'; or 'slave', and a child born there being considered the heir of the legal first wife. A literal reading of these biblical passages suggests that the pattern of the fulfilling of God-given sexual desire is sometimes via polygamy, and that polygamy was acceptable at that time, at least for the providing of an heir. What is not easy is the question whether or not, by later progressive revelation, God's will was shown to be against polygamy.

That is clearly a question for modern times as well as one concerning ancient times, since it leads on to the question of how far apparently clear 'literal' understandings of biblical passages concerning sexuality (whether polygamy or homosexuality) really are so straightforward, or perhaps, rather, need careful and hard work done on a variety of factors involved.

There seems currently to be a good element of simplicity in the way in which many interpreters are picking on just two main types of factor as vital for understanding meanings in this area of interpretation. The first types may be called 'tradition-based factors', which take seriously the study of the data which we have from the past, in the form of the scriptural texts and versions. The duty to keep our eyes open and our attention given, in continuing to give importance to them, however much the need to be aware of culture-gaps between the ancient centuries and modern centuries demanding changes of idiom and expression in translation, presses upon us (not simplified by the fact that in some respects human nature does not alter all that much as between then and now).

The second types of factor that obviously emerged in the twentieth century can loosely be called 'humanising factors'. Thiselton gives us the imaginative phrase 'the horizon of human experience' as one of the horizons on which to keep our eyes fixed, since people's very different human experiences – whether the experiences of oppressed human beings across the world, or the personal experiences of human beings belonging to different cultures, or any human experience whatever of disability or alienation – have been making their contributions increasingly to the business of biblical interpretation and the understanding of meanings. Experiences of being exiled in modern centuries have fed in notably into the study of, say, the *Book of Exodus* or the *Old Testament* prophetic writings arising out of the Jews' Babylonian exile years, touched on earlier. Technically some of 'the humanising factors' have been known as the importance of 'reader-response' ways of interpretation. And Thiselton's phrase about horizons is a good passing on to English readers of a development of the thinking of the philosopher Hans-Georg Gadamer. The 'horizons' phrase, however, and talk of horizons of meaning, can, in ways not too complex, make real for us the respective importance of tradition-based factors in interpretation, humanising factors, and transcendent factors: including, as they do, both what is past, what is present, and what is future, just as a landscape-painter may have his or her foregrounds from the present-day near at hand, and maybe some ancient historic buildings taking us far back in time, and then some distant scenes as the painter looks ahead into the future.

Can we see any resolution, then, between what some have phrased as 'the claims of truth as evidenced by Paul's blunt statement in *Romans* Chapter 1' and 'the claims of love as evidenced by the overall *New Testament* emphasis being loving and charitable'? It may be that the phrase 'two integrities' ties up in a way with Thiselton's 'the two horizons', which he took as the title of an earlier book that he wrote, in 1980. I realise that 'integrities' is a less poetic word than 'horizons'. (I mention 'two integrities' as only a possible way forward on the issue here being examined, since in our own minds we may not at the moment see the term 'an integrity' as applicable to same-sex relationships.) But 'two integrities' can be a good strong phrase, and certainly takes us back to thinking about what I have called the 'twin truths', such as justice and compassion, lying at the heart of some central paradoxical couplets validly used in discussing human life, ultimate reality and the Kingdom of God.

Colin Morris, who was formerly head of religious broadcasting and BBC Controller in Northern Ireland, has recently drawn attention to an interesting difference of conviction which arose between two BBC figures in positions of importance, when the BBC decided to go ahead with showing the programme *Jerry Springer: The Opera*, in spite of receiving 63,000 complaints on the grounds that it was blasphemous and full of swear-words and insulting remarks about Jesus made by characters in the programme.[204] One of the BBC figures was Mark Thompson, the BBC director general, and a practising Christian. He decided to let the programme go out. He said he found nothing blasphemous about it. The second BBC figure was Anthony Pitts, the Radio 3 producer and also a committed Christian, who resigned in protest at this being allowed to happen. He said 'Jesus is my friend.' Colin Morris said in his article that he fully understood both stances. He understood Anthony Pitts' distress and honoured his willingness to pay the price for it. But he also understood Mark Thompson's decision, and commented that 'for the BBC to apply his' (Anthony Pitts') 'valuation of Jesus to its output would turn it

---

204. The Rev. Dr Colin Morris, *Jerry's Last Judgement. The Guardian*. March 2005.

into a confessional Christian station which John Reith refused to countenance long before Britain became a multi-religious society' and at the Corporation's founding.

Colin Morris also added that Springer is a vicious satire on the American way of life with many important theological issues raised. The satire's song where God sings 'It's hard being Me!' '… parodies with deadly accuracy the theological liberal deity who appears to look on in anguished impotence when tsunamis strike…,' and the satire contains strong language and shocking imagery. But, says Morris, in present-day cultures and societies, although some Christians may be offended and the figure of Christ becomes 'fair game for artistic interpretations', the offended Christians 'can't have it both ways by claiming that Jesus was a real man, while expecting society to treat him with kid gloves.' He concludes with these words: 'It would be curious if Christianity, having survived 2000 years of martyrdom and mass persecution, were under threat from a barrage of swear-words.'

Descriptions of situations such as that are strong stuff, but I believe they drive home the point that within Christian 'communions', and among Christian people, both parties in some clashes of conviction between two sides can be said truly to have their own integrity about them. Such an integrity can be part of a twin-truth that is an apparent contradiction, but paradoxically not a real contradiction. And the resolution of that apparent contradiction may be beyond our minds on earth at present to compass. But we stand in hope like people in an antechamber waiting to pass into an inner sanctum and a nearer understanding of the fullness of some mysteries. Some resolutions of course come even quicker.

Jesus' paradoxical phrases: warnings and encouragements

A brief concluding note follows concerning paradoxes and severities in the Gospels.

One cannot omit here a brief further reference to Kierkegaard's thought, already discussed in Chapter 6. He seemed determined to emphasise Jesus' use of paradox.[205] Only so, he was convinced, could be driven home the severity of some of Jesus' teaching and yet also the gentleness of other parts. And only so, with the severity, could the gulf between God's goodness and human depravity be recognised, even if the phrases used by Jesus may seem exaggerated and perhaps be seen just as part of Hebraic idiom. Otherwise, Jesus' opposites of an extreme of generosity and an extreme of prudence would be missed: 'sell everything you have and give to the poor': 'be wary as serpents, and harmless as doves'.[206] But, as noted previously, all this was accompanied in Kierkegaard by a deep piety and held together in prayer.[207]

Personal choice and the old religious narratives

Are the so-called 'grand' religious narratives to be abandoned as guidance in life, in favour of our own personal choice and discernment? Are the narratives in the *Bible* now to be seen, in a post-modern age, as a thing of the past, and no longer as having prescriptive and definitive value? Undoubtedly the narratives have often been used through the centuries in authoritarian or hierarchical ways that are flawed, and, say, used as unchallengeable

---

205. Lovis Dupré, *Kierkegaard as Theologian*. 1964

206. *Luke* Chapter 18. verse 22: Matthew 10.16

207. Kierkegaard. *Journals* translated and edited. A Dru. Oxford University Press.1938. p.73, and Bishop Kenneth Cragg *Alive to God*. OUP 1970 p.167.

authority to keep oppressed minorities or groups in society in subjection. But does that mean that the narratives now have no authority? And what about the alternative authority, 'choice', on which all the emphasis now tends to be put? While the emphasis on 'choice' by individuals or modern societies is obviously made in the name of freedom and of modern adulthood, and while 'choice' is an important element in arriving at decisions, is it to be the only element?

Currently, the focus on 'choice' is seen by a number of theologians as having considerable dangers, and likely to lead to considerable chaos. For example, Professor Timothy Gorringe writes in a book-review that such an exaggerated focus can only lead to a wilderness of endless individual, unilateral choices: 'an endless pluralism, a market-stall of ethical views and life philosophies.'[208]

As discussion continues on this topic, it is probably useful to consider various distinctions between the word 'narrative' and the word 'story'. A 'narrative' can get associated, in the modern multi-media world, with something presented by a skilful narrator pressing his own slant on the subject. Whereas in biblical narratives it is the human 'story' and experience in what is being related that is arguably of greatest significance. 'Story' is the fruit of human experience, and brings stories alive for us, someone or some group being human and 'becoming human'. Those last aspects of the story or narrative certainly have authority in the present-day.

---

208. A book-review in *The Expository Times*, October 2005.

9

ARTISTIC AND OTHER APPROACHES TO BIBLICAL MEANING

Two centuries ago the landscape painter J.M.W. Turner was professor of perspective at the Royal Academy in London. (His father was a barber in Covent Garden.) He wrote, 'without the aid of perspective, art totters on its foundations'; and taking architecture as an example in art, said that only perspective 'could bring out the extent, height, dignity and towering majesty of architecture.' Modern writers seem to tend to say that although some of Turner's earlier paintings contained picturesqueness, the overall impression left with the viewer is a mingling in Turner of 'a tragic vision' [209] ('apocalyptic visions of turbulence') and an undoubted presentation of light and sunlight bursting in. His fine watercolour of the town of Luxembourg perched darkly on the winding river gorge is outstandingly dark. On dark blue paper, we see just a crescent moon and a few pale yellow wisps of light. Apparently, the art critic Ruskin admired Turner, and pointed out Turner's similarity to Goethe, who regarded blue-

---

209. The phrase is used by Graham Reynolds in *Turner* Thames and Hudson. 1969 and reprinted 1992. The final chapter is headed 'The Tragic Vision'.

ness as melancholy and yellow-ness as depicting light and sunlight. But, of major importance, we are told we should notice these words of Turner: 'The interest of a landscape consists wholly in its relation either to figures present or to figures past or to human powers conceived,' 'not in rocks and water and sky.' In other words, it was links with humanity in a landscape and in history, and in natural phenomena in their direct relation to humanity, that counted for Turner. In one sentence Reynolds writes of Turner's lifelong preoccupation with the frustration of human plans.[210]

That glimpse of Turner's perspectives in wide-ranging senses seems to be relevant to the importance of perspective as a realm where religious belief can contribute to join scientific and historical contributions on issues of nature, tragedy and creative transcendence.

In the century following, a few interesting similarities can be found between the landscape painter John Piper, who died in 1992, and Turner. The strong light-darkness pattern stands out notably in both. And Piper had the added development of direct church and religious involvement through such things as windows in Coventry Cathedral and the designing of the magnificent new stained glass windows in the war-damaged south aisle of St Margaret's Church, Westminster, adjoining Westminster Abbey. This and other stained glass work linked up artistic perspective with institutional 'Church' expression of religious faith. The St Margaret's windows let in plenty of light, and have an overall uprush of the vertical about them: one window has just a few marked vertical lines of blue and yellow, and is characterised by a delicate but distinctive rock-like, angular, geometrical and wedge shaped design throughout. Over a good many years in the 1940s and 1950s Piper was visiting Snowdonia, living especially in a

---

210. Reynold's *Turner*. p.205.

farmhouse opposite Tryfan and above Llyn Ogwen. Often his paintings there were of the big mountains such as Snowdon or Cader Idris featuring in the distance or the centre, large masses of light to focus dramatically on their great semicircular rings of crater-like, rock ridges in the two mountains just mentioned, and centring in the foreground, again with a mass of light, on some large flat boulder surface; these features were offset by darker surrounds. But one entitled *Ffynnon Llugwy* is of a scene that would have been high up in the mountains above his farmhouse, and that was of almost unrelieved dark crags and cliffs with only a few streaks of light on any side. The light-dark pattern seemed to be a pronounced emphasis in so many of the mountain watercolours. In one of his books, however, he shows how that pattern was supplemented by a more personal perspective.[211] The latter described his emotions up among the rocks on the Glyderau, also above Ogwen. There his perspective seems to have held together, without bitterness, the foreground slabs or rock-boulders and the wider mist covering the mountain all round him. 'The affectionate nature of the mountain... not changed by the acute loneliness and closed-in feeling induced by the mist...' This is followed by fascinating passages (that are hardly able to be trodden down by any phrases about 'pathetic fallacies' from dismissive critics). 'Each rock lying in the grass had a positive personality; for the first time I saw the bones and the structure and the "lie" of the mountains, living with them and climbing them, as I was lying on them in the sun and getting soaked with rain in their cloud-cover and enclosed in their improbable private rock-world in fog... The rocks can only look grey in a leaden light and then do not, commonly. The same kind of rock can look utterly different and changed equally violently in colour according to the light and time of year.'

---

211. Piper. *Piper's Places*.

That seems to see perspective as of real importance and to be of interest for anyone trying to come to conclusions in the face of 'violent' changes of many sorts.

The perspectives of poetry, and the Gospels' perspective of authoritative truth and vulnerability

One way of looking at the poetry of R.S. Thomas is to say that it brings out verbally and poetically what has underlain much of the visually artistic thrust of the artists just looked at. One modern writer on R.S. Thomas has described him as 'the great Wordsworthian poet of our time',[212] and Wordsworth famously wrote in his *Prefaces* that the great thing about poetry is that it is 'truth carried alive into the heart by passion.' A mid-20th century preacher of a university sermon in Oxford followed this with the comment that 'Poetry is the language of religion: it is that heightening of language which enables us to hint at the incommunicable. If men do not understand poetry, how shall they understand religion?'[213]

Reference has already been made briefly at the beginning of this present book to R.S.Thomas as a poet of paradox, and to the figure of Christ in the Gospels as a figure always of surprise and of the unexpected. As mentioned in Chapter 3, this is clearly and characteristically brought out in his poem 'The Bright Field' from the 1970s: a poem which also touches on the perspectives of eternity, and here lines from the poem are printed out, and lines from two of his other poems:

---

212. Walford Davies in *Autobiographies*. Phoenix. 1997
(A translation of R.S. Thomas' NEB and other Welsh writings)

213. William Greer in 1946. He later became Bishop of Manchester

'I have seen the sun break through
to illuminate a small field
for a while, and gone my way
and forgotten it. But that was the pearl
of great price, the one field that had
the treasure in it. I realize now
that I must give all that I have
to possess it. Life is not hurrying

on to a receding future, nor hankering after
an imagined past. It is the turning
aside like Moses to the miracle
of the lit bush, to a brightness
that seemed as transitory as your youth
once, but is the eternity that awaits you.'[214]

In contrast to the light and delight there is the darkness and bleakness of much of his poetry, which provide the short-term, immediate and earthy foreground of his perspective. His autobiographical writings admit that when he looked out across the coastal sea round the Lleyn Peninsula in North Wales he could never forget the hidden cruelty going on underneath the waves, of 'seals and cormorants and mackerel hunting like rapacious wolves.' His austere and sometimes bitter lines about some experiences of times of prayer are well-known: 'it is this great absence/that is like a presence, that compels/one to address it without hope/of a reply.' [215]

But nearer the end of his life, the imagery of nature from both full incoming tides and ebb-tides held together for him his sense of long perspective. He describes himself as 'I who/have been made free/by the tide's pendulum truth/that the heart that is low now will be at the full tomorrow.' [216]

---

214. *Collected Poems 1945-1990*. Dent 1993. Phoenix 2000. p.302

215. *Collected Poems*. 'The Absence.' p.361

216. The poem 'At the End', *No Truce with the Furies* Bloodaxe. 1995. p.42

The poetry of Martyn Crucefix, and the poem 'An English Nazareth',[217] which provides the title of a 2004 collection of his poems, present a different sort of perspective. It is not fed by images from the created world of nature, but from a holding together of two different English pictures and visions of the figure of Jesus the carpenter of Nazareth, visions separated in time by centuries – first, the visions of a devout 11th century rich lady of Walsingham, Lady Richeldis, who, in her contemplation, received instructions to build a replica of Christ's home, and, secondly, the reverent respect that Christ the craftsman and worker attracts from a modern craftsman. The poem appears to give us a holding together of both the Christ of eternity and also the Christ in relation to time and the modern world.

The poems in the collection from which the Nazareth poem is taken all have something to do with the poet's concern over human beings' loss of innocence in childhood, felt with distress growingly as childhood passes to adolescence (echoes of Wordsworth's 'shades of the prison-house begin to close'). The poet feels that this loss of innocence continues as a sense of distress in our world, and sees it standing out clearly from the writings of Graham Greene and the book *The Quiet American*. The saying of Jesus, 'Whoever does not accept the Kingdom of God like a child will never enter it,' [218] seems not far away from what the poet is talking about. In the poem 'An English Nazareth' we get the conviction of a modern man being expressed, that there is something near innocence, simplicity and naivety in the straightforward modern carpenter's focussing on Jesus the fellow-worker. The 11th century lady's honouring of Jesus is 'a witness to the original' and 'her dream has weight', and so have 'we', says the modern poet; though we may not be rich 'we give praise to God

---

217. Enitharmon Press, 2004
218. *Mark*. 10.15 (REB)

for the gift of work; we have our strength'; this, our 'honouring of Jesus', too has weight in all 'its simplicity', it is implied.

But the poem must speak for itself:

'We – who have only our strength to sell
and so little here to be thankful for –
we know well she has never risen
from that embroidered footstool
where she embroiders her mornings.
Yet she has stood in his simple home,
she says, the woodshavings obvious
on the clay floor, the cramp, the cool.
And because she has power over us
to manufacture walls out of English
ground, to her specifications
(though she insists, not hers at all;
she's only a witness to the original),
because of this her dream has weight
Here a slant of evening sun, the saw
still warm in the red-grained wood.
Here, the hammers shout on the nail
each time bursting and then dying off
as she passes a door out of Palestine.'

A few lines more follow on the lady 'tall and swaying/ richly through Christ's small house' before we come to the complementary picture of the modern carpenter's house where the craftsman finds that the presence of Christ the fellow-worker becomes real to him:

'… no matter how vivid her dream,
local men build as we have always built:
English wood upon English earth.
The best we deliver is a mockery,
A cacked version of our own poor homes
(those shambles she's never visited)
yet this is the one she will have us deck
with flowers, have us light, keep warm,

proof from rain, since this is the roof
under which she expects to dwell
long in grace, in that other real place.
While we – who have only ourselves to sell –
give praise to God for the gift of work.'

Music's perspectives

As mentioned in Chapter 4, St Augustine of North Africa in the early centuries of the Christian Church believed there to be a close relationship between religion and music. One of his sentences was 'He who sings, prays twice.'[219] I take this to mean: 'Putting into song something you want to express helps to make that something really your own and helps you to express it with warmth of emotion, and takes advantage of the fact that music has ways of expressing what is inexpressible in words, or is almost inexpressible.' Music can sometimes express and hold together such emotions and experiences as pathos and joy. To describe situations in life where both are present more or less at the same time can involve one in paradox and apparent contradiction, in ways that can be helpful expression, but seem to fall short of fully adequate expression. And this can apply of course to any interpretation of the Gospels, and to the combination of authoritativeness and vulnerability and of challenge and compassion in their picture of Jesus, focussed on in earlier chapters of this book.

Nearer our own day, Richard Strauss argues vigorously that music should rely on no religious 'crutches' (in an aggressive form of the sort of viewpoint put less aggressively in many more modern comments about Christianity being for those who want

---

219. Since St Augustine's mysticism had its early background in the Platonist conviction about God as Truth, Beauty and Goodness, he seems to have taken music as a good parallel to prayer in the mystical intuition of God. Music's focus on beauty holds hands with prayer's focus on truth? And goodness?

just a 'comfort' message). In 1911 Strauss wrote in his diary: 'It is absolutely clear to me that the German nation can only attain new vigour by freeing itself from Christianity.'[220] But the last half-century has shown some strong examples of composers moving in another direction. Stravinsky, in his later period, added to his earlier revolutionary styles musically and general outlook, an emphasis on something more traditional. More recently there has been a diversity of figures ranging from Messiaen and Tavener to some in the world of English cathedral music, such composers as Jonathan Harvey; and composers, in, for example, Poland, Estonia, Georgia and Russian circles, showing that religion for them has returned as a vibrant force. Prominent in spreading the word about new vibrancies is James Macmillan, with such compositions as 'Magnificat' and 'Nunc Dimitis' and 'The World's Ransoming', meeting with wide acclaim.

But that is only to focus on the composers or on those composers. Mention, in the context of this chapter's focus on perspectives, of two figures from the middle of the 20th century must be made: they were two people who both found certain musical perspectives to have been vital in their religious perception and growth. One was a famous music critic (and cricket writer) for many years on a national broadsheet newspaper, Neville Cardus. In his 1947 autobiography he wrote this:

> 'For years I was as dogmatic an atheist as could be. It was when I understood for the first time the later quartets of Beethoven that I began to doubt my rationalism... There is for me no accounting in terms of evolution or survival value for the sense of beauty, for laughter and tears that come and go without material prompting, for the ache after the perfect form and the ineluctable vision.'[221]

---

220. James Macmillan in *The Guardian*. Oct. 2003.
221. Neville Cardus: *Autobiography*, Collins. 1947

In 1961 Alec Robertson, already mentioned in Chapter 4, organist and director of music at Westminster Cathedral for many years, also wrote his autobiography, adding the following sub-title to his book: 'one man's testimony to a source of peace and strength.'

As noted in Chapter 4, Alec Robertson refers to Vaughan Williams' *Fifth Symphony*, which was dedicated to Sibelius, whose setting geographically, and background, could be said to be characterised by distant landscapes, far horizons and long perspectives. Intriguing and interesting because the *Fifth Symphony* has close links throughout with Vaughan Williams' early music for his opera *The Pilgrim's Progress*, with its emphasis on pilgrimage, journeying and route-finding. The symphony's slow movement was headed in the manuscript, one learns, by a quotation from Bunyan: 'Upon that place there stood a cross and a little below a sepulchre'. Then he said, 'He hath given me rest by his sorrow and life by his death.' In both Bunyan (who wrote in a foreword to his book 'This book will make a traveller of thee') and here in Vaughan Williams there is an anguish and an Alleluia perspective; in Vaughan Williams' case, passages of anguish were followed, in his concluding Coda, by the murmur of Alleluias, as mentioned by Robertson, and a mood of serene radiance.

A not dissimilar perspective is there in Stravinsky's *Symphony of Psalms*, which appeared in 1948 in a revised form. He highlights verses from *Psalm* 39, and *Psalm* 150. There is the same journeying, through anguish, to Alleluia. Among the words sung are 'Lord, hold not thy peace at my tears: for I am a stranger with Thee, and sojourner, as all my fathers were ....', 'He brought me up also out of a horrible pit, out of the miry clay, and set my feet upon a rock, and established my goings... and many shall see it and fear, and shall trust in the Lord' with, finally, 'Alleluia, praise ye the Lord... praise Him with the sound of the trumpet..., praise him in the timbrel and dance, ... let everything that hath breath praise the Lord'. Far from the ancient Jews' Jerusalem Temple or the Babylonian exile, the *Symphony of Psalms* was composed as a commission from the conductor Koussevitsky for a symphony to celebrate the 50th anniversary of the Boston Symphony Orchestra. Stravinsky said of the work: 'The psalms are poems of exaltation, but also of anger and judgement, and even of curses.' But the serenity of the last movement, which Robertson mentioned, was that to which the prior anguish won through. As one writer wrote of it; it was 'one of the most extraordinary accomplishments in Western music of this (20th) century in its suspension of time in static adoration and incantatory contemplation.' In what I have called the anguish and Alleluia perspective in all the above, there stands out a holding together of what another author calls the Hebrew psalmist's deep combination of 'lonely questions and fragile trust.'[222] And together with that, Stravinsky's desire to give expression to the anguish of humanity and yet the courage and hope of the human spirit.

In connection with paragraphs above about the creative work of painters, poets and musicians, and their precious perspectives in communicating truths concerning the anguish and courage of humanity in the face of life's challenges, a further quotation from the philosopher Wittgenstein may be recalled: 'There are things that cannot be expressed. And yet they show themselves.' R.S. Thomas quotes that in his *Autobiographies*.[223] It seems a particularly significant statement since Wittgenstein overall was no mere sentimental discarder of the role of human rationality.

R.S. Thomas' own poem *Gradual*, published in the 1980s, moves along similar lines, and the following lines from the poem go some way to sum up its gist:

---

222. Gordon Mursell. *Out of the Deep (Prayer as Protest)* DLT. 1989. p.55

223. Op.cit. p.165 and 166.

I have come to the borders
of the understanding. Instruct
me, God, whether to press
onward or to draw back.
… I need a technique
other than that of physics…
… for registering the ubiquity
of your presence… Call your horizons
in. Suffer the domestication
for a moment of the ferocities
you inhabit, a garden for us to refine
our ignorance in under the boughs of love.'[224]

In direct connection with creativity, a few lines of poetry from Julia Cameron, author of *The Artist's Way*,[225] encourage artists to persevere with creative work in spite of the creative tension that so often seems to accompany or precede creativity:

'We are ourselves creations.
We are meant to continue creativity by
being creative ourselves.
This is the God-force extending itself through us.
Using creativity is our gift back to God.'

The phrase 'God-force' may sound to some to be a much too vague phrase from a Christian point of view. But in fact, I think, it stays very close indeed to Jesus' central phrase 'The Kingdom of God,' as touched on already in an earlier chapter of this present book. When a foremost biblical scholar such as Bruce Shilton sees the major meaning and theme of God's kingship and kingdom, both in the Jewish *Psalms* and then in Jesus' teaching, being 'God in his strength', that reminds us that words and phrases such as 'force', 'dynamic', 'thrust', and 'creative energy' are central to understandings of the biblical phrase 'The Kingdom of God'.

---

224. *Collected Poems*. P.411.

225. Macmillan. Pan Books 1994.

That is, central to its message of the dynamic of values and standards of justice, mercy and trustfulness – Jesus' 'weightier matters of the law' – and the dynamic of Paul's nine fold 'gifts of the Spirit' and 'harvest of the Spirit' – 'love, joy, peace, patience, kindness, goodness, fidelity, gentleness and self-control'.[226] These standards and values and thrusts may surely well be named 'God-force': in other words, the creative energies of God's love. 'God's force' may sound close to the philosophers' more general terms of 'élan vitale' and creative evolution, but it is close also to the creative message of the Kingdom.

The territory of the artists is not, of course, limited to those painters, architects, poets and musicians to whom we normally apply the word 'artist'. It includes all those who have the touch of the artistic about all they do, or all they write down. It is said truly that creative artists teach us how to see: to look, to spot, to be aware. An example of this for many people in recent years, chiefly in the United States but also across the world, has been Henri Nouwen, through his many books and through his life. He died in 1996, and one of his biographers since then[227] has put 'An Artist, Not a Scribe' as the chapter-heading of one of his chapters about Nouwen. Nouwen certainly seems creatively to have helped people to see in the sense that he has helped his readers and his very large number of individual contacts and friends to get a picture of life helping them to cope with life's changes and chances, lonelinesses and potentials, dilemmas and challenging turnings in the road. In this way he was an artist. Another writer about Nouwen recently has put it more vividly; 'By sharing his own struggles he mentored us all, helping us to pray while not knowing how to pray, to rest while feeling restless, to be at peace

---

226. *Matthew* 23.23, Galatians 5.22

227. Michael O'Laughlin. *God's Beloved (A Spiritual Biography of Henry Nouwen)*. Orbis. 2004.

while tempted, to feel safe while still anxious, to be surrounded by a cloud of light while still in darkness, and to love while still in doubt.'[228]

Nouwen was a Dutch-born American, a Catholic priest, a writer and university lecturer. He was in fact also artistic in the far from vague sense of identifying strongly with art and artists, studying and enjoying paintings and other artwork. Also, a fellow-Dutchman, Vincent van Gogh, was a great source of inspiration to him. More personally, both Nouwen and van Gogh for all their gifts and fame of different sorts, lived troubled and lonely lives, both suffering from some element of low self-esteem, insecurity and feelings of shame and rejection. In Nouwen's case this was the tension that lay behind his creativity in helping people in books and life. It would not be easy, it seems, to say what part his family background lay behind the sense of rejection: his father never questioned his son's desire to become a priest, but the father was an energetic member in the Dutch business world and (as in van Gogh's case also) Nouwen felt to some extent rejected. It should be added that some have been completely put off by the fact of his homosexual temperament, made public only very recently: and maybe the temperament contributed to the sense of rejection. Anyway, Nouwen was a wounded healer in his helping of others and what he wrote so effectively was often due to the fact that he was writing out of his own experience and vulnerability. One of his books was called *The Wounded Healer*, referring to Christ.[229]

It is there that Nouwen helps in the interpreting of the Gospels' picture of Jesus, for readers of the Gospels. He was particularly, though not exclusively, fond of *The Gospel of John*. Typically focussed on by him was the scene where two of those

228. Ronald Rolheiser. *The Holy Longing: the Search for a Christian Spirituality*. Continuum. New York. 1999.

229. *The Wounded Healer* (Ministry in Contemporary Society) Doubleday 1979. Darton, Longman and Todd. 1994.

who were to become disciples of Jesus were pointed towards Jesus by John the Baptist and sought Jesus out. 'Rabbi' (which means 'Teacher') 'where are you staying?' and Jesus replied, 'Come and see.'[230] Nouwen found this invitation by Jesus a great inspiration, and wrote that 'making a home in Jesus' (cf the New Jerusalem Bible's 1985 translation of *John* 14.23: Jesus replied: 'Anyone who loves me will keep my word, and my Father will love him, and we shall come to him and make a home in him') is a theme running through the Gospel. Related to all this is Nouwen's focus on Jesus' reaching out to individuals. Another of his books is entitled *Reaching Out.*[231] Nouwen's whole approach tends to be highly personal, subjective and impressionistic; but another description, not unconnected with that trio of words, could be passionate, related to life, and full of an artistic and contemplative sense of sensibility and sensitiveness. In 1986, for the last ten years of his life he joined one of the L'Arche communities of the network of communities containing a combination of disabled and non-disabled people – the network inspired by Jean Vanier's influence. There he both fulfilled his desire for truly feeling himself to belong to a community on the one hand, and able on the other to serve others in a reaching-out movement of his own. In fact there he gave himself to serving one particular very disabled man and to being responsible for taking on the man's basic needs for help in down-to-earth respects such as toilet matters, feeding, and the business of dressing and washing. He reckoned that what he called this 'downward mobility' of his made his life richer and deeper.

---

230. *John* 1. 37-39 (REB)

231. *Reaching Out.* Doubleday. 1966.

Problems presented by coded language in the Gospels

This chapter ends, after having described above some of the understandings of Jesus' teaching given by imaginative, artistic, and sometimes mystical people, with a more questioning, not to say complaining, comment of someone whose life has been that of an electrician. He was someone whom I got to know when his life had had its troubles; and later, after he had moved a long way away, he was in the habit of ringing me up around Christmas-time for some years, just to keep in touch. One year, in a parting sentence before ringing off, when I had been, I think, mentioning briefly a parable of Jesus from the Gospels which I had just been reading, I concluded by saying 'That's in rather coded language, I'm afraid, and needs a bit of de-coding and unpacking': to which he replied, referring to the Christian faith, 'Cecil, the whole thing for me still needs de-coding.'

But, as we all know these days, with our pin-codes, post-codes and perhaps tax codes, a code-word or code-phrase or code-formula is a very helpful, quick, shorthand way of providing briefly a great deal of more detailed information hidden within its small compass. One definition of the word 'code' given in the Shorter Oxford English Dictionary (a definition which, it seems, came into use along with telegraphic communication) is 'a system of signalling'. Tax-codes are a brief way of signalling whether a person is earning, say, £18,000 a year, or, say £80,000. However, in the wider world of, say, literature, the word 'code' has come to be used in more complex ways: for example, codes are seen as important not just because they secure and provide brevity, but because they secure and provide an element of secrecy and mystery. Books are written entitled *The Great Code: the Bible and Literature*.[232] These aim to describe a sort of genetic code which holds the programme of a book or a collection of books,

---

232. Northropp Frye. 1982.

much as the scientists have isolated the hitherto unknown DNA code. And at least one biblical scholar has suggested that verses 5-9 of the first chapter of the *Gospel of Mark* 'hold the book's genetic programme'.[233]

It is interesting to note that in the Gospels' account of Jesus' sayings and conversations, in some situations he used uncoded and more simple explanatory language, and in other situations he used coded languages. The first type of situation there was his usual way when speaking to crowds of people. He usually gave them explanatory illustrations in terms of everyday life situations that were familiar to them: for example, about a farmer who sowed seeds in his field, and how, miraculously and wonderfully whether he is in a bed asleep or not, the seed goes on growing silently, till the great day of harvest and fulfilment comes. So is the Kingdom of God in its growing, says Jesus. 'He gave them his message, so far as they were able to receive it. He never spoke to them except in parables.'[234] There is not the faintest hint that these crowds found Jesus' message to be coded. We read on another occasion that 'the large crowd was listening to him with delight'.[235] In the second type of situation, however, when, for example, Jesus encountered opposition to what he said from 'a deputation from the Pharisees', he used a more challenging type of parable of a traditional Hebrew sort which took the form of 'a riddle story': in this would be a story of someone facing a difficult dilemma or choice which challenged him or her, and this type of parable challenged the listener to make some choice in life, and this, from Jesus' point of view, included making up their minds whether they were going to listen seriously to what he was saying

---

233. John Drury in *The Literary Guide to the Bible* ed. Robert Alter and Frank Kermode. Collins. 1987. p.409.

234. *Mark* 4. 26-29 and 33-34. (REB)

235. *Mark* 12.37 (REB)

or going to insist on sticking to their own position. That must have been the situation lying behind Jesus' words about some of his opponents, when he said: 'everything comes in parables, in order that' (if they insist) 'they may indeed look, but not perceive... and not turn again and be forgiven.'[236] In that sort of situation Jesus could certainly be said to be using coded language, through a story with a hidden personal message.

There was another group of people, of course, his disciples, to whom Jesus could be said to have spoken both in uncoded language and coded language. Of the crowds, it is recorded, 'he never spoke to them except in parables; but privately to his disciples, he explained everything.' But the 'everything' contained secrets and mysteries: Jesus told the disciples 'To you the secret of the Kingdom of God has been given, but to those who are outside, everything comes by way of parables.'[237] And as the gospel story develops in later chapters Jesus will tell the disciples that the coming of the Kingdom in its fullness is going to be accompanied by suffering and that he himself will have to die. That was clearly a hidden, coded part of the message they were given.

However, out of all this the two truths emerge clearly: first, that Jesus' language for much of the time was uncoded and clear to his listeners, and my friend with his difficulty and complaint was quite right to expect to find something 'unpacked' and decoded somewhere in Jesus' message, and secondly that Jesus' language was also often the language of mystery and secrets (even if we hasten to add that the secret part is now an 'open secret' in the fullness of good news revealed in Jesus' life, death and resurrection). As we have seen in the previous section of this chapter, the work of poets, visual artists and musicians is one of the guides that can lead us into moments of creative vision, and

---

236. *Mark* 4.11 and 12 (NRSV)
237. *Mark* 4.34, 4.11 (REB)

into a sense of wonder and of ultimate realities and mysteries that are bound not to be fully understood within the compass of our human understanding in this life. In an earlier chapter, of course we have seen that even one of the most central phrases in Jesus' message, 'The Kingdom of God', is in a sense coded language; for, as well as signalling splendidly in many minds the thought of such central sentences as 'Blessed are the poor in Spirit; the Kingdom of Heaven is theirs' and other Beatitudes in *Matthew* Chapter 5, the phrase 'The Kingdom of God' or 'The Kingdom of Heaven' is a phrase whose true meaning is easily misunderstood. As Jesus pointed out, it is not a kingdom of this world,[238] but (as mentioned earlier) rather a kingdom of values and right standards, such as 'justice, mercy and good faith'[239] or, as Paul listed them (within 'the harvest of the Spirit'), 'love, joy, peace, patience, kindness, goodness, fidelity, gentleness and self-control.' Those and other listed qualities were, in the Christian message, following in the line and heritage of the Hebrew psalmists who basically meant by God as 'king', in kingship and kingdom, 'God in his strength'. The Kingdom of God was God in the dynamic and thrust of the values spread to all.

A fairly brief postscript. We sometimes impose coded language quite unnecessarily, in a way specially unhelpful to younger generations in school or family. This is when in readings from the *Bible* we may like to choose to read from a version of the Bible written in the language and idiom of several centuries ago. The latter is laudable in the sense that the language of those times may provide a good sense of mystery and have a good poetic and literary ring to it, not unsuitable in worship in a church. But communication of the biblical word which conveys meaning to the listener or reader in a language and idiom well understood by

---

238. *John* 18.36 (REB)

239. *Matthew* 23.23 (REB)

them is even more centrally important. When King Alfred was translating parts of the *Latin Vulgate Bible* in the 9th century into Anglo-Saxon, he had this rule for his translation: 'sometimes word for word, sometimes meaning for meaning.' And when Martin Luther was translating biblical passages from the *Vulgate* in the 16th century, he wrote in a letter to a friend that for translation of the *Bible* in Latin into a more modern European language a good rule was: 'Figures of speech and the liveliness of sentences and arguments can be rendered in a free translation only.' The delicate matter of biblical translation will always be a matter of controversy and discussion, which is no bad thing. But language used in idioms no longer used or understood by hearer or reader presents an unnecessary barrier often to the understanding of the meaning of a passage, and, without a suitable idiom, the language can anyway lack 'bite' and directness. Many of us may find that the *King James Bible* translation of Paul's *Letter to the Church in Philippi in Philippians* Chapter 1, verse 10, 'I pray that... ye may approve things that are excellent', sounds a noble and clear statement, but a rather undefined one; and may be glad to be told that for the first three words there ('that are excellent') the most literal English translation of the original phrase used by Paul is probably 'that are worth more'. And the lexicons tell us also that the English words 'that really matter' express a meaning of the original phrase found in the centuries when this was written. So when the *Revised English Bible* translates the whole verse in the following way, using an idiomatic phrase of modern times, its modern translation is likely to be found accurate, in modern idiom, and to have a definite directness, meaning and bite to it:- 'this is my prayer... (that you)... may learn by experience what things really matter.'

Questions about whether Jesus' route-plans for human behaviour have now been superseded by genetic programming

A century and a half ago the Christian Church in Britain was deeply affected by Darwin's scientific discoveries and evolutionary conclusions. A.N. Wilson's 1999 book *God's Funeral*[240] (a title taken from Thomas Hardy's poem with the same title, written between 1908 and 1910) writes of 'the Victorian disease, Doubt' growing strongly from the 1860s onwards, in spite of the presence of what Wilson describes as such 'pious revivals' as the Evangelical revivals through the Clapham Sect. He writes of Darwinism as a huge reinforcing of movements of a very different sort, such as 'the death of God' presentations of Nietzsche (born in 1810) and the influence of Thomas Hardy (born in 1840); and at the very end of his book gives a comparison between the loss of Christian faith late in the 19th century, and what he finds to have been a much more positive religious situation in the second half of the 20th century. He writes of 'the immense potency' of many factors in the 20th century British situation.

'One of the most extraordinary things about the twentieth century has been the palpable and visible strength of the Christian thing, the Christian idea. Just as Nietzsche's generation were declaring the death of God and Thomas Hardy was witnessing his burial, religious thinkers as varied as Simone Weil, Dietrich Bonhoeffer, Nicholas Berdayev and Teilhard de Chardin were waiting in the wings.' As well as saying that 'the Catholic idea played a demonstrable role in the collapse of the Soviet Communist system,' he added:- 'the roles played in the spiritual war against racism by the Southern Baptist minister Martin Luther King and by the church of England monk Father Trevor Huddleston showed that there was immense potency, not just in the Christian

240. John Murray 1999

ethical ideal but in their biblical sense of God coming to earth with His winnowing fork in his hand, ready to clear his threshing floor. These world-changing men and women decided to ignore the death of God in the nineteenth century. They spoke in the name of a God who was First and Last. They put their trust in One who said, "I was dead, and see, I am alive for evermore." (The fact that the above statements of A.N. Wilson were written by a man who is a well-known journalist regularly writing abrasive comments in London evening newspapers criticising the Church of England establishment, and archbishops of Canterbury, gave the statements added force. One thing, however, should be added: that he wrote in *The Spectator* magazine at the end of 2004 about Archbishop Rowan Williams: 'In all the essential things, he is just what the Church and the nation most need.')

The Church of England's response in 1860 to Darwin's and T.H. Huxley's scientific and evolutionary discoveries was notoriously negative. The then Bishop of Oxford, although a keen ornithologist, with a first-class university degree in mathematics, and a Vice-President of the British Association for the Advancement of Science, dismissively asked Huxley at a big conference whether it was through his grandfather or his grandmother that he claimed his descent from a monkey, as he had previously also castigated Huxley for his 'foul speculations' about the age and origins of the universe.

People of authority in the modern Church of England, however, have taken a different attitude to Darwin and Darwinism. Keith Ward as Regius Professor of Divinity in Oxford has debated vigorously with Richard Dawkins concerning the latter's 'selfish gene' type of Darwinism. And John Habgood, a recent Archbishop of York, who trained and worked earlier in life as a scientist in the field of biology, wrote a chapter entitled 'A Vote of Thanks to Darwin' in one of his books. He also wrote a contribution to a 'Face to Faith' column, in a broadsheet newspaper, headed 'I'm

More than My Genes'.[241] His writing of this sort, and that of other contemporary writers who are also priest-scientists, is good to listen out for, in a world where a predominantly 'scientific-only' approach is all that most people hear.

As Habgood's title makes clear, his main point is that none of us as persons is defined only, or determined only, in terms of genetic programming. His book *Being a Person*[242] makes the same point. And 'A Vote of Thanks to Darwin' may be briefly summarised as emphasising four or five reasons for the 'thanks'. He points out that not long after Darwin's announcement of his discoveries, one or two Christian writers had said that the discoveries had been of help to them concerning some of biblical scholarship's difficulties at the time over the undoubted fact that many of the *Old Testament* situations described showed the Israelites involved in barbarities: in other words, the 'revelation' of God's purposes had to be seen to be 'progressive revelation' evolving slowly. He points out that in many ways Darwinism's discoveries about natural processes in the universe fit in well with what modern biologists know about the growth and structure of crystals, which show both rules and structures at work ordering the whole process but also a principle of freedom, creativity, and something more 'random' than ordering, at work. So, not unlike the crystals' processes, he says, we may find, in the processes of continuous divine activity and creativity in the universe as a whole, a not dissimilar combination of both an ordering and controlling hand of God, but also such things as human creativity, freedom, choice and initiative. The tensions, perversity and suffering that enter the processes along with human freedom and initiative are not left out of consideration in Habgood's presentation, but are seen

---

241. Habgood: *Faith and Uncertainty* 1997 Darton, Longman and Todd. *Also Face to Faith*. Guardian. November. 1998.

242. Hodder and Stoughton. 1998.

as developments and burdens 'of which God bears the weight'. Finally, it is pointed out that in considering the whole evolutionary theory, 'we must welcome the long-term implications for science in having to take time, history and development seriously.' In a sense, the above 'welcoming' note seems to look at science and at religious faith with a deep sense of perspective.

Habgood, however, is far from being 'starry-eyed' about any deterministic idea of genetic programming. He writes 'Unless its limitations are made clear, its tendency in the long run is to undermine moral responsibility and our sense of independent personhood.'[243] Or again 'Genetic determinism makes no sense in creatures as complex, as open to our environment, and dependent on social action as human beings have always known themselves to be... Genetic systems are often mistakenly described as blue-prints,' but are 'more like bundles of instructions, setting in motion and controlling a process which does not depend wholly on the genes themselves, but which depend in part on what else is happening.' For instance, 'on the relationships, physical, personal, and ultimately transcendental, within which our lives develop.'

A similar approach is found in another well-known priest-scientist, priest-theologian, John Polkinghorne, who, as a theoretical physicist, was for ten years a professor at Cambridge University. His phrase is to see a principle of both 'order and openness' at work in evolution and in the universe. He sees evolutionary changes as having to work both through order, 'or nothing persists', and through openness, 'or nothing changes'. He mentions Irenaeus, in the early Christian centuries, calling the Son and the Spirit 'the two hands of God' and he sees something of that two-handedness in relation to divine creativity.[244]

---

243. Habgood. *I'm More than My Genes. Guardian*. November. 1998. See also Habgood *Being a person*. Hodder and Stoughton. 1998.

244. Polkinghorne. *Warfield Lectures*. Princeton Theological Seminary. 2003

Yet another well-known priest-scientist, from the field of biology, and priest-theologian, Arthur Peacocke, mentioned already in an earlier chapter, has a passage in one of his books that helps to bring us back explicitly to the figure of Jesus in relation to the above paragraphs, and leads on towards recalling how Jesus defined human beings: 'Jesus manifested the kind of human life which... can become fully life with God, not only here and now, but eternally beyond the threshold of death. Hence, for Christians, his imperative "Follow me" constitutes a call for the transformation of humanity into a new kind of human being and becoming. What happened to Jesus, it was thought, could happen to all... Jesus represents the consummation of the evolutionary creative process that God has been effecting in and through the world of matter.'[245]

Peacocke's mention of 'a new kind of human being' reflects of course Christianity's belief in Jesus as having brought in a new humanity (to supersede, as 'the last Adam', in Jewish phrasing, the first Adam and first human beings at the beginning of creation, the *Genesis* Adam). Adam's disobedience had marked the entrance of sin, and a distortion of God's gift to humanity and human beings, the gift as recorded at the beginning of *The Old Testament* when God created human beings in his own image... and likeness. It was as a call to realise all the precious potential of God's gift to humanity in the creation that the early Christians spread abroad their message. In writings and letters in the tradition of Paul to Christian Church members the encouragement to grow in humanity's new nature, with Christ and in God's likeness, comes across loud and clear: 'You must put on the new nature created in God's likeness,' or the reminder: 'you have in baptism put on the new nature which is constantly being renewed in the image of the Creator and being brought to know God.' These calls and

---

245. Peacocke. *Paths from Science towards God*. One World 2001. pp.147, 148.

reminders were of course a handing on of the whole spirit of what Jesus' teaching had been about what his followers' conduct and new ways of living were to grow into being. Not only 'Love God and love others', but as when he challenged a group of Pharisees over what 'the weightier matters' of the Jewish Law were; and defined the following, as what it meant deep down to be 'a person': it meant growing in 'justice, mercy and faith'.[246]

---

246. *Romans* 5.12,14: 1 *Corinthians* 15.22: *Ephesians* 4.2: *Colossians* 3.10: *Matthew* 22.37,39:23.23

10

WIDER AND GLOBAL
UNDERSTANDINGS OF JESUS

It's useful to remember sometimes that one of the main directions
in which Christianity first spread from Jerusalem in the early
centuries was eastwards – through regions of northern Syria,
Iraq (as we know it now) and areas of Persian rule for centuries
– our modern Iran. At the first Pentecost in Jerusalem the first
four named out of twelve regional groups present in *Acts of
the Apostles* – i.e. Jews of the Dispersion come to Jerusalem,
and devout enquirers or 'proselytes' – were from this eastward
direction: 'Parthians, Medes, Elamites and from Mesopotamia.'[247]
And noticeable among the other regional groups named were
those from 'Egypt' and 'Arab' lands. Those who returned
home from Jerusalem after Pentecost to all these regions and
who had taken Christian influence with them in a lasting way
were to be called by historians of later centuries, up to our day,
Christians of 'the Eastern Churches' – Orthodox, Coptic and so
on. Those Churches, with others more widely (for example in
Greece and Russia) were together to bring some most distinctive

---

247. *Acts*. 2. 9.10 (NRSV)

and special understandings of Christ, as also special mystical, poetic, contemplative and worshipping gifts, to contribute to the worldwide Church. Most of the stories in *Acts of the Apostles*, it is true, direct our attention to the more westward direction of spread out from Jerusalem, and to Christianity's spread towards Rome and the many places around the Mediterranean coasts under the Roman imperial rule. The Church in these areas of Christianity's spread early on have, in turn, come to be called by historians since then 'the Western Churches'. However, the eastward spread remains highly significant.

Profiles of Jesus from eastwards out of Jerusalem

The significance of the spread eastwards is well seen in more detail by looking at the early centuries of one Church, the Christian Church in Iran, in 'the Persian regions' that the names 'Parthians, Medes and Elamites' in the *Bible* refer to. The Church seems to have its origins there in the second century CE, with Christianity handed on from what the historians call 'the main missionary centre of Edessa'[248] in northern Syria, known as a big Jewish-Christian centre not far north of Jerusalem, and having many cultural and trade routes and channels spreading out from it. The Nestorian Church in Edessa, separately, doctrinally and organisationally, from other 'Eastern Churches', was to spread geographically very widely indeed, and is known today in Iran as the 'Assyrian Church'. Its missionary movement is described by Dr Frend as 'one of the great missionary movements of all time' which 'nearly changed the history of Asia and the Middle East.'[249] Missionaries were sent in the early centuries up till the eighth century to Turkestan, India and China: to Siberia, Mongolia,

---

248. W.H.C. Frend, in *Religion in the Middle East*. Cambridge University Press. 1969 p.286

249. *Religion in the Middle East*. P.286

Arabia: to Java, Korea and Japan. By the third century twenty bishoprics were established in Iran, and by the early fifth century no less than sixty-six. In none of these countries was it ever easy for Christianity to settle, because of other existing religious faiths firmly established there, and the later spread of Islam increased the difficulty. But the movement was a great pioneer movement in hazardous settings.

A well-known Russian orthodox leader and writer of the twentieth century, Nicholas Zernov, made articulate the 'Eastern' tradition, and its distinctive features and insights. He wrote about the 'Eastern' and the 'Western' Churches, 'When the West wants to explain... the meaning of salvation it usually speaks about the pardon of the sins of an individual reconciled to God through the passion and death of his Son... For the East Christ is the Saviour because he showed the way of a new life and proved by his Resurrection the power and truth of his teaching.' Or again, 'The East does not think about salvation in terms of the individual soul returning to its Maker; it is visualised rather as a gradual process of transfiguration of the whole Cosmos' and 'In the West the Christian acts, feels and thinks as an individual... In the East the Christian thinks of himself first of all as a member of one big family of all Christian people both living and departed:... the Church for them' in the East 'is a living community, but not an institution: it includes the whole cosmos...' The writer adds further: 'The Western mind is analytic: ...Eastern Christians... are more interested in synthesis'[250]

Many years ago the writer of those words visited India and spent a year there, mostly in the Syrian Orthodox Church of Malabar, and in lecturing. In a book which he wrote while there, he gently suggested that, although he was aware of India's historic ties with the West, surely both Christian and Hindu circles in India

---

250. Nicholas Zernov. *The Church of the Eastern Christians* SPCK. 1942. p.53-54

ought to know more about the Eastern tradition of Christianity which is the religion of a large number of people inhabiting western and northern Asia and the eastern half of Europe. It was a suggestion that seemed to make a great deal of sense to those who heard it or read it. It may seem odd, in turn, that in our discussions nowadays on many vexing issues between parts of our various Christian church networks and denominations in different continents, these sorts of issues about 'Eastern Church' tradition in Christianity do not get much attention, other than in the World Council of Churches.

Two points need to be mentioned about the terms 'eastern' and 'western' used above about church traditions. First, it will be obvious, but may need raising, that these two positions should not be taken as used in a mutually exclusive sense and as though opposed. They stand for two truths and understandings of the significance of Christ which between them give a depth, richness and vision (two-eyed vision), the legacy of the two traditions.

Secondly, it will also be obvious that, going on from that useful Christian church-distinction, lines drawn and distinctions in the West made more generally between, for example, emphasis 'in the West' being on suffering aspects of the figure of Christ and emphasis 'in the East' on something very different, are bound to find their lines and distinctions become somewhat blurred in what we observe in various countries. As noted later in this chapter, a well-known Christian artist in India is fond of bringing out in his writings how it is the sufferings of Christ on which Indian painters, whether Christian or not, tend to focus very often. In other words, their 'eastern' emphasis in their case is on the sufferings. The same point applies also in West Asia, in Iran, though in relation to poetry rather than painting, often. In his 1994 booklet *Christ and Christianity in Persian Poetry*,[251] Bishop Hassan Dehqani-Tafti,

---

251. Sohrab Books 1994, 3 Crown Gardens, Oakham, Rutland LE15 6JN.

formerly the Bishop of the Episcopal Church Diocese in Iran, himself a poet, quotes from Persian poets, Muslim and Christian, past and present. It is clear that the theme of Jesus' suffering appears frequently. As well as the fact, of course, that the Shi'a tradition in Islam is to the fore in Iran, with the theme of suffering central in its beliefs, the focus on the sufferings of Christ must be seen as of distinctive importance. The bishop describes how, before the Islamic Revolution, on many evenings, groups used to collect in the Goethe Institute in Teheran, listening to poems recited by modern poets. One Muslim poet, Ahmad Shamloo, the bishop writes, was especially popular. A poem by Shamloo called *The Death of the Nazarene* is described, and some lines quoted in an English translation. It describes Christ carrying his Cross; the cruelty and injustice of the soldiers and of humanity; an onlooker, 'Lazarus', who is overcome by the love and mercy of Jesus on the Cross but, more than that, feels as he walks away finally, that the power of the love and mercy have taken away the power of the evil injustices, and redeemed some debt to Jesus he himself had felt he owed. The line 'Make haste, Nazarene, Make haste!' resounds through the poem twice over; a mixture, perhaps, on the one hand of the soldiers' impatience as they cried 'Scourge him!' to weaken him, and, on the other, of Lazarus' longing for Jesus' suffering to be ended. The first four lines are: 'The burden's wooden tail/Drew a line/Heavy and trembling in his footsteps,/ "Crown him with a wreath of thorns!"' and the last four lines: 'The mourners walked up the hill/And the Sun/And the Moon/Darkened.' Movingly, the booklet includes a hymn from their modern Persian Hymnal, with the words written by the bishop and the tune composed by his son Bahram: Bahram was to be killed and martyred in the times when the Revolution was at its height, and those who killed him had earlier shot at but failed to kill the bishop. The hymn was on Jesus' pain and the world's pain. One or two of its lines are: 'You, oh my God, gifts of knowledge give to me,/that hidden mysteries/

may clearly see/Free me from inward fights, life's tangled skein/ My torn heart heal, Oh Lord, make me glad again': and 'Spirit of Jesus reaches our pain,/Consciences weak through guilt, He'll make whole again'.

Christian mission in later centuries and its sequel

With the global spread of trade and shipping in the last five or six centuries from West to East and West to America (Dutch, Portuguese, Spanish, French, British, German) and the accompanying spread of colonial and imperial power, new modern movements of Christian mission developed with them. The understandings of Christ and Christianity as formed and given shape in the 'western Church', and, originally, Mediterranean thought, were taken across the world in this new sweep; and not only into the wide area of the world already penetrated by the pioneering missionary movement from Jerusalem in the early centuries, which had had so many setbacks in its spread, due not least to the rise of Islam

After the spread of political independence in many countries of the world in the twentieth century and the decline of political power (though not necessarily of continuing economic power) in those countries on the part of the colonial powers, Christians in those countries who had only rarely till then been able to find a voice of their own in expressing their understandings of Christian faith, began to find a voice. The founding of the World Council of Churches in Amsterdam in 1948 had its deepest significance in its giving of a voice to the voiceless. The language used in Christian circles globally in the decades following had an air of excitement about it. In 1983 two Christian theologians and thinkers, Virginia Fabella of the Philippines and Sergio Torres of Chile, edited the report of one of the international conferences, held two years earlier in New Delhi, of the Ecumenical Association of Third World Theologians, bringing together Asian, African, Latin American and other theologians from the Third World (a designation which the Association has officially accepted, and did not seem to find demeaning). The report was entitled: 'Irruption of the Third World: Challenge to Theology'.[252]

This excitement is found also in the writings of Ursula King, professor of Theology in Bristol University:

> 'It is in the Third World... that Christianity is
> at its most diverse, its most creative, its most
> vibrant. Most Christians now live in the Third
> World, often in a minority situation, challenged
> by the otherness of surrounding religions and
> cultural differences. Historically, most of Christian
> theology has been produced in the West... It is
> this dominance of European thought-forms in
> theological discourse that Third World theologians
> now call radically into question.'[253]

Equally clear, and strong, are the words of R.S. Sugirtharajah, Professor of Biblical Hermeneutics in Birmingham University, in various writings which include such chapter headings as 'Biblical Studies after the Empire' and 'Moving beyond the Mediterranean Milieu'. In one sense he is writing, as he says, in the tradition of the Arab scholar and writer Edward Said who urged people 'to read texts about the experiences of the exploited and the exploiter together'.[254] But Sugirtharajah makes a clear and distinctive transferring of that into the biblical field:

---

252. Orbis. 1983

253. *Christ in All Things* SCM Press. 1997

254. Said. *Culture and Imperialism* London. Chatto and Windus. 1993

'When Jesus made his belated second visit to the
eastern part of Asia' (i.e. the Western Church's
missionary movements in the last six centuries,
and their presenting of Jesus) 'he did not come
as a Galilean sage, rather he came as an alien
in his own home territory,... as a clannish
god of the "parangis" (a term used by Indians
during the salad days of the empire to describe
the foreigners) sanctioning the subjugation of
the peoples of Asia and their cultures. He was
projected and paraded as the totem symbol of
the privileged and the powerful. Since then
there have been a number of attempts by Asian
Christians to counteract this imperial, supremacist
and absolutist understanding of Jesus. These
discourses try to re-Asianize and refashion Jesus
in Asian terms to meet the contextual needs
of Asian peoples.'[255] And again 'the challenge
present-day Asian Christians face is to refashion
in a fresh way the claim that Christianity would
make for Jesus without being unfaithful to his
Jewish milieu, and at the same time making
accessible the mystery of Jesus to different faith
communities without sounding superior.'[256]

It is often rightly pointed out that Mahatma Gandhi greatly
treasured the Sermon on the Mount, and the Beatitudes especially.
But when an American asked him, soon after his return from
South Africa in 1915, 'How can we make Christianity naturalized
in India, not a foreign thing, identified with a foreign government?
What would you, as one of the Hindu leaders of India, tell me, a
Christian, to do in order to make this possible?' Gandhi replied,
'I would suggest that all of you Christians must begin to live

---

255. *Asian Faces of Jesus* Orbis. 1993. p.viii,ix

256. op.cit. p.263

more like Jesus Christ.'[257] Clearly it is this particular question that Dr Sugirtharajah is, nearly a century later, putting before us strongly, in terms of these later years and looking to the future.

Vibrant voices from Africa

A generation ago one of the voices that best articulated some of the sorts of new expressions of faith mentioned above, for many people, was that of Desmond Tutu in Africa. He was at that time Secretary of the African Council of Churches, later to be Bishop of Johannesburg, and then Archbishop of Capetown. I make no apology for quoting a rather substantial fine section at the close of an address which he gave in 1975 at a conference of African and Black American theologians in Ghana:[258]

> 'Why should we feel that something is amiss if our theology is too dramatic for verbalization and can only adequately express itself in the joyous song and movement of Africa's dance in the liturgy? Let us develop our insights into the corporateness of human existence in the face of excessive Western individualism; about the wholeness of the person when others are concerned for hellenistic dichotomies of soul and body, about the reality of the spiritual when others are made desolate with the poverty of the material. Let African theology enthuse about the awesomeness of the transcendent when others are embarrassed to speak about the King, high and lifted up, whose train fills the temple. It is only when African Theology is true to itself that it will

---

257. E. Stanley Jones, *Mahatma Gandhi* Hodder. 1948. pp.69,70

258. Printed in *Journal of Religious Thought*, 1975. vol.2. and reproduced in *A Reader in African Christian Theology* ed. John Parratt. SPCK 1987.

go on to speak relevantly to the contemporary
African – surely its primary task – and also,
incidentally, make its valuable contribution to the
rich Christian heritage which belongs to all of us.'

Those words about the corporateness of human existence
were spelt out more fully in some words of his twenty years later:
'There's a southern African concept called Ubuntu that says a
person can only be a person through other people. You can't know
you're beautiful unless you can see your beauty reflected in me.'
That's a welcome way of thinking for the West, because technology
has created an environment in which we don't need to depend on
other people, and we're each turning in "on ourselves".[259] That
conviction from southern Africa is echoed in the Kenyan John
Mbiti's and the Ghanaian Kofi Appiah-Kubi's writings. As the
latter puts it: 'In the words of John Mbiti it may be said, "I am
because we are and because we are therefore I am".' This idea
strikes the great chord of African solidarity and the sacredness of
the human community. The Akan proverb – 'Oba se Ose nanso
owo nkyi' (the child resembles the father but he has a clan) sums
up the cardinal importance of the genealogical tables of Christ
in *Matthew* 1, 1-17, among African Christians. In the African
concept of man, a man is truly man in community with others.[260]
Although the above paragraphs talk most in terms of 'theology'
in general, they seem to be all related to Bishop Kenneth Cragg's
dictum 'It takes a whole world to understand a whole Christ.'[261]

Desmond Tutu has, of course, not only written about 'the
corporateness of human existence', but lived out his conviction,
notably from 1994 onwards by his leadership in the 'Truth and

---

259. Words quoted in the *Church Times*, London, in December 1994

260. Kofi Appiah-Kobi's *African and Asian Contributions to Contemporary Theology* WCC Geneva, 1976.

261. Cragg. *The Call of the minaret*. Oxford University Press. 1956.

Reconciliation' Commission and the years of its meetings after the end of the apartheid regime in South Africa. His account of the meetings in *'No Future without Forgiveness'*[262] must surely stand as one of the most remarkable books written by him, as well as being a record of a huge pioneering venture of those times. It is customary, after a country has passed through a time of strife and cruelty, for trials to be held. But the 'Truth and Reconciliation' venture's procedure was to encourage those from either side who were conscious of having committed wrong to come forward and confess to the Commission what they had done, but not for the Commission to proceed to punishment. This obviously called for tremendous patience for all concerned, and caused much anguish and often tears for them, including for Archbishop Tutu himself. That enterprise and experience in peace-making has understandably been listened to seriously by those involved in their own political times of violence and strife, though so far a similar route does not appear to have been followed anywhere else. It remains as a beacon-route: where there were of course those who did not confess their crimes and where the reconciliation was in that sense incomplete; a route not for perfectionists, but for any willing to work away at a possible way ahead. The story of the Commission is covered rather more fully in Chapter 12, in a section on justice and compassion.

Other African voices

Lamin Sanneh, from Gambia, and now professor of Missions and World Christianity, and Professor of History at Yale, has in his 2003 book *Whose Religion is Christianity? (The Gospel beyond the West)*[263] given a salutary reminder to Europe and North America that there are now far more Christians in Africa than in

---

262. *No Future without Forgiveness* Rider. Random House, 1999.

263. Eerdmans. 2003

European and North American Churches, as a result of modern missionary movements from the West in recent centuries. The way he puts it in his opening pages is that 'the contemporary confidence in the secular destiny of the West as an elevated stage of human civilisation is matched by the contrasting evidence of the resurgence of Christianity as a world religion.'[264] And the closing words of the book flag up some of the book's main points: 'Bible translation enabled Christianity to break the cultural filibuster of its Western domestication to create movements of resurgence and renewal that transformed the religion into a world faith.' Lamin Sanneh has for many decades been usefully reminding the West of the power of Islam in Africa, but the above quotations show his message of confidence in Christianity's strength today, as he focuses on its current African 'resurgence' and vitality.

He sees the translation of the *Bible* into African languages as having been basic in helping Christianity to take root in Africa. Although the early translators were well aware, he says, e.g. in Nigeria, that the name of the Yoruba high god, Olurun, in Yoruba culture and religion, had some links with polytheism, they adopted his name as a translation of the divine name. 'Bible translation has thus helped to bring about a historic shift in Christianity's theological center of gravity by pioneering a strategic alliance with local conceptions of religion,' making possible not just a foreign handing over of Christianity but what Sanneh calls 'the indigenous discovery of Christianity.' (This may be compared in some ways with Christian translators in Asia, e.g. in Chinese situations, who found the very different type of word 'Tao' very possible for translating the scriptural word 'Logos' or 'Word', as Christ is described.)

Sanneh's emphasis on Third World freedom, and freedom from 'Western domestication', is also prominent in his book,

---

264. *Whose Religion is Christianity?* p.3

as shown above. He cites the Masai of East Africa as described in Vincent Donovan's *Christianity Rediscovered (An Epistle from the Masai)*[265] and describes 'their so-named African Creed' as a creed 'of believing as a community rather than as individuals.' The first seven lines of that creed (printed in Donovan's book) are as follows:

> 'We believe in the one High God, who out of love created the beautiful world and everything good in it. He created man to be happy in the world. God loves the world and every nation and tribe on the earth. We have known this High God in the darkness, and now we know him in the light. God promised in the book of his word, the bible, that he would save the world and all the nations and tribes.'

Sanneh has recurring passages in the book, controversially, on the Enlightenment movement in European history, and he has long-held views on this. He seems to find important about it only its undoubted results in extremist rationalism, and to have no room for its significance also within the whole Renaissance and Enlightenment movement as partly an expression, rebirth and re-voicing of emphasis on creative truth. However, as said above, his book is obviously a crucially challenging reminder to all of us of realities that are now globally there for us to see. It is not a happy thought that so many local Christians in certain parts of the Third World seem to be doing the opposite of what Lamin Sanneh writes about in this new book of his. He writes movingly about Third World 'resurgence' and its own 'discoveries of Christianity', but many local Christians in the world mentioned above seem to be moulding their songs and spirituality on still-imported ways of thinking, such as the 'theology of success' found in some of our prosperous western countries.

---

265. Fides (Indiana) 1978, Orbis 1982, SCM 1982

In the same year a book came from southern Africa, from the Archbishop of Capctown, Njongonkulu Ndungane, with the title *A World with a Human Face*.[266] The message and the voice to be heard in the book do not mince words. It is, he says, a 'call to the rich nations, and the multinational corporations, which must recognize that they cannot continue on the present course of economic growth and exploitation which disregards the consequences upon fellow human beings and the natural world.' In the face of Africa's immense problems of poverty, AIDs and globalisation, with the latter implementing a system of a single, lucrative, world market which is strongly competitive, and a global economic system with terms of inclusion dictated by and in favour of the wealthy, 'there are serious questions over whether developing states will be able to survive these globalization processes at all.' The writer Salvadore Marcus is quoted: 'A new world war has begun, but now it is against humanity as a whole, in the name of "globalization".' And the following words are added, from which the book's title comes: 'We need to engage now in combating this war by putting in place strategies to create a world with a human face.'

We will all be aware that some countries such as China, and some sections of Indian opinion, have viewed globalization much more favourably; but Archbishop Ndungane's voice and message cry out in prophetic terms and in a way that demands to be heard. The book deals not only in generalisations but also in detailed suggestions and challenges, which he describes as 'route markers on our journey towards wholeness.'

But Archbishop Ndungane also gives detailed attention to the whole question of biblical interpretation. He sees this matter as having been sadly neglected in the Anglican Lambeth Conference of 1998 and in current discussions and decisions in the Anglican

---

266. World Council of Churches, Geneva, and SPCK London. 2003 pp.39,63-65 and 93

Communion. He writes that 'biblical texts were seldom examined in their contexts' at the 1998 conference and subsequently, and he comments that we need to discover what 'the leading themes of the scriptures' are, 'which can help to control our interpretation.' He says that in South Africa the following brief summary of such themes have been suggested; first, 'the loving faithfulness of God, and God's righteousness, resulting in effect in the supremacy of the two commandments of love of God and love of others'; and secondly, 'liberation and mercy as the key to interpretation.' He has strong words to say about 'the embarrassing refusal' of the Lambeth group looking at the whole issue in 1998 'to listen to the stories of homosexual persons' and notes that 'medical and psychological evidence was not considered either', or feminist approaches to patriarchal cultures, and so on. In view of the fact that from other parts of Africa a predominantly hard-line and one-line type of approach was presented in discussions, Ndungane's giving voice to the above wider coverage of *New Testament* and biblical material on the subject is naturally particularly valued.[267]

A section on the significance of symbolism in Africa, when issues of religion and culture are being addressed, is added. This touches on what the book calls former 'colonial models' and illustrative symbols 'which intended to entrench control' from the side of one particular culture only. Also added are these words: 'The Christian symbol of the cross, while not especially African, is central to Christianity and stands at the centre of Christian worship. Where contextualisation has taken place is in the replacing of the Caucasian-featured Jesus on the cross with an African figure; underlining an African focus on the suffering Christ.' (The same 'replacing' of course may be seen in Britain where multiracial groups worship, and on one wall in St Matthew's

---

267. *A World with a Human Face* p.39 and pp. 112 to 122

Church, Willesden, in north-west London, there is a large crucifix depicting Christ as an African.)

In Chapter 1 I have already touched on how a group of readers in Southern Africa have interpreted one biblical passage, finding a liberating message for themselves in *Isaiah* Chapter 61. That can be matched, not only by very many other past instances of biblical interpretation from South Africa in relation to liberation from apartheid, but also from further north in Africa. Jean-Marc Ela is a Cameroonian scholar, and writing from the University of Yaounde in the 1980s, he made the following comments about the *Book of Exodus* and its interpretation. He applied its message about God's deliverance of the Hebrews from oppression in Egypt to the situation of oppression experienced by the Kirdi people in North Cameroon,[268] and not only generally in relation to God's deliverance of human beings from the oppression of sin and fear. He says that in colonial times the *Bible* had come to people in Cameroon in European form and had been passed on by those who had a very different cultural setting and background from that of Cameroon; the result being that the *Book of Exodus* was a book 'terribly absent to us', because the God of missionary preaching was a God so distant, so foreign, to the history of the colonized people. The biblical book's message about a future of hope and salvation including the possibility of the colonized people criticising their own existing social situation had not emerged. Ela adds that in the *Book of Exodus* God is portrayed as a God journeying with his people; and it is pointed out that this emphasis is in line with a modern scholar such as Jürgen Moltmann using phrases about God's name being, in the *Bible*, 'a wayfaring name, a promise that discloses a new future'.[269]

---

268. Ela. *African Cry* Maryknoll. Orbis Books 1986. And a passage from it included in *Voices from the Margin* edited R.S. Sugirtharajah. Orbis/SPCK 1991, 1995

269. Moltmann *Theology of Hope* Harper and Row. 1967. p.30

Powerful voices about the biblical message from the Afro-Caribbean region cannot be forgotten. One such voice was that of Philip Potter in the 1970s. Born in the Caribbean island of Dominica, trained and working in Jamaica, with five years of mission work in Haiti, he went on to give notable leadership both in Methodist ministry in his own region and in West Africa and then as General Secretary of The World Council of Churches. He described himself as 'a Caribbean person containing in myself many cultures', which was a reference to what a colleague of his described as 'his mixture of African, French and Irish ancestry which made up his birthright.' (In his own island the local people spoke a French Creole; but Jamaica was different; the English-speaking and French-speaking influences, and the links between Caribbean and West African countries reflected colonial history and the diverse influences of the French and British empires.) In tributes to him at the end of his career, Dr Adeolu Adegbola, Director of the Centre for Applied Religion and Education in Ibadan in Nigeria, summed up Philip Potter's work by saying that his great concern was for a more relevant, more intensive and more inclusive 'participation of all Christians in the sufferings of Christ for the salvation of our broken, divided world.' And Dr Emilio Castro, from Argentina, who succeeded him as WCC General Secretary, wrote this: 'Philip is a man of the Caribbean; he knows only too well how the powerless peoples of the world have been exploited by the powerful nations. His missionary calling has been to raise his voice on behalf of all the exploited of the world, and to say clearly and loudly to the powerful of the earth: "Repent; see the whole reality. Stop saving my soul – and crushing my person".' Emilio Castro then went on to say that whereas in the past 'evangelical perspectives on spirituality and on theological convictions' for Christian witness had 'come basically from theologians in the North Atlantic region; but now had to be supplemented by the perspective of the poor' in an 'evangelicalism' that came also from 'those of a more spiritual and activist nature developed in the third world.' The latter clause reminds us of some of the inner springs of conviction that lay behind much of Philip Potter's witness to the biblical message of good news for all those experiencing oppression and indignity in any form.[270]

Listening to Latin America

The name of Emilio Castro leads us on to other Latin American voices. As is well known, some of the earliest writing on liberation thinking came, during the 1960s, from Latin America. And not only the earliest, but writing that was full of the most surprises, not to say shocks, for the thinking on the interpretation of the *Bible* and on theology in the Third World and beyond. The theme of Jesus and the Gospels showing 'an option for the poor' was presented over the subsequent decades in book titles such as *Subversive Scriptures: Revolutionary Reading of the Christian Bible in Latin America*, from Lief Vaage in 1997.[271] It is not one of the earliest expressions of the movement's thinking. English translations in the 1970s and 1980s of some of the 1960s' books originating in Mexico, Peru, Argentina and other countries, obviously came already with a challenge; viz. from José Miranda's *Marx and the Bible (A Critique of the Philosophy of Oppression)*, Gustavo Gutiérrez' *Jesus Christ, Liberator*, and José Miguez Bonino's *Faces of Jesus in Latin America*.[272]

---

270. Much of the above material on Philip Potter is owed to Pauline Webb's edited volume of tributes: *Faith and Faithfulness*, World Council of Churches 1984. Especially to her own chapter pp. vii-xviii, and to pp. 8-17 and 52-60. Philip Potter's brief, quoted description of himself is from his own book *Life in all its Fullness* WCC 1981 p.9

271. Trinity Press International

272. Miranda, SCM Press, 1977: Gutierrez, Orbis, 1973: and Bonino Orbis, 1985

As Gutierrez later wrote: '... the conviction arose in Latin America that poverty, in which the immense majority of its population lives, is not only the most serious social issue of the continent but also the greatest challenge to the announcement of the Gospel, and in consequence, to reflection about the Christian faith.'[273]

To get an idea of how the Latin American movement of liberation started, a good way is to read one or more of the papers read to a conference in Brazil in 1980, the International Ecumenical Congress of Theology in Sao Paulo. Here I summarise some of the points made in, and give a few quotations from, a paper entitled '*The Challenge of Basic Christian Communities*'.[274] It was written by a Dutch Carmelite priest and theologian, Carlos Mesters who had worked in Brazil for 12 years, in Roman Catholic parishes and communities, and it describes how the *Bible* came alive widely among rural communities and farm-workers, and so on, in those times; in particular through 'grassroots' Bible study sessions among Brazilian Catholics. He describes how previously he had been familiar with groups meeting for Bible-study in such communities where the group's questions collected beforehand for answering on the study course were usually questions such as these; 'How do you explain the *Book of Revelation*? What does the serpent stand for? What about the fight between David and Goliath?' The questions were all limited to the *Bible* as such. 'No hint of their own concerns, no hint of real-life problems;... no hint of problems dealing with economic, social and political life.' But, by contrast, he says, he remembers a very different group where he had been asked to give a course of Bible-studies. There were about ninety farmers 'from the backlands and the river-

---

273. *Dictionary of Third World Theologies* eds Virginia Fabella and R.S. Sugirtharajah. Orbis 2000. pp.131-132

274. *The Bible and Liberation* eds. Norman Gottwald and Richard Horsley. SPCK/Orbis. 1993. pp.3-16

banks; most of whom could not read and the questions which they had prepared beforehand were very different. What about their current fight with landlords, or fights on other issues? One priest gives us, they said, a Gospel-message that could touch on our land-problems but saying that the landlord was right, but another priest nearby gave a Gospel-message that could also touch on the land-problems and would say that the tenant-farmers were right: what does the *Bible* have to say on all that? Is the second priest's conclusion 'communism'? Those were the sort of questions asked, though the questions also said 'Please tell us the stories of Abraham, Moses, Jeremiah, and Jesus,' which he did. In that place, said the writer of the paper, the *Bible* gradually seemed to come alive for them, bringing together God's Word and real life, and the Bible-studies in new ways became a stimulus for hope and courage. As became clear in the discussions that followed the speaker's presentation and listening to the *Bible*, to use the speaker's vivid words – they did not just use their heads on the biblical stories and come 'fairly close' to Abraham, but felt their feet following in Abraham's company. A farm-worker who was in the group said to the speaker: 'Now I get it. We are Abraham, and if he got there, then we will too.'

A few lines after his sentence quoted above, Guttiérez defined 'the main and concrete expression of the theology of liberation' in the following way: '... the preferential option for the poor.'

But how has the questioner's question 'Is the second priest's conclusion, about the tenant-farmer's being right, communism?' been answered? Liberation theology has certainly been dismissed as 'Just Marxism' not only by uninformed people but also by some Christian leaders. Pope John Paul II gave us a courageous witness to conviction about non-violent-resistance and about an 'option for the poor', illustrated by visits to 'the poor', but at the same time was cautious about and critical of liberation theology, on the grounds that the slide into Marxist ideology presented for that theology a huge and known danger. José Bonino, in what he wrote, said that 'particularly in Marx's early thinking' he had 'taken up the Judeo-Christian prophetic tradition' and that Marxism had built its own 'secular theodicy of progress towards a good life'. But Bonino admitted that Marxism went on to 'develop a critique of religion in general and Christianity in particular as an alienating theology'... 'While popular movements related to liberation theology have been inclined to socialism and co-operated with Marxism in terms of social change, they have rejected Marx's atheism,' and have been strongly critical of much of the socialism in their times.[275]

José Miranda, in turn, in the book mentioned above about Marx and the Bible, points out that in the *Gospel of John* there is a strong emphasis on 'struggle' and says that when Jesus speaks about loving one another, he is referring above all not mainly to fellowship in an inner group, but, in a very *Old Testament* prophetic manner is speaking about justice, brotherhood and the struggle against all mercilessness. Miranda sees 'love' in the *Gospel of John*, as meaning 'love-justice for the brother in need'. (Admittedly echoes of biblical scholars such as Bultmann may be heard here, in what they say about *John* Chapters 5-8 being 'conflict-chapters'.) Miranda's aim is to define the main theme of the *Gospel of John* as 'God's justice for the oppressed.'[276]

As will be clear elsewhere in these pages, concerning Indian Christian writers and theologians, this issue of Marx and Christianity has had to be tackled often at the level of practical personal experience and conviction, and not just at the level of theological thought in general. M.M. Thomas, the noted Indian

---

275. *Dictionary of Third World Theologies* Bonino's article on Marxism. pp. 137-8

276. *Marx and the Bible* pp. 88, 127-137 and p.223

Christian lay theologian and writer, wrote in the 1980s that in 1945, in working out what looked like his role in Christian mission, being a youth-work-leader at the time in his state of Kerala in India, he asked at the same time for ordination in his Church, the Mar Thoma Syrian Church, and for membership in the Communist party, and that both of the requests were rejected, for opposite reasons. 'I was convinced that' (in my situation) 'the Christian had a double task..., convinced that Marxism was a necessary ideological basis for political action for social justice in India, but that its utopianism , which elevated it to a scheme of total spiritual salvation, was a source of tyranny. Here class politics for justice and evangelistic witness to justification by faith became equally central to my understanding of Christian mission in India.'[277] It has to be added that people who strongly warn about Marxist dangers often forget that Jesus could be called a social and political activist at times, as the Gospels' story about the Temple moneylenders shows.

In the second half of the 20th century, two of India's states – Kerala and West Bengal – have had Indian Marxist governments over many years, and Kerala, of course, contains a very large number indeed of Christians, by whom an atheistic type of Marxism is not accepted. And responsible reporters on land-reform in India have said that the two above states have the best record in regard to that in India. Jonathan Power, writing in the British journal *Prospect* in July 2004 does not underrate continuing problems overall, but says: 'India has changed profoundly in the last 30 years. The number of poor has been halved.'

In a somewhat different way, in a post-colonial age, more new challenges are not absent. Liberation thinking is seen by some as not having yet 'achieved its potential': and the call comes

---

277. M.M. Thomas. *My Pilgrimage in Mission.* Reproduced in *Frontiers in Asian Christian Theology*, ed. R.S. Sugirtharajah Orbis 1994

to people in a post-modern age not only to 'disconnect from their colonial past', but also to be 'willing to divest themselves of their colonial intentions to make all of Asia Christian';[278] in the sense of expanding into wider 'contours' of vision (horizons?) and of former colonial powers taking other faiths and their theologies more seriously, and people being listened to as 'subjects' in their own right, rather than as 'objects'. A call, clearly, for looking not, or not only, towards a universal church but radically towards a global cultural humanity, with the superseding of an age when the 'subject's convictions and experiences have been regarded, very often, however graciously, within only Christian and biblical contours and horizons.

This clearly raises large issues concerning dialogue between faiths and cultures, and how far that dialogue so far has been felt to have reality. On the question of how far 'room for faith' can still continue and be taken seriously in the case of all concerned, in the light of the above challenge and in a post-modern age, alternative viewpoints naturally exist. Vernon White, the British theologian, seems to express himself in a way that cannot be considered extremist, yet that touches well on where the real heart of the issue lies. Near that heart, certainly, lies discussion not aimed at perpetuating old and strongly hierarchical and authoritarian anchors, but aimed at establishing the validity of there being other authoritative guides for human behaviour than just individual choice and rational guidance. In a recent review of a book about the philosopher Wittgenstein and the theologian Stanley Hauerwas,[279] Vernon White, who describes them, respectively, as 'an austere, reserved linguistic philosopher' and 'a feisty, polemical Christian ethicist', says that, as it were surprisingly, he found the book

---

278. R.S. Sugirtharajah in *Dictionary of Third World Theologies*. Orbis. 2000. p.131

279. The journal *Theology* for July/August 2002 p.315

'immensely illuminating', and he describes the book as 'a very good book indeed'. Not least, one gathers, because both of these two very different types of thinker held together both mystical theology plus its faith, and philosophy plus its rational wisdom. He applauds, in other words, their joint stance in holding these two sides together rather than polarising the issue on one side or the other. (White adds a note to say that he himself admits the strength of the rational side in relation to the whole post-modern situation, considering the provocation of many eras of 'scandalous religious wars'.) All this, for me, seemed to be very relevant on the question of establishing validity in the sense referred to above. 'Mystical theology' and, for example, the sacramental principle, may undoubtedly look impossibly narrow and non-relativistic in the eyes of much post-modernity, but has its place in true dialogue and in continuing discussion.

Further voices, mainly from the Indian subcontinent

In previous pages the themes both of suffering, or oppression, and also of hope can hardly be said to have been absent. But in Christian thinkers and writers in Asia there seems to have been a very distinctive and special strength in approaching the figure of Jesus through a patient awareness of the reality of human suffering and also through a dynamic undercurrent of hope.

In one sense, one could say that that strength was possible through the long experience of Asia's particular cultures, religions and civilisations. Both in its early experience of Vedic and Hindu religion, but also through Buddhism's strong hold on considerable parts of the Indian subcontinent under Asoka's empire in India in the third century BCE, and Buddhism's subsequent spread into other parts of Asia (rather more quickly than Hinduism's spread there), Gautama Buddha's convictions about the basic significance of human pain and misery and of the meaninglessness and emptiness of life were underlying influences and were summed up in his phrase: 'Only one thing do I teach; sorrow and the uprooting of sorrow.' Though accompanied by the belief that right living offered a way of hope, his convictions seem to have underlined some sort of Asian special awareness concerning the reality of suffering that could never be dismissed from human understanding.

When I first joined a college-staff in India, I remember that I had a long conversation early on with a colleague on the staff, Emani Sambayya. He said he had just been reading Reinhold Niebuhr's Gifford Lectures (*The Nature and Destiny of Man*)[280] and was impressed by the way that he brought out how full of anxiety America was. India, Emani Sambayya said, despite many problems and bad physical circumstances in many places, had more people 'resting in God'. He said that as someone who came from a Telegu Brahmin family, who had been led into the Christian faith through American and English missionaries, who had himself studied in America, and who got on very well with Americans. My point here is that it is not all that fanciful or difficult to see a link or an echo between Gautama's century's unrest and awareness of the reality of life's meaninglessness on the one hand, and a modern awareness of the unrest and anxiety of many in modern centuries, on the other.

But we need to go beyond background, and it may be the artists and the poets who give us the briefest, best lead-in to the subject. Jyoti Sahi, the Indian Christian artist, poet and theologian, has a 1981 poem and a black and white drawing with the title '*Sign of Hope*'.[281] His poem is prefaced by some lines from *Job* Chapter 14: 'There is always hope for a tree:/When felled, it can start its life again;/its shoots continue to sprout./Its roots may be

---

280. Two volumes 1941-1943

281. Christian Literature Society, Madras

decayed in the earth.../But let it scent the water, and it buds,/and puts out branches like a plant new set.' The drawing is of the trunk, branches and roots of a tree, and with a foetus-shaped, curved Christ-figure pictured in its roots, as a sort of Indian 'cave in the heart', and as symbolising the new life coming to birth at Bethlehem. The poem's ending is this: 'the Word entered the cave,/ stirring the roots of death to life.' And the poem begins: 'This was the tomb and the aperture/through which he came/Hope's prayer, most pure...' Tadao Tanaka's painting *Elijah and the Crow* from Japan comes from a little earlier in the 20th century, and is also centred on a tree – starkly painted, but with the figure of Elijah prominently below, reaching out to food being offered by a raven (or 'crow' as in Tanaka's title). The biblical reference is *1 Kings* Chapter 1, where Elijah is in hiding, fleeing from threats to his life and in the middle of a great drought and famine: 'and the ravens brought him bread and meat morning and evening, and he drank from the stream.' Tanaka is a Christian artist who was widely respected among Japanese artists and chaired the Japanese Artists Association for some years. In the above ways, Job's questionings of God's creation with its paradoxes and sufferings and his awareness of springs of hope, and Elijah's desperate and anxious experiences of forsakenness yet also provision from God, are reflected in the work of Jyoti Sahi and Tadao Tanaka.

Then, beyond that, Jyoti Sahi's book called *Stepping Stones*[282] has the sub-title *Reflections on the Theology of Indian Christian Culture*, and the double focus on suffering and hope is spelt out in ways that reflect the viewpoint of an artist but also the viewpoint of a thinker and a theologian. The artist in him and his paintings aim to show that Jesus taught through gestures rather than words, or that alongside the words 'Do not be afraid' there can be seen to be in the Gospels what Indian culture calls the

---

282. Asian Trading Association, Bangalore. 1986.

'abhaya' gesture of the hands; in the story of the transfiguration of Jesus on the mountain, Jesus found his three disciples with terror on their faces, and he 'came up to them, touched them, and said, "Stand up; do not be afraid".'[283] Jyoti Sahi has been fond of pointing out that Indian Christian art was initiated, in its most 'consistent' forms not by Christian artists but by Hindu artists. He has written of one such well-known artist all of whose paintings in a 1980 New Delhi Exhibition had had a Christian theme. That same artist, he added, though describing himself as someone who had lost faith in all forms of traditional religion, also said that 'he saw in Christ a figure who opposed historically two terrible forces: one was the prevailing colonial empire of Rome, and the other was the narrow religiosity of his fellow Jews. Between these two opposed interests Christ had been pulled apart, and crucified. He felt, as a modern Indian, that we could find the same two power systems in India today. On the one hand were the colonial interests of multinationals, and so on. On the other hand there was the narrow, parochial religiosity of Hindu conservatism. In the figure of Christ he wanted to celebrate man's ultimate longing for freedom...'[284]

As for himself, Jyoti Sahi writes this: 'Increasingly I came to realize that the Image which Christian art has to offer to India is the image of the prophetic, suffering servant.'[285] And on the theme of 'the faces of Jesus' he has produced much in painting and writings during the 1990s. However, along with all that, the 'hope' side in the Prophet image has been expressed by him, in his writings and paintings about justice, peace and a dynamic Christian message. 'We meet Christ not just statically, sitting as it were in our armchairs, but dynamically, as we ourselves

---

283. *Matthew* 17.7 (REB)
284. Jyoti Sahi *Stepping Stones* p.138
285. Jyoti Sahi *Stepping Stones* p.133

are pilgrims, or fugitives, travelling homeless through this world.'[286]

Another Christian artist from the subcontinent, Nalini Jayasuriya from Sri Lanka, has written passages of distinctive significance for the understanding of Jesus. Commenting on a meditational painting of hers, a 'Christ Mandala' of Jesus within the Trinity, she writes:

> '"Mandala" in Sanskrit means Centre and Circle. It is an Asian concept based on the circle which is the prime symbol in Asia, as a form that has neither beginning nor end, and is suggestive of Totality, Perfection and Ceaseless Renewal. Since we in Asia do not believe anything is final or conclusive and therefore static, a centre radiates outwards to become, incessantly, circles. This is believed to symbolize the whole process of life, death, and ever living lives, or Renewal.'[287]

Such explanations of Asian 'circular' thinking can clearly shed light for us in the West, and provide a salutary reminder in relation to common western dismissals of eastern 'cyclical' thinking in connection with philosophy or religion as mere fatalism or as a despairing absence of any sense of a future destination or goal about human history. Nalini Jayasuriya, as described above, obviously presents a very different outlook, and one of her emphases is on the significance of early and contemporary Christianity's symbolism. She sees the Asian symbols just mentioned (Centre and Circle) as 'vital expressions of truth and life, enabling me to see beyond the immediate present into a spiritual reality and self-knowledge.'.[288]

---

286. Jyoti Sahi *Stepping Stones* p 68

287. The painting forms the front cover of Keith Ward's *A Vision to Pursue*. SCM. 1991.

288. from a 1980s article in *Image*, the newsletter of the Asia Christian Art Association

For many of us this may be seen to give further insights into topics in Christian belief such as that of God and time. It may be seen to link up with thinking about biblical words for 'time' in recent decades. That is, the special significance of the Greek word 'kairos' in the *New Testament*. Out of the two Greek words for time, 'chronos' means roughly 'clock-time' or 'a period of time', whereas 'kairos' means 'a point in time', or 'the right, proper, favourable time'. In *Paul's Letter to Titus* (Chapter 1. verses 2 and 3 in the *Revised English Bible*), 'kairos' is used, and the sentence is about the good news of the Gospel, promised by God long ago, but 'now, in his own good time', given by God in Christ's saving work and entrusted to Paul's preaching. So Christians can believe both in the timelessness of God's unending love and also in the timeliness of God's rescuing and enabling grace in history and human lives. Nalini Jayasuriya's talk of the circle as symbolizing both eternal life and also 'ceaseless renewal' at countless points of time may be seen as especially illuminating here.

This same Asian focus on the 'circle' has also, interestingly, been brought home to us in Britain by Ivor Smith-Cameron in London, and his recent book.[289] Born and brought up in Madras (Chennai), he has lived and worked in Britain for 50 years: 15 years as a university chaplain, and 35 years in parishes. In recent years, he has received an honorary degree as Doctor of Divinity in Serampore University in India. In his address and response to the Serampore Senate on that occasion he took as his subject 'Culture and Creation: The Circle and The Revolving Door' (*Insights and new Symbols for Theology*). In his book he not only draws attention to his feeling close to Celtic spirituality and its sense of the relationship of humanity to the whole created order, and draws attention to David Adams's writings (e.g. the latter's prayer 'Circle me, O God; keep peace within: keep turmoil

---

289. *The Church of Many Colours* 1998. Published from 100 Prince of Wales Drive, London SW11 4BD

out'.) but, in what is also a very down-to-earth and practical book, has many memorable sentences of his own about the all-surrounding presence of God:- 'The Creator God is not distant, aloof or impersonal... God's centre is everywhere and God's circumference is nowhere.'

There are, or have been, of course, many other Christian thinkers in India who contribute distinctive angles on world-wide themes where their angles of contribution are badly needed. On biblical interpretation the late George Soares-Prabhu, the biblical scholar, emphasised that any reading and interpretation of the biblical text in India must be an Indian religious reading, an Indian social reading, and a single integral reading, in an emphasis that could obviously have corresponding and similar patterns in other cultures. He was of the view that any interpretation had 'to avoid the academic barrenness which afflicts "scientific" exegesis today'. Those words were written in 1981 and he was writing till his death at the turn of the century. He wanted the kind of interpretation that would be informed by India's rich religious tradition, and uncover resonances and creativities missed by, say, western interpreters with very different sensibilities. He wanted a social reading that would uncover the biblical liberating message of relevance in India's context with the many socially oppressed. And, finally, he wanted an interpretation where India's 'liberationists' and India's 'ashramites' would 'not be indifferent to one another' in their life, work and thinking.[290] Another badly-needed angle, too, is shown in such writing as the Indian theologian Christopher Duraisingh's article on 'Syncretism', which reminds us, in relation to inter-faith matters not least, that pronouncements about syncretism in

---

290. George Soares-Prabhu's 'The Historical Critical Method' article in *Theologizing in India*. Theological Publications in India, Bangalore, 1981. Edited M. Amaladoss. Reproduced in *Readings in Indian Christian Theology* SPCK London. 1993. Eds. R.S. Sugirtharajah and Cecil Hargreaves.

these matters are too easily made by those in religious settings in the west, and elsewhere, where there are strong syncretisms as between religion and culture. Duraisingh has a sentence about 'unwitting accommodation of the Gospel to individualism and capitalist consumerism among many Christians in the West'.[291]

Indian Christian understandings of Jesus in the second half of the 20th century came to focus in a major way, through Christian participation in the 'dalit' movement, on the 'God-forsaken' Jesus. ('Dalit' means 'downtrodden', 'broken' or 'oppressed', being the name chosen for themselves by the old 'untouchables' in Indian society.) It was on behalf of a considerable number in the population, probably about 20%, who have been kept out of the Hindu caste system. Arvind Nirmal, himself of a dalit family, raised his voice and gave great leadership during the 1970s and 1980s in the dalit movement cause, and in his writings had the reminder that between 80% to 90% of people in the Christian Churches in India were of dalit origin. In his book of edited chapters *A Reader in Dalit Theology*,[292] a book written when he was finally Professor of Systematic Theology in a Lutheran Theological College in Chennai (Madras) he himself spoke of his understanding of God as 'on the side of the dalits': 'the God whom Jesus Christ revealed and about whom the prophets of the *Old Testament* spoke is a dalit God', and in describing Jesus as 'the God-forsaken Jesus' he meant that not only was Jesus sympathetic to the dalits and downtrodden of his day, but that the cross of Jesus 'symbolises the dalitness of his divinity and humanity'.

One more Indian Christian thinker and theologian must be mentioned again, from the later 20th century decades. M.M. Thomas, a figure of supreme importance, was a member of the

---

291. *Dictionary of Third World Theologies*. Orbis 2000. Eds. Virginia Fabella and R.S. Sugirtharajah

292. Gurukul Theological College, Chennai. 1991.

Mar Thoma Syrian Church, a lay theologian with a background and training in sociology and economics. Internationally known, he became chairman of the Central Committee of the World Council of Churches, and late in the 1980s Governor of Nagaland, in North East India. Fully committed to a theology of personal, individual conviction, he pleaded also for 'a theology of society' and 'a spirituality of hope'. He saw Christian mission as including a struggle for 'the humanizing of the secular structure of existence', a struggle 'for personal existence', and a struggle for 'The new Asia'. A book which he wrote in 1976 had the title *The Secular Ideologies of India and the Secular Meaning of Christ.*[293] In it he based his spirituality of hope on Jesus' involvement in history and the world, as seen in his life in 'Palestine', his Crucifixion, his Resurrection and the Promises of the End-time and the Fullness of Time. Then the book examined what 'history and the world' meant in terms of India's liberal nationalism, socialist humanism, Marxist-Leninism and anti-Brahmanism. M.M. Thomas can thus be seen to have been prominent among those who in India at that time tried to go deeply into the significance of Jesus, alongside those who pointed to that significance through poetry and visual art, and in many other ways. One further point may be noted. In one of his books[294] M.M. Thomas touches on the question of the influence of the figure of Jesus and of salvation, as applying to those in other faith-communities and outside the Church. He himself could be said to prefer to speak of the 'decisiveness' of Christ and his work of salvation rather than use such phrases as the 'uniqueness' of Christ. The latter word can of course so easily

---

293. Christian Literature Society. Chennai (Madras). M.M. Thomas' phrase 'a spirituality of hope' comes from his article 'The Pattern of Christian Spirituality' in the journal *Religion and Society* for June 1969. Bangalore

294. *The Acknowledged Christ of the Indian Renaissance* CLS Madras 1970 p.308-309

get used in ways that sound to those of other faiths patronising or superior in tone. The word 'decisiveness' in these contexts is certainly preferred by other notable Christian theologians in Asia such as Choan-Seng Song in his writings, as in the article 'The Decisiveness of Christ'. M.M. Thomas quotes in full some words of the American theologian Schubert Ogden: 'the claim "only in Jesus Christ" must be interpreted to mean, not that God acts to redeem only in the history of Jesus and in no other history, but that the only God who redeems any history (although he in fact redeems every history) is the God whose redemptive action is decisively represented in the word that Jesus speaks and is.'[295] Also quoted are the words of the Sri Lankan theologian and missioner D.T. Niles, 'those engaged in the Church's mission must be prepared to encounter in their work the result of God's free initiative, the previousness of Jesus Christ in every situation, the all-embracing work of the Holy Spirit within which the mission of the Church is set.'[296] Thomas comments on those two quotations: 'Probably this is the only form of universalism which can be ultimately called Christian.'

Asia: voices from further East

Although this part of the chapter, on Asia, should not concentrate only on the theme of 'suffering and hope', and although the voices of Christian thinkers in east Asia in very recent times such as the Chinese feminist theologian Kwok Pui-lan have notably concentrated not only on what one might call 'suffering liberated by hope', but especially on the liberation of oppressed women, yet in general, also, the theme of suffering and hope has had very wide attention given to it in countries in east Asia just as in India, during the second half of the twentieth century. In 1946

---

295. Schubert Ogden *The Reality of God*. 1967. p.173
296. D.T. Niles *Upon the Earth* London 1962 p.86ff

Dr Kazoh Kitamori, professor of systematic theology in Tokyo, published a book entitled *Theology of the Pain of God*.[297] He said that Christians needed to tackle that and not spend all the time, as western thinkers tended to do, on theologies of the Word of God. He cited the Japanese word 'tsurasa', meaning 'pain-love', the basic principle in Japanese tragedy, as highly significant. Similarly, a little later, the Taiwanese theologian, Dr Choan-Seng Song, wrote of how in the languages of China the words 'love' and 'pain' are interchangeable, saying 'a mother pain-loves her child'. He went on to say how he saw Jesus as embodying that pain-love of God and as being involved in the pain of Asian people through the passion of his own pain on the Cross. In his 1979 book *Third-Eye Theology*[298] he goes on to amplify what he says in two of the chapters, headed 'Suffering unto Hope' and 'The Rice of Hope'. Again, the Japanese missioner in Thailand, and theologian, Dr Kosuke Koyama, reminds his readers that South Korean Christians have a theology of 'han', meaning the brokenness and 'the pain of oppressed people', and that village-people in Thailand found special significance in Jesus' words 'Now is my soul troubled': and that for him, Koyama, in his own experience, the message of pain-love was most made real in the breaking of the bread in the Eucharist. 'When the bread is broken a new "painful" space appears between the two pieces of the bread; making Jesus' own brokenness and pain real for us and making us commit ourselves further to sharing in some way in service and brokenness.'[299]

It is surely not without significance that Kitamori's 1946 book came in the year following the Hiroshima and Nagasaki

---

297. Published in English by SCM Press

298. Lutterworth press. Eng. Edition. 1980.

299. Koyama. *The Ecumenical Movement as the Dialogue of Cultures*. Included in Pauline Webb's edited book Faith and Faithfulness. World Council of Churches. 1984. pp.49-50

bombs. And Koyama has acknowledged that the experience of Japan's tragedy and defeat in 1943 was one of the main things that fashioned his thinking. The word 'power' is given prominence in his writings and he sees modern culture as 'predominantly power-orientated'.[300] Dr Sugirtharajah describes Koyama's book *Mount Fuji and Mount Sinai* as 'an absorbing investigation of the relationship between East and West, leading to a theology of the Cross against the menace of the nuclear threat.'

A large number of those mentioned above have been described as 'theologians' and the Chinese Kwok Pui Lan is no exception. But she wrote as well, in 1992, an autobiographical article entitled *Mothers and Daughters, Writers and Fighters*,[301] which is very personal and autobiographical, and supplements her theological writings as a member of the staff of the Episcopal Divinity School in Cambridge, Massachusetts and previously in the Chinese University of Hong Kong. Well-known as a radical feminist theologian, she concentrates also on biblical interpretation and on issues of religion and culture, her radical views on these subjects offering an important Asian contribution in relation to topics currently to the fore in non-Third-World parts of the world.

Her autobiographical writing puts a strong emphasis on her 'story', her experience and her Asian family background, which she wants to see integrally bound up with the Christian biblical story handed down traditionally among Jews and Christians. Elsewhere she writes that modern people's stories of their own in different cultures share in a dialogue 'to search for a collective new religious imagination'. The *Bible* 'offers us insights for our

---

300. Koyama. 'The Crucified Christ Challenges Human Power' article is from his *Your Kingdom Come: Mission Perspectives* 1990. WCC. Reproduced in *Asian Faces of Jesus* ed. R.S. Sugirtharajah. Orbis 1993.

301. Reproduced in *Frontiers in Asian Christian Theology*. Ed. R.S. Sugirtharajah. Orbis. 1994.

survival.' 'It represents one story 'of the Israelites' struggle for justice in Egypt, and in many other of their situations. But 'Asian Christians are heirs to both the biblical story and to our own story as Asian people'.[302]

Her family background and 'story' was this. Her mother was a devout Buddhist and her mother-in-law 'did not follow any particular religious practice', but, she says, had 'a profound trust in life and an unfailing spirit for survival.' And she admired both of them. Then she had what she calls her 'spiritual foremothers' among Christian women pioneers of the earlier twentieth century, and others later, including in particular, Deaconess Huang Xianyun (Jane Hwang). Huang Xianyun and Joyce Bennett were ordained as the first women priests in the Anglican Communion in 1971, by Bishop Hall.

Kwok Pui-Lan has, as mentioned, a feminist emphasis at the heart of her theology and thinking. It is 'doing theology from a Chinese woman's perspective' that she writes of as her guiding line, while respecting the fact that the deadening hand of a patriarchal tradition has been struggled against both by brave Christian Chinese women whether the tradition is in Chinese culture or in Christianity, or by brave Chinese people like her mother and mother-in-law wherever they found the tradition. So a feminist emphasis is centrally determinative for her. She writes that a critical question for women theologians is that of who Jesus Christ is for Asian women, giving the answer that he is seen as 'a fully liberated human being whose prophetic ministry challenged the status quo and transgressed' (and crossed) 'the religious and ethnic boundaries of his time'.[303]

---

302. Kwok Piu Lan. *Discovering the Bible in the Non-Biblical World*. Orbis. 1995. Reproduced in *Voices from the Margin* ed. R.S. Sugirtharajah. SPCK London. 1991: Orbis. 1995, pp.303,294

303. Kwok Pui-Lan in *Dictionary of Third World Theologies*. Eds. Virgina Fabella and R.S. Sugirtharajah. Orbis. 2000

As pointed out earlier, her position on biblical interpretation is both religiously and culturally formed. She explicitly states that the relationship between those two factors has been especially difficult in the case of the Chinese because 'Christianity came to China together with the expansion of western military aggression' – the latter being a cultural factor in western human behaviour at that time.[304] And she refers to Koyama's focus on dangerous extremisms of political totalitarianism or religious absolutism which show the complex mixture of the cultural and the religious, a focus touched on above: she refers also to C.S. Song's writings. The latter had the sentence 'culture affects spirituality', in connection with how the arrival of a spiritual mission in the seventeenth century into Japan was seen as something power-related, since foreign.[305] In the present age, when China is regarded as one of the two super-powers now emerged, Kwok Pui-Lan's contribution among Asian writers on culture, religion and power can hardly be unrecognised.

This section perhaps suitably closes with Kosuke Koyama again. He has seemed to have, in a warm-hearted and distinctive way, both a religious, devotional, theological thrust and also a poetic intensity of expression. He has a brief passage centring on the phrase 'Our God is a transitive God'. That is, a God whose eyes are on long routes with his creatures: a God of the long perspectives of both what is near at hand and what is distant: a God of 'three miles an hour, the speed of love', and the speed of his people in their wanderings: and a God who wants humanity to try and follow their routes in a similar way. Or again, Koyama writes that he himself wants to see things as Jesus did. 'I want to

---

304. *Mothers and Daughters*. p.149

305. C.S. Song. *Third-Eye Theology*. P.8. Lutterworth Press, London. 1980

see his eyes.[306] I ask no theologians to stand by when I meet Jesus, to give me a theological exposition about his eyes. In silence, I just want to see his eyes by myself.'

One last comment in this chapter returns us to Kwok-Pui-Lan, and is this. Reflecting on her emphasis on our human stories as central elements helping us not least to bring life and imagination into dialogues across cultures, many of us will be tempted to see something almost absurd about much western discussion recently on the need to turn our backs in a post-modern age on the traditional hold of 'narrative', especially received religious narrative. Admittedly, as mentioned in earlier pages, narrative may justly come under fire if its role has become authoritarian and imprisoning. But that is only one aspect of narrative, and a wholesale dismissal of the importance of narrative, for example, in favour, solely, of individual choice, is clearly disastrous.

---

306. Koyama. *Three Mile an Hour God.* SCM. London. 1979. pp.8-10 and *Fifty Meditations*. Christian Journals, Belfast. 1975. p.25

11

A MODERN SON OF NAZARETH AND
OTHER ROUTE-MAKERS

Hosam Naoum, whose father was a carpenter from Nazareth, has been recently, as a young priest, Rector of St Philip's Episcopal Church in Nablus and the Church of the Good Shepherd in Rafidia, in the Diocese of Jerusalem. Nablus (the biblical Shechem in Samaria) is about halfway between Jerusalem to the south and Galilee to the north.

In an article for the summer 2004 issue of *Christians Aware*, Hosam Naoum describes his calling as a priest, and how he understands the path of spirituality on which the whole Church of Christ is called to follow, in the following words: 'We all belong to each other as people, black, white, Christian, Muslim, Jew. Our only enemy is hatred and discrimination, and not being human to the person who stands in front of my eyes. Look for the good in each person.'[307]

He says that most of his life has been spent in Galilee (though it may be important for us to notice that throughout he uses the designation '<u>the</u> Galilee' and not 'Galilee': and some

---

307. Published from 2 Saxby Street, Leicester LE2 0ND

242

biblical commentators remind us that 'Galilee' in Hebrew means a 'ring' or a 'circle', and is a contraction of a fuller expression, 'Galilee of the nations'; and that originally the district was a frontier district surrounded on three sides by foreigners). But though he has been mostly in Galilee, he spent three years, after his schooling and upbringing in Nazareth, in South Africa, training for the priesthood at the College of the Transfiguration, of the Mirfield tradition, in Grahamstown. That was clearly a hugely important period for him; it is described by him as 'a wonderful experience, challenging and enriching. Keeping in mind the situation of apartheid in South Africa, and coming from Palestine, it inspired my life and my spirituality.' Plainly, that period's experience lies behind the three sentences of his about his vocation and calling which I quoted earlier.

He says further that before those three years he had been looking at the conflict in Palestine and Israel from a secular point of view, and now he came to look at it 'from a Christian point of view', which was 'the bottom line' of what he learned in the seminary. That bottom line is also described as learning to look 'at the whole issue of life. All life is transfigured in God's image. We must be transfigured'. Mention is also made of how the college was known for its academic excellence, and how he received a degree in theology.

Three other points may be said to emerge from what is written. First, on his vocation, he writes that he did not have a Damascus road experience at the start, but describes himself as having loved the Church since childhood, and is conscious and grateful of how 'God, one way and another, has put in my heart the love to serve him in his church and to be an ambassador for Christ in the world'. He says that his calling is not finished, but is reviewed each day through meeting people, talking to people, serving the church.

Secondly, on his parish work, he writes 'I am first of all a priest. I do the work of any priest...' of his time in Nablus and Rafidia. He expresses delight at the fact of the building of a new church in Rafidia, adding that it is not every day that a new church is built. And he gives news of his own marriage in 2002.

Thirdly, he expresses his sense of the importance of being able to rely on the mutual prayer for each other in different parts of the world Church, especially when 'the Church is aching'. That clearly touches on the situation of his own part of the Church in the conflict in Palestine and Israel, referred to above. He adds words, too, about what he terms the mission of the whole Church and our need 'to restore God's image by reconciliation, peace and how to make this out of conflict'. He is encouraged by the help that e-mail gives, in keeping in touch with believers and friends across the world.

Route-finding through opposites, ambiguities and paradoxes

Esther de Waal is a writer, lecturer and conductor of retreats, who lives now in the Welsh borders where she grew up. One of her books is entitled *Living with Contradiction*.[308] Her approach is a Benedictine one, and another book, *A Life-Giving Way*, is a commentary on the Rule of St Benedict.[309] Her interest is also in the Celtic tradition.

In the second of her books mentioned above, she writes that it was when she lived in Canterbury, in a house that had been in the Middle Ages the prior's lodging of the great medieval Benedictine community, that she first discovered St Benedict's Rule and started reading it. And then she adds: 'I had thought

---

308. Fount paperbacks, London, 1989, and published in 1997 by Canterbury Press

309. Mowbray/Cassell 1995

that I would pick up the rule in order to increase my historical understanding. Instead it changed my life.'[310]

In the first of the books mentioned, she describes how the Rule's help and guidance have been her support in facing the contradictions and complexities in life: in particular how St Benedict's teaching on paradox (she calls him 'a master of paradox') has helped her to see that between and beyond the two extremes of naïve optimism or meaningless despair, which may seem to be the only choices before us in the face of life's opposites and contradictions, there can be found the secret and the possibility of 'a creative holding together of opposites' as found in paradox and a middle way between two extremes. Esther de Waal says that this finds a positive response in her; 'in my heart of hearts I know I grow by opposites', and 'this polarity, this holding together of opposites, presents us not with a closed system but with a series of open doors'.[311] She likens a paradox and its opposites to a mediaeval architectural arch, with the two sides of an arch seen as a creative holding together of tensions, leading up to a stone boss at the top which carries the thrust of the two sides in a stability for the whole building.[312]

St Benedict belonged to the sixth century and brought together the two monastic traditions, that of St Basil and his humane leadership, and that of the desert fathers with their more ascetic character. Benedict wrote of the regulations which were to set the tone for his community: 'We hope to set down nothing harsh, nothing burdensome', though adding: 'the good of all concerned, however, may prompt us to a little strictness in order to amend faults and to safeguard love'. He avoids extremism, and is open to differing and even divergent aspects of the truth, though

---

310. *A Life-Giving Way* p.221

311. *Living with Contradiction.* p.38 and p.22

312. *Living with Contradiction.* p.iii of the Preface

there is not necessarily any resolution of the tension between them: simply avoiding mutual antagonism. Again, as touched on above, such points have reality for Esther de Waal, because, as she says, her prayer to God is 'to be an honest expression of the person that I am', and the contradictions which she finds within herself 'are the basis from which she approaches God'.

She backs up her convictions here by referring to the *Psalms*, declaring that 'Benedictines are people of the *Psalms*', and outlining the *Psalms* as expressing (as some have put it) the psalmist's patience and praise, but also his complaints and protests. Though she does not specify this psalm, *Psalm* 55 exemplifies this aspect. Its two opening verses are scarcely veiled complaint ('Listen, God, to my prayer. Do not hide yourself from my pleading. Hear me and give me an answer, for my cares leave me no peace'). But the last verse of the psalm is this: 'Lord, I shall put my trust in you'. de Waal adds: 'I stand before God as I really am, or at least that is what I want to do.'[313]   Enlarging on this, she writes of how dilemmas for many of us take the form of the two inner extremes referred to earlier: on the one side, contradictions, despair and knowing oneself on the darker side of one's nature, and, on the other side, a naïve optimism, perfectionism and idealization: the latter as known on the 'nicer' side of one's nature, and as encouraged, it may seem to us, by well-meaning exhortations from those who have guided us. The middle way of facing those dilemmas, the way of holding the two sides together, is not seen by the Benedictine approach as any sort of way of weak and soft compromise, but as a positive, though paradoxical, 'two sides of the arch', approach, offering a healthy way of moderation and balance. (Within other aspects in Anglicanism, one may be reminded of William Law's warnings about the 'extreme of zeal'.) An earlier chapter of this present book

---

313. *Living with Contradiction.* pp.129, 130

refers to R.S.Thomas' words of how, in his experience, times of difficulty have led to creativity; out of the tension of opposites in life creative work often seems to be born.

Is the whole of the above 'approach' biblically-based as well as prayer-based and monasticism-based? Esther de Waal replies strongly in the affirmative. She not only cites the central paradoxical emphasis of the Cross, seeing the Christ on the Cross as 'the ultimate contradiction', holding together the vertical looking up to the Father and the horizontal looking out, and arms stretched out, to the world. She also sees the Gospels and their teaching, and the rest of the *New Testament*, as full of paradox; the triumphal Victor who rides on a donkey, the Saviour 'who is executed like some common criminal', 'the God whose promise is that in losing my life I shall find it', and so on. All this she sees as shining through the Benedictine approach. As for the paradoxical significance of the figure of Jesus, what was written in previous pages about Jesus' ancient Jewish background and heritage (born out of the Jews' early experience of pioneering, of providential guidance, and of paradox), as also what was written about Jesus' calling to both authoritativeness and vulnerability in his baptism and in Nazareth, the closeness between the Benedictine way and the biblical good news in Jesus, in the *New Testament*, can hardly be questioned.

Mentioned above is the word 'perfectionism'. The teaching of Jesus contains one verse that can sound like nothing but perfectionism: as given in some translations into English (both traditional and some modern translations), it is 'Be perfect, as your heavenly Father is perfect'.[314] But some of the most acclaimed English biblical scholars in the twentieth century translated it as; 'There must be no limit to your goodness, as your heavenly Father's goodness knows no bounds', the translation to be found

---

314. *Matthew* 5.48 in *King James Bible*

in the *New English Bible* and the *Revised English Bible*. The point at issue is the meaning here of the original Greek word 'teleios' which (based on the word 'telos' meaning 'end') can be used of someone who is 'fully-grown', or 'perfect', or is complete. The *New English Bible* and *Revised English Bible* translators have clearly wanted to bring out the general meaning of the verse as a call by Jesus to his followers to be people who have completed God's end-purposes for them, rather than a call to be 'perfect'. To avoid the word 'perfect' is not to lessen the demanding nature of the teaching, but is to avoid the sense of a perfectionist meaning which the word can in English convey in modern parlance, while retaining a true meaning of the original word.

A domestic problem over choices and options

Margaret Killingray is linked to the London Institute for Contemporary Christianity. Her book *Choices*, with a sub-title *Deciding Right and Wrong Today*,[315] combines two things usefully: the stories of people confronting very practical dilemmas in their everyday life with good, serious, readable discussion about ethics, and a tackling of her sub-title's theme.

One point in particular that seemed to me to come across in her book is her central concern that the issue of maintaining the distinction between right and wrong receive serious discussion, along with her clear emphasis on the challenge involved in many of the 'opposites' with which life confronts us. In the context of this present book's obvious dwelling a good deal on the importance of paradox, and of paradox as 'apparent contradiction' (as exemplified, say, when we talk of someone as paradoxically combining anger against injustice and yet also compassion for all), it seems valuable to note what I take to be one of Margaret Killingray's main points.

---

315. Bible Reading Fellowship. 2001

One of her stories of people facing dilemmas is her story of a married couple, John and Peg. Their children have grown up and left home. They are having a conservatory built on the back of their house, and have finally decided on what seems to them a good estimate for the work from a builder. A moment then comes when the builder mentions that he would like to be paid in cash, and obviously in that way will avoid paying income tax. He thereby also offers them the chance not to have to pay value-added tax on the bill. Later, when the couple were discussing between themselves those last points from the builder, their younger daughter arrives unexpectedly. Looking around at the signs of preparations going on, by way of curtain samples and carpets and so on, and hearing more about the building plans, she comes out with challenging questions about why they are spending so much money on themselves when there are empty bedrooms upstairs, homeless people in the street, and much need, hunger and suffering across the world.

That clearly presented the couple with a growing dilemma. At first they had regarded the builder's mention of paying in cash as a generous offer which it would be rather discourteous and embarrassing to refuse to take up. Then, as they had thought about it, they had wondered whether in fact the builder's apparently generous offer was not sitting lightly to the fact that a builder is bound by law to be taxed on the money he earns, and that the builder's suggestion might, in the view of many people, be seen as tantamount to stealing. Now, on top of all that, their daughter had complicated the dilemma further; her comments were liable to sow in their minds other options and routes than their original plans, in the direction of seeing if there were any students in a local college who might be needing accommodation, or in the direction of sending money to a charity currently making an appeal through the post.

However, their daughter's comments were equally liable to produce resentment in the couple's minds, for being criticized, but Margaret Killingray, being concerned with the dilemmas involved, does not seem to continue the couple's story further. In fact, however, the story of one couple's dilemma has itself pointed up the chief focus of her book, on the good options and the bad options, like a fork in the road, confronting any couple in a situation like that couple's. In one chapter of her book, she asks the question 'What is morality?' and looks carefully round that general topic. Noting, importantly, that some recent philosophy, concentrating on a linguistic approach, has concluded that words like 'good' and 'bad' have no moral force, 'They are simply expressing personal preference, and to say that something is "good" is meaningless.'[316] Hence the modern tendency to concentrate only on personal choice and individualise the whole subject, and to want to discard all such things as guidelines and signposts. The second part of her book is subtitled 'Is there a Christian way to live?'

A foreword to the book by Rob Warner refers to the 1960s as an era of 'moral libertarianism', and to the 1990s as a time of 'moral' anxiety: mention of the 1960s of course raises large questions which take one on to matters which Margaret Killingray's book has not the space to cover. The legacy of the 1960s' gets more discussion in Adrian Hastings' massive paperback *A History of English Christianity 1920-1990*,[317] where he saw the 1960's crisis as 'a crisis of secularisation' in both a negative and positive sense. There was a contempt for structures, whether religious or secular, and for structures of received belief. But also what Hastings calls an 'impressive' relating of religious institutional bodies (in danger of domestication) to 'the totality of the secular'. Christians got more involved in politics and

---

316. *Choices*. P.59
317. SCM Press. 1991. especially pp. 580-586

economics: distinguished economists and lay theologians such as Barbara Ward and Fritz Schumacher gave a great lead in Britain in the 1960s; and, in a slightly later decade, David Sheppard was saying that to be a bishop in inner-city Liverpool one had to get involved in politics. But the book *Choices* is very much a part of the total wide discussion.

The Eucharist as transition out of brokenness into renewal

John Drury, the biblical scholar and theologian, now Chaplain and Fellow of All Souls College, Oxford, in his book *The Burning Bush,*[318] starts from the burning bush event in Moses' life. Moses was described as being given a glimpse of the abiding presence of God staying with him and his people through all transitions and upheavals. He saw in the bush the miracle of a bush that was on fire, but was not burnt up.[319] At one stage in his book he takes the above glimpse to lead us splendidly into the mysteries of what I like to think of as the timelessness and unchangeableness of God, and yet also the timeliness of God, interwoven with power and love at every needed time into the mundane earthly changes and transitions in the lives, delights, failures and achievements of his human creatures.

Drury then proceeds to show the reader how he or she, at every occasion of their sharing in the Eucharist and the breaking of the bread, can be given, in spite of all their acknowledged mortality and perversity, a transition across into God's presence and activity in the covenanted meal, shared with the worshippers, of the sacrament. The Eucharist, says Drury, 'begins with tragic reality', and moves towards and fosters 'communion' with God,

318. Collins, Fount. 1990
319. *Exodus* Chapter 4. w.2-8

and others.[320] Ritually there are opening moments of confession and forgiveness of sin and failure, for ourselves, our society, our world, and then the central focus on the death of Christ, rehearsed at the beginning of the Eucharistic prayer. 'And at the end of it all', writes Drury, the Eucharist moves into communion, and the worshippers' self-commitment and self-offering, in thanksgiving, hope and renewal.' St Paul's words to the Christians in Corinth are quoted, in which Paul writes about the tradition handed down of the breaking of the bread.[321] The Christian tradition was that the brokenness (as well as the truth of Christ raised) lies behind every worshipper's ability to face his or her own brokenness and to take hold of the healing of it, with life and energy for subsequent service and outreach. Christian life was a 'carrying about, in one's body, Jesus' dying', so that the life and power of Jesus may also be shown and revealed in lives and bodies.[322]

It was a sacrament, in other words, in which believers are invited to make their own crossings, that is, from a submerging to a being raised, and from a joining in fraction and brokenness into a sharing and a belonging, in relation to God and to others. The Eucharist's pattern is seen as a route between two extremes: despair, guilt, solitude, exclusion and tragedy on the one hand, and on the other, the extreme of utopianism and cocksureness. In a strong passage, Drury writes:

> 'Tragedy' (like classic tragic dramas) 'and
> Eucharist are representations that enforce on us
> our participation in death.' 'And our culpability…
> We would like to get back to The Garden of Eden,
> without its snake. Utopias and cocksure sects
> beckon… The results of acting on that dream are
> familiar to our century and marked at Auschwitz

---

320. *The Burning Bush* pp.65-68

321. *1 Corinthians*. Ch.11. verses 23-26

322. *2 Corinthians*. Ch.4. verse 10 (REB)

and Katin. The Eucharist is crucially important
because it speaks of better things. Beginning with
tragic reality rather than flattering dream, it fosters
communion rather than crusade.'[323]

The sacrament's invitation deepens, as said above, into a
final partaking, self-offering, and the promised experience of the
presence and activity of God.

Elsewhere in his writings, Drury comments on biblical
meanings to be found in the *Gospel of Luke's* account of Jesus'
visit to the house of Martha and Mary in Bethany, as illustrated
in the seventeenth century artist Velasquez' painting *Kitchen
Scene with Christ in the House of Martha and Mary*. The painting
shows both Jesus talking to a group in the background and also
a 'Martha-like' woman telling a worried maid, who is wrestling
with some cooking, that Jesus has said that they must not be too
anxious about household details and difficulties. Drury notes
that the maid's 'deeply troubled face'... 'is close to tears'. The
contrast, of course, is with Jesus' words to Martha: 'only one
thing is necessary; Mary has chosen what is best'. And a general
comment of Drury on '*Luke's*' presentation of Jesus' activities
sheds light on the deep meanings within such paintings as those
of Velasquez in Spain: 'St Luke's imagination twisted eternity
together with our historical world of times, people and places.
In the fabric of his' (*Luke's*) 'work the two are woven together.
Mundane existence is shot through with the golden threads
of divinity'. The last few words there may perhaps provide us
with a good final phrase to describe how Drury's writing on the
Eucharist shows the sacrament vividly as an occasion when time
is 'shot through with the golden threads' of eternity.[324]

---

323. *The Burning Bush*. Pp. 65-68. 1990.

324. John Drury. *Painting the Word (Christian Pictures and Their
Meaning)*, Yale University Press, New Haven and London, and
National Gallery Publications, London. 1999. pp.41, 156, 159.

A philosopher's journey through the claims of reason and love

Route-making in *Love's Work* and *Paradiso* by Gillian Rose lies between the good claims of both reason and love.[325]

As philosopher, as someone of Polish and Jewish family with a tragic background of Holocaust persecution and loss, and as someone known to her friends as a radiant, passionate person who saw love and relationship as the heart of life, she acknowledges the vocation to wrestle with the claims of mind and heart, and with what she called 'quandaries'. 'My Judaism helps me to develop a perspective on quandaries,' she wrote.

In the years immediately before her death in 1996, she was Professor of Social and Political Thought at the University of Warwick. She strongly maintained that reason had a very positive role to fulfil in facing life and all its 'hells'. On paradox, she was attracted to one of Aristotle's distinctions which she had been pointed to, the Aristotelian extremes of 'aporia' (perplexity) and 'euporia' (a way out), though he put the emphasis on the middle term 'diaporia' (the way through): she describes 'diaporia' as 'exploring various routes, different ways towards the good enough justice, which recognises the intrinsic and the contingent limitations in the exercise'. But, alongside this, the claims of love are faced. She fully accepted the fact of vulnerability, in herself, in human nature, and of 'a trauma within reason itself'. The route lies between mind and emotion, power and vulnerability. In her last years and months before her death from cancer, and with the companionship and help from others, which she describes and welcomed, there was a continuing movement towards integration.

---

325. *Love's Work*. Chatto and Windus. 1995. pp.52, 74, 116, 133, 135. *Paradiso*. Menard Press. 1999, posthumous: editor's preface p.7-8. The first two paragraphs that now follow are mostly reproduced verbatim from my article in the journal *Theology* Sept/Oct 2003.

She wrote: 'love and philosophy may seem to have had the most say, but friendship and faith have been framing and encroaching by night and by day.'

Following up the preceding paragraphs mostly on the claims of the mind and the reason, it is good to find in the last book of Gillian Rose[326] that she includes some more personal references, to her contacts during the 1990s, and to the 'friendship and faith' which played a significant part in her life, and continuing thought, in her last years.

She found the medical consultant in a Coventry hospital to whom she was referred in her illness to have, as she saw it, just the sort of philosophic approach that helped her, which at its simplest, meant 'the ability to pay attention' to his patient, and truly listen. She adds that, for her, his approach 'incorporated the nursing definition of care into that of the specialist'. And one of her descriptions of him is simply to write of his 'goodness'. Her phrases are striking. She says that he helped one, without doing it in a way that made you feel you had lost all control of your condition, but in a way that handed back to one 'the knitting of body and soul' that was necessary. He did this by 'presenting knowledge about critical illness without arrogating authority, but also without relinquishing it'. She seemed to sense that he wanted to share 'control' of her illness with her. It certainly seems to have established for her a deep feeling of mutual trust.

Another contact during those years was a member of an Anglican contemplative religious community in the Benedictine tradition, Sister Edna. She met her first at an Oxford event in 1992 centred on a lecture on the Hebrew Scriptures, since Sister Edna did much researching into Jewish mystical theology and, for example, the Hebrew Talmud Torah. As a contrast Edna had a background of ballet-dancing in earlier life, and continued to

326. *Paradiso* (Menard Press 1999 published posthumously): pp.15-36, 42-47

have what is described as 'a passion' for the Hebrew biblical book *Song of Songs*. Her parents had started as what is described as 'impecunious Bohemian parents' on the continent. The friendship clearly became a deep one, with many mutual interests. Gillian Rose in 1995 stayed briefly as a guest at Sister Edna's convent, and describes how impressed she was both by the disciplined life of Christian prayer and by the accompanying openness and social friendliness of afternoon times of conversation. It became clear to her, and Edna made it clear, that behind the interest in, and the attraction to, *Song of Songs,* 'the life of prayer and the hiddenness' was everything for Edna, just as that life of prayer 'was everything' for the community. Since Gillian Rose was already familiar with St Augustine and other Christian mystical thinkers, she writes that Edna's whole life-story seemed 'to parallel and modernise the dilemmas and the goodness of St Augustine'. She discerns in her a 'continuity' of both 'integrity and brokenness'. She likes Edna's mystical theology and her combination of 'keen intellectual presence' and 'unfathomable piety'. She is reminded of St Augustine's early life and his different later life; also of Augustine's emphasis both on the knowledge of God, doctrinally thought out and taught, and on an accompanying emphasis on mystical friendship with God, as in his *Confessions.*

Of one other contact, whom she had known already during her Warwick years, she writes when describing her final stay in the hospital ward, and he was visiting her. He was Simon Barrington-Ward, the Bishop of Coventry at that time. In a paragraph of hers about the authority belonging both to doctors and to nurses, and touching on a point already mentioned above about her good fortune in having found a doctor who 'incorporated the nursing definition of care' into his own specialist care, she has some moving sentences about the bishop and his visits. He seemed, she says, to have 'an inviolable authority' as he came carrying in his hand some simple 'posy of fragrant garden flowers'. She adds that 'he came to help me push gently forward', in the task perhaps best described in a phrase already referred to as the knitting of body and soul. In a tribute written by Simon Barrington-Ward after her death, he said that in her last few weeks she asked for baptism and was baptized, finding reality in the figure of Christ, the Word, 'the Logos become human, as wholeness for us in our brokenness'.[327]

Some will find the focus in the above sections on route-finding between two extremes, with references to R.S. Thomas' poetry of paradox, to be somewhat paralleled in Karen Armstrong's book *The Spiral Staircase*.[328] Her painful journey to find the spirituality she had long sought contained an early tackling of the experience of extremes (p.91) with clues to a resolution of problems found in T.S. Eliot's poem *Ash Wednesday*, and perhaps, underlying that, the well-known lines from his *Four Quartets*: 'the end of all our exploring / Will be to arrive where we started / And know the place for the first time'.

A risky route-making in challenging times

The heading above relates to the well-known Iona Community, based in the West of Scotland. We have already in Chapters 5 and 8 made brief references to it and to its message of 'holy restlessness'. The Introduction to the book *Wrestling and Resting*[329] quotes a verse from one of the community's 'Wild Goose Songs', as giving us a good reminder 'of the urgency in the Gospel, the holy restlessness which urges us on into the Kingdom'. The verse, described by the Introduction as an example of 'grounded, earthed spirituality', is this:

---

327. *Church Times*. July. 1996.

328. Harper Collins, 2004.

329. *Wrestling and Resting (Exploring Stories of Spirituality from Britain and Ireland)*. CTBI Inter-Church House, 35-41 Lower Marsh, London SE1 7RL. 1999. ed. Ruth Harvey.

'Heaven shall not wait
For the dawn of great ideas,
Thoughts of compassion divorced from cries of
       pain:
Jesus is Lord:
He has married word and action;
His cross and company make his purpose plain.'[330]

(John Bell and Graham Maule)

The phrase 'holy restlessness' matches well, of course, the wild goose symbol which the Community has taken as its symbol, and which is the ancient Celtic symbol for the Holy Spirit. Ron Ferguson, a member, and for some time leader, of the Community, has written a classic (paperback) book on the community, with the title *Chasing the Wild Goose*.[331]

The sight of a flock of wild geese, powerful birds with a wide wing-span, flying across the sea in formation, has been a special feature of the Hebrides over the centuries and remains so. Ferguson says that wild geese 'flying in flock' together have a seventy-per cent greater range than a single goose on its own: and geese in formation fly seventy-five per cent faster than single geese. So it is that the wild goose has been seen as a symbol both of travelling with a strong forward thrust and with a pattern of community and formation, and seen too as a symbol for any band of pilgrims on pilgrimage. While the riskiness of such a journey in a wild area must be admitted, and the risk that it might turn out to be what the modern use of the phrase means by a wild goose chase, yet Ferguson says that within this chase, Spirit-led, 'the clues of our true destiny are to be found'. While the companion-

---

330. *Wild Goose Songs* Volume 1. 1987. Wild Goose Publications. Publishing Division of the Iona Community, Pearce Institute, 840 Govan Road, Glasgow G51 3UT

331. Fount. Harper Collins. 1988

symbol of the dove for the Holy Spirit has been the traditional symbol in the Western Church, the more 'turbulent' sign of the wild-goose is the one, he writes, 'appropriate to living the faith in our day'. He adds 'We live on a roller-coaster'.

So – just as 'the wings of the Wild-Goose were beating' when St Columba and his twelve followers came to Iona in the sixth century, and when, in the 1930s of the 20th century a team of present-day St Columba pilgrims came from Glasgow to Iona, in a modern Iona Community, to help rebuild and repair the buildings of Iona Abbey, it could be said (as Ferguson says) that that has been 'one contemporary attempt to listen for the beating of wings, and to venture into the following of the Holy Spirit's Chase, a sacred chase'.

The venture from Glasgow in 1938 was part of the result of George Macleod's leadership as a minister in the church, and as someone who since 1930 had been minister of Govan Old Parish Church in one of the great shipbuilding centres in Glasgow. But the great national Depression of the 1930s was hitting Glasgow, the shipbuilding yards were silent, many craftsmen with a variety of skills were unemployed, and social deprivation in Govan was described as appalling. The parish church became extremely active: its team of volunteers climbed tenement stairs in visits to housing estates, and Macleod invited some of the unemployed craftsmen to repair a broken-down mill at nearby Fingleton, so that their skills could be used and morale lifted in turning the place into a leisure centre for Govan families.

Meanwhile, from 1935, Macleod had been floating the idea that Iona and its ancient Abbey should be given new life, its buildings repaired, ordained Church ministers in training should spend time each year living in the community and at the same time unemployed craftsmen should go there too and start rebuilding work. Macleod's vision was that the Church of Scotland should be helped to recapture some of its ancient calling to be a Church for the whole community and not just a collection of congregations of church-members liable, as he felt, as in all Church-bodies, to become inward-turning. His vision for the Abbey was a new 'blend of worship and work in the context of shared Christian community' (Ferguson's words) that would also 'forge a new vocabulary and style for the Christian life'.

As time went on and when Macleod had been eight years in Govan, he followed suggestions that a follow-on to the Fingleton venture should be undertaken in Iona, and he left the Glasgow parish for Iona. The latter is described as having been a difficult decision to make. Some of the members of the parish in Glasgow, it seems, and others in Scotland, regarded the experiment with suspicion, as 'Roman' or 'playing at being monks', or whatever. The way ahead, for the *Wild Goose* journey and the community to undertake it, was seen, as ever, to be risky and full of hard decisions at forks in the road.

But the establishing of this ' "brotherhood" within the Church of Scotland, of no permanent vows, into which men of such a mind could come for the first two or three years of their ministry' went ahead in 1938. (The quotation there is from Macleod's original proposal.) The *Wild Goose* travellers did not seem to be put off with fears of possible negative developments that might arise on the way ahead. They seem to have trusted in the assurance that lies at the heart of Christianity. That is, in the wonder and mystery of how the positive can be born out of the negative, and of what religious and theological terminology has called the wonder and mystery of the redemptive, creative and re-creative potential of times of tension, uncertainty, adversity and suffering.

What followed between then and now in the story of the Iona Community, much of which Ferguson gives in his book, can only be briefly touched on here. Community members and associate members for lay and ordained ministries within and outside the traditional Church, in Britain and overseas, now make up the Community, and have brought into it their diverse practical and professional skills and experience. Women, of course, have long joined fully in the membership of what was styled above as 'the brotherhood'. Young people have been active in work-projects, in 'programmes' and conferences in the Abbey, and so on. The importance of musicians and song-writers such as John Bell and Graham Maule, mentioned briefly earlier on, and their work very widely in enabling and bringing new life into the provision of aids for prayers and patterns of worship, have been one important feature of worship in many churches and of much of what is gathered up centrally in worship in the Abbey. Among the places across the world mentioned by Ron Ferguson as some of the places where Community members have been working since the early days, in addition, of course, to the places in urban Scotland such as the huge Easterhouse housing-scheme in Glasgow, are the following ten countries: 'Pakistan, South Africa, Kenya, Zambia, Nigeria, Malawi, India, Gibraltar, the USA, Canada'.

Ron Ferguson has a mild but fine phrase about the moment when the Community first settled in Iona in 1938, commenting that for Macleod and his companions, 'it felt right to be living in continuity with the Columban and the Benedictine communities'. And the book's closing words are just this; that 'Patrick Cavanagh' (the 20th century Irish 'poet of the mundane', who continued to try and stop certain excessive pressures of mundane pulls in his own life from hiding the realities of the Christian faith in which he had been brought up) 'says it beautifully':

> 'Then I saw the wild geese flying
> In fair formation to their bases in Inchicore
> And I knew that these wings would outwear the
> wings of war
> And a man's simple thoughts outlive the day's
> loud lying.

Don't fear, don't fear, I said to my soul.
The Bedlam of Time is an empty bucket rattled,
'Tis you will say in the end who best battles.
Only they who fly home to God have flown at
all.'[332]

---

332 The poem Beyond the Headlines, written during the Second
World War. Patrick Cavanagh *Collected Poems* 2004, Penguin Books.
P.111

12

FOUR CURRENT DILEMMAS IN HUMAN ROUTE-FINDING

What follows are merely brief probings into huge dilemmas, but hopefully they may provide some material for reflection or discussion. Here are the predicaments and dilemmas:

1. Religious Extremism and Some Extremities of Cynicism.

A remark commonly heard in Britain is that 'It's religion that causes very many wars.' At the same time we hear the additional statement: 'It's religious extremisms that are the trouble: be modern, and remove religious factors like that and adopt a secularism that focuses on morality and humaneness'. (That viewpoint was of course voiced in an earlier chapter.) Then if we add to the cleft-stick implied in the second statement the undoubted fact that the healthy scepticism and scrutiny provided by much secularism has shown a habit widely, in the last century, of sliding into cynicism and an almost despairing malaise about life, we land up with something like a three-forked predicament about the way forward. A way with no clear world view, apparently leaving us just to concentrate on the individualist level of personal choice, and otherwise without any wider prospect for humanity's way ahead other than a possible bleak wasteland along the lines of Thomas Hardy.[333] He wrote to someone 'Altogether the world is such a bungled institution from a humane point of view that a grief more or less hardly counts.'

For many now, naturally, since '9/11', and suicide-bombings and violent killings in Britain and elsewhere, the issue is inevitably seen in terms of religious extremism - 'Muslim extremists', 'Arab extremists', with perhaps the word 'fundamentalist' coming into it, or 'al-Qaida' and 'Osama bin Laden'. That obviously claims the centre of our attention and concern. But we will know, if only from the 1990s' years, that religious extremism is not limited to the Middle East or the Muslims. In the conflict in Bosnia in the 1990s both the Serb leader and the military commander, Radovan Karadzic and Ratko Mladic, were Serbian Orthodox Christians honoured at the time by their Serb fellow-countrymen as true and loyal Christians, and they were honoured as examples of leaders who had chosen to follow 'the thorny path of Christ'.[334] Yet both of those leaders currently have charges against them of leading the most violent, ruthless and 'extremist' massacres of thousands of Muslims at that time, and both men face an international tribunal. The dilemmas become steadily more complex.

A Saudi Arabian diplomat has recently said that the underlying point at issue concerning suicide-bombings is that the vast majority of people in the Muslim world hate America, and he says that for him that last fact is more tragic than 9/11 itself.[335] So we see here America's 'feeling wounded' by the undoubtedly cruel means of expression from the Arab or Muslim

---

333. Hardy. *Collected Letters*. Oxford 1978, 1988.

334. Oliver McTernan *Violence in God's Name*. (Orbis)

335. Mark Hollingsworth, author of *Saudi Babylon,* in an article in the *Guardian*, July 2005.

world in 9/11 matched by that world's feeling that it too has been cruelly 'wounded' by what it sees as the USA's exploitation of, and interference in, the Middle East. However, it seems that the American government since 9/11 continues to say 'We don't know why they hate us here in the West, except perhaps out of envy.' So the issue of the causes of the hatred is usefully pinpointed as one of the big questions of the present time (the suggestion of 'envy' hardly meets the case, of course, for, as any nation eventually knows which has formerly been an imperialist or colonialist power, or any wealthy nation which is currently among the big investing nations knows, it is their 'dignity' that any 'protesters' are talking about rather than an 'envy' of them).

A few answers concerning the cause of the hatred have indeed been forthcoming. Meic Pearse's 2003 book *Why the Rest Hates the West*[336] gives useful pointers towards an answer, though, somewhat surprisingly, he seems to regard his pointers and viewpoint to be likely to be unfashionable. Meanwhile Bishop Kenneth Cragg, a noted scholar in Islamic Studies, who for many years has lived and worked in many countries in the Muslim world, has written a book *A Certain Sympathy of Scriptures,*[337] which is, as its title shows, about the affinities which he has found between Islamic phrases and vocabulary used in the Quran and in Muslim prayers on the one hand and in Christian phrases and vocabulary used in the *Bible* and Christian prayers on the other. And, in that book's preface, there are deep passages in which Cragg sets, alongside the precious affinities, the truth also that Muslims 'resent and dispute many attitudes in the West', including its 'cultural arrogance', the near-satiated consumerism, the blatant materialism, the over-indulged world of gross advertising and the consequent neglect of others' poverty, and the crude imbalance of

---

336. SPCK

337. Sussex Academic Press. 2004

the world's economies'. These are seen, he says, as 'symptoms of an abeyance of the will to worship and of the capacity for wonder'. To this are added further words about how, 'though Christianity may seem, to Muslims, to be "failed religion" at least in respect of its western territory, the factors are seen to lie in a gathering western lapse of confidence in the human situation as truly a delegacy from Allah' (that is, a custodianship over the divinely created world of humanity). The West is 'seen as astray, in the grip of delusion and "the secular".'

Cragg proceeds then to two other points. First, that there has been what may perhaps be described as a shared perception between Muslims and many in the West over the above 'lapse of confidence', in which many people are seen as in a situation where 'they no longer believe in belief'. And T.S. Eliot's weary post-first-world-war poem *The Wasteland* has had a powerful impact on twentieth century Arabic writing, 'perhaps in part because it shaped a mood of desolation around the Palestinian tragedy'. Echoes of *The Wasteland*, it seems, run through the prose and poetry of Muslim communities – Arab, Turkish, Urdu, Malay – alike in East and West. The Islamic dispersion in Europe and America shares the factors directly. Secondly, the great influence of the growth of modern science and technology is noted, and 'the multiplying devices' able to be harnessed by those aiming at increased power – all of these being 'patterns of change more than religions have ever been or ever will be able to re-order or control'.

I have given the above quotations at some length because Bishop Cragg's writings[338] here must surely articulate and gather together in a uniquely cogent way the major dilemma posed by, on the one hand, the extremisms and mistaken 'fundamentalisms' that can grow like a flower gone to seed out of the convictions

---

338. The references in Cragg above are to pp.xii and xiii in the preface to *A Certainty Sympathy of Scriptures.*

of faith-communities, and on the other hand the extremisms of cynicism that can grow, again like a flower gone to seed, out of the healthy scepticism and work of scrutiny in secularism.

In addition to those descriptions of the Muslim world's criticisms of western loss of religious belief and 'lapse of confidence', in European thinking generally, the voice of other acclaimed theologians such as Jürgen Moltmann are to be heard. In Moltmann's 1997 book *God for a Secular Society (The Public Relevance of Theology)*[339] he uses very strong terms to describe what he sees as having been a growing increase in 'cynicism' about religious belief ever since Nietzsche's 'God is dead' views, and both the massacres of World War One and the later Auschwitz cruelties. He says that this cynicism 'expresses itself' in 'a contempt for God'. He adds that Christians must 'go deep into the discovery of the Kingdom'. And encourage Christian congregations to develop a 'mature' wrestling with these movements in secular society.[340] Moltmann's writing on all this clearly presents the modern situation as one of hard dilemma as between the path of cynicism and the path of trust and faith.

Part of the dilemma, of course, appears in sharpened form in fundamentalism, the term that first emerged out of early twentieth century American Protestantism. Such twentieth-century definitions as the following were to emerge: 'historic fundamentalism is the literal exposition of all the affirmation and attitudes of the Bible and the militant exposure of all non-biblical affirmation and attitudes'.[341] A much less militant understanding of the term 'fundamentals' was to be found in Britain in the *'New English Bible'* of 1970. There the heading 'Recall to Fundamentals'

339. SCM Press. English translation. 1999.

340. Moltmann. Pp.16 and 216-225

341. George Dollar of Bob Jones University in his *History of Fundamentalism in America*, quoted by Malise Ruthven *'Fundamentalism'* Oxford. 2004

was put as a description of *The First Letter of John* with its opening verses declaring 'Our theme is the word of life… made visible in Jesus Christ'. Referring to the more adversarial use of the term 'fundamentalist', Bishop Ian Cundy, now Bishop of Peterborough, could write near the end of the twentieth century:

> 'Most Evangelicals here' (i.e. in UK) 'would both disown the label "fundamentalist" (and did so when James Barr published his similar evaluation) and also recognise the complex interplay of authoritative scripture, the Church's evolving understanding and the use of reason in discerning truth…' [342]

Fundamentalism and literalism in our global world strongly affect worldwide discussion on biblical interpretation, but in North America currently its widespread, mainstream influence is obviously on politics. Michael Northcott's book *An Angel Directs the Storm: Apocalyptic Religion and American Empire* [343] makes clear just how strongly apocalyptic the current tone of American Christianity is and he is very critical of the current trend. He says that some in the American scene identify the Kingdom of God with the free-market: and others, who include top generals and White House members, think that all-out nuclear conflict might precede the Second Coming. Prof. Timothy Gorringe had a major review article on it in *The Expository Times* for December 2005, and supports the view that the current apocalyptic religion deforms American Christianity by American imperialism. Rather, he writes, 'Christians must resist this new religion of violence and affirm belief in the true apocalypse, which is a message of hope to the victims of history, not to their imperial overlords.'

---

342. *Church Times,* February 1991.

343. Taurus. 2004.

In Britain, Bishop Cragg's discussion in his book, though only slenderly represented in my attempted summary of part of it, seems to me to have underlying it those two priorities of authoritativeness or firmness, and vulnerability or sensitivity that stand out in the priorities of what Jesus lived out in face of the dilemmas with which he was presented.

2. Sensuality and the Celebration of the Senses.

This, to me, is a clear choice and a real dilemma. But first, a word about the phrase 'the celebration of the senses' which may sound perplexing or vague. What sensuality is being contrasted with is all the good and precious ways in which our bodies and the human five senses (listening with the ears, seeing with the eyes, touching with the hands, tasting with the lips, and smelling with the nose) can play a part in Christian life. For example, music can give us a great deal via hearing, and visual art via seeing. We have a need for a balance between heart and mind; the senses can bring alive for us many of the things that the mind serves up to us often in a colder and more analytical way.

Kathy Galloway has given us a clear description of how the Christian view of the body and the senses has often sadly been misrepresented, as though it is saying that everything to do with the body is bad. And she protests about the following misrepresentation:

> 'It has allowed all that is sensory and feeling, all
> that is instinctive and intuitive to be despised,
> and the intellectual and "spiritual" to be idolized.
> It has deprived countless men and women and
> children of the experience of much of what is
> most delightful, most hopeful and most joyful
> about being human. It has divided people against
> themselves, against each other, and against
> God.'[344]

---

344. Galloway. *Dreaming of Eden*. Wild Goose. Glasgow. 1997

But as for 'sensuality', we know exactly what that means. It means 'binge-drinking' and 'wife-swapping' and so on. We are told that 44% of violent crime in Britain is now alcohol-related. It is to be seen widely on the streets in many inner cities and is displayed fully on television. *Men Behaving Badly* was apparently watched by fourteen million viewers at Christmastime in 1998. And in 2004 *Footballers' Wives* was watched by six million. In one episode in the series, it seems, an annual team party was shown, including the filming of a closeted gay footballer having sex with a male prostitute, watched by all the team. The Archbishop of Canterbury, Rowan Williams, did not keep silent, and apparently said at that time, of the series or the episode, that it was promoting the kind of selfish behaviour that was now commonplace in contemporary Britain.

It is of course pointed out sometimes about some 'explicit' theatre productions that they are to be seen as modern 'morality plays' and as good satire, and that they do the same job as, say, Shakespeare's tragedies about human cruelty, sin and fear, making us think hard about a human situation. Or that the productions are a sort of 'fun' satire. (This was touched on in an earlier chapter.) But the explicit plays and dramas mentioned in the preceding paragraph surely hardly come into the same category. An early-adolescent viewer of *Footballers' Wives* is hardly likely to see it as having serious nuances, but more as an invitation to things not so healthy, - the sort of 'fun'-nuance that Aldous Huxley in his *Brave New World* early in the twentieth century envisaged that humanity was going to focus all its attention on and grow into: that is, that human happiness consists just in 'having fun'.

It would be less than transparent if I did not mention here one instance of a dilemma with which I myself was confronted many years ago. I had a family background that presented us with a salutary and notable challenge and reminder about how morally corrupting and dangerous such aspects of sensuality as the unbridled use of alcohol and smoking could be both personally and socially. My Dublin grandmother's immediate forbear Anne Jane Carlile founded, with a Roman Catholic and Baptist colleague, the organisation called 'The Band of Hope' in Dublin, Cork, Ulster and Leeds in the nineteenth century. It provided activities encouraging children to avoid alcohol problems, and included Christian teaching.[345] Anne Carlile had early on founded a temperance society for sailors in Dublin. Her temperance concern had come from visiting women's 'penitentiaries' and prisons for men and women. She realised that alcohol lay behind a huge area of crime and illness. However, in my father's generation, though he was almost entirely a teetotaller, he smoked a pipe all his adult life, and it was often considered inhospitable at certain levels of society not to offer guests a cigarette. Dilemmas presented themselves frequently, however, then and later. I myself, in an early nine-year period of work in a theological college in a city in India, long ago, in a decade before definite medical bans on smoking, joined a close friend and colleague on the staff at that time in some moderate smoking for some years.

Many of us, including myself and my Indian colleague, in our city setting, were well aware that, especially in rural and village areas, many families with very little to live on often had their family life and well-being damaged or destroyed by the father spending most of their small earnings on drink or smoking in the village. And, for that and other reasons, one or two of our students in the college who came from large rural areas found my smoking offensive, though they said nothing about it. Anyway, it was a clear tie-up with what St Paul was writing about when he urged some of his congregations and followers who ate meat

345. Its modern successor is the organisation 'Hope' which works for drug and alcohol education and is based at 25(f) Copperfield Street, London SE1 0EN

(which might have been first 'offered to idols' in non-believers' temples) to stop doing so if it offended a Christian brother or sister who did not eat meat.[346] My friend and I, in our smoking, were clearly, in our acknowledged overall aim of attempting to follow the Nazareth route, taking a wrong turning at this fork, or dilemma, in the road. We were aware of potential dangers in general and in villages and so on, but not aware enough on the personal side. It was a good and salutary reminder that personal choice is not the only factor in making decisions over choices and dilemmas; personal choice often has to be balanced by what others see as the right choice.

But trying to follow the Nazareth route on other issues, for example on sex, remains centrally a personal matter in human existence at many points. The human sexual pull for gratification being so extremely powerful a feeling, there has to be, for its control, something even more powerful in terms of a commitment and an inward pull in a person. Here again it is in *St Paul's* writings and letters that we find what that more powerful pull and commitment can be, spelt out in practical terms related to the senses and personal sexual matters. The Pauline tradition as found in the *Letter to Christians in Colossae* is of particular modern relevance here. It invites and urges the readers to centre their lives on commitment to Christ and on trust in the assurance of his living presence now. 'Be rooted in him, be built in him, grow strong in the faith...' Don't be distracted, it says, by those who are currently enticing you with supposedly helpful clues to the truth, such as ascetic disciplines, and getting in touch with visionary cosmic powers and 'elemental spirits of the universe' controlling human existence, and 'angel-worship'. No, says the *Letter to the Colossians*; such things may have 'an air of wisdom' but are 'of no use at all in combating sensuality'. Fix your eyes

---

346. *1 Corinthians* Chapter 8. verses 7-13

and your commitment on Christ: 'all things are held together in him'.[347]

I said that the above is of particular modern interest. Phrases used above from the *Colossians' Letter* about false ideas by which Christians in Colossae were being enticed, and against which they were warned find parallels in modern warnings of another sort. They are almost identical with some phrases used today by some scientists, it seems, who oppose Christian beliefs on the creation and who have extremely controversial 'Intelligent Design' theories. A biochemist, Michael Behe, recently interviewed in Britain, agreed that although he found it congenial to think that God is the designer, he believed it to be quite possible that the universe was designed by 'some kind of evil alien', 'some satanic force', or 'an angel', or 'some new age power'.[348]

After all that, it is good to turn again to 'the celebration of the senses', and to see how the senses can bring alive for us many of the issues just looked at and can help us in the growing process by which the figure of Christ has reality for us. One theologian has given us a thorough discussion of desire as central in any consideration of many issues including sensuality. Professor Timothy Gorringe's book *The Education of Desire* has the sub-title *Towards a Theology of the Senses*.[349] He writes in effect that although, for example, capitalism attempts to restrict unfettered grasping of profits, we have in Christianity an alternative way of giving the education which desire needs. He says that desire in the Christian sense also has a positive side and that its full meaning for us should not just be dominated by 'evil desires' meanings, such as 'lust' or 'greed', but we should also go beyond that to look overall

347. *Colossians* Chapter 1 verse 17, and Chapter 2.7, 18, 20, 23 (R.E.B.)

348. A scientist interviewed by John Sutherland in *The Guardian*. 12.9.05

349. SCM Press 2001, especially on pp. 92-93 and 97-98

at 'desire', e.g. in relation to finance, and to let 'desire' overall be seen as just one part of what is a large and deep phenomenon within human life, a phenomenon which in one's life includes the desire deep down for God, and for truth, beauty and goodness. The climax of this small section of Gorringe's book is found when he mentions the way in which St Paul describes the human body, and human desires of the body, when he wrote to some Christians in the notoriously 'permissive' city of Corinth: 'Do you not know that your body is a temple of the indwelling Holy Spirit...?' (*1 Corinthians* 6.15.) Gorringe also adds that part of the education of desire is the liberating of it from the damaging link with egoism, an alliance into which it easily strays in human nature.

That section in Gorringe ties up closely, of course, with what many writers, from *St Paul* and the *Gospel of John* write about how 'Christ Jesus' became human; 'he was in the form of God, ... but made himself nothing' and 'bearing the human likeness, sharing the human lot, he humbled himself'; or, in the words of *John*, Jesus' saying to his followers 'You have only to live on in me and I will live on in you'.[350] Gorringe has a notable phrase when he says that this was 'God exploring God's creation', a theme seen as leading on from the verse in *Proverbs,* 'The Lord shines into a person's soul, searching out his inmost being'.[351] Gerard Hughes also gave us the notable phrase 'God is within my own being, constantly creating it'.[352] In all these wordings, and in all these 'humble' areas of life, where our human desires and senses lie, God is seen creatively at work.

In addition to those senses of hearing and seeing that can be celebrated and used by us, many other gifts of the senses come

---

350. Paul in *Philippians* ch.2. verses 6-8. (REB) and *The Gospel of John* ch.15. verse 4. (in Ronald Knox's translation).

351. *Proverbs*. 20.27 (REB)

352. Hughes. *The Surprises of God*. DLT. (1985)

to mind. Standing in the middle of his local countryside and its landscape, Thomas Traherne summed up his celebration of what he received from nature (a quotation referred to earlier) in the words 'I... did little think such joys as ear and tongue/to celebrate and see'.[353] Here I just choose two aspects of the senses to touch on slightly more fully: those to do with the hands and those that can express themselves in movement and dance.

In 1971 Henri Caffarel wrote a booklet which was translated a few years later as *The Body at Prayer*.[354] Starting from the Psalmist verse: 'My heart and my flesh cry out for the living God' in *Psalm* 84, it urges the reader to let the body share in the responsibility felt by so many to increase all ways of making prayer real. He writes that he knows people who, when their spirits are low and they are finding it hard to pray, happily leave the ultimate responsibility with the body, its movements of expression and its postures. He goes through some of the ways that the hands are widely used in prayer, combined with different postures such as standing, sitting, and kneeling, commonly used. Three or four examples are these:

> Standing with one's hands together in front of
> the chest, to express, from the start, reverence, a
> readiness to listen and obey

> Standing with one's hands stretched out above
> one's head, either fully stretched or with the palms
> of the hands facing the front

> Standing with the open palms of one's hands,
> perhaps cupped together, in a gesture of either
> composure, or gratitude, or praise, or offering, or
> entreaty, penitence, and a giving-back

353. Traherne. *The Salutation*

354. *Editions du Feu*, Paris (1971), and SPCK London (1978). Translated by Bob Burn and Heather le Dieu.

> Using similar movements, but sitting or kneeling,
> perhaps sitting back kneeling on one's haunches,
> or kneeling with straightened back to express
> thanksgiving, attention and for meditation, with
> deep breathing maybe.

In the 1960s, Sydney Carter wrote *The Lord of the Dance* which became well-known and was widely sung. 'I came down from heaven and I danced on earth; at Bethlehem I had my birth. Dance then wherever you may be, I am the Lord of the Dance, said he.' Carter wanted dancing to be seen as a spiritual activity, and many people agreed that in the singing of his song, they rediscovered their own spirituality, through an image that suggested life, energy, grace and movement. Just short of forty years later, Michael Mayne, a former Dean of Westminster Abbey, wrote a remarkable book called *Learning to Dance*,[355] on the theme of the dance as running through numerous aspects of the world's life and of personal lives in their relationships, their faith and spirituality. A passage, movingly told, near the end of the book came across to me as a splendid reminder that in dancing, for example ballet dancing, with all its skilful but easy and supple flexibility and rhythmic smoothness, we have a powerful message of the importance of 'loosening' up, and of disciplined but relaxed 'letting-go' in life. Michael Mayne expresses that much better, in some humble words about his own life: he wrote that in retirement he had seen more clearly 'how much time I have wasted in a kind of anxious perfectionism; how aware I have been of the beauty both of nature and the arts, but how much I have simply taken for granted; and, while I have always tried to put pastoral care at the top of the agenda, how much more loving I might have been.'

There will be more than a few people who do not like the idea of dancers in cathedrals and churches (in spite of *Psalm*

---

355. Darton, Longman and Todd. 2001.

150's 'Praise him with tambourine and dance', about the worship of God):[356] but very recently there was a display of Kalai-Kaviri dancing from South India in Gloucester Cathedral and St Paul's Cathedral in London; and in the Cathedral in Kurunegala in Sri Lanka there is a well-known crucifix which is given the name 'The Dance of Triumph on the Cross'. The range of the celebration of the senses can be a wide range, from giving thanks through watching a sunset, or listening to the quietest of music, to giving thanks in the context of a joyful and energetic dance.

3. The Claims of Justice and the Claims of Compassion.

A third great current dilemma is lit up for us by Archbishop Desmond Tutu's 1999 book *No Future without Forgiveness*, about the South African 'Truth and Reconciliation Commission' in the 1990s, following the ending of apartheid, [357]a book already touched on. The dilemma which that lights up, and sheds light on, is of course part of the whole dilemma in general, in humanity as we know it, of how to meet the claims of both justice and compassion. Anyone for whom the Calvary, Good Friday scene of the Cross has profoundly deep meaning can hardly help seeing the 'Truth and Reconciliation Commission' as a signal modern living-out of Calvary's significance, or as the truth of the Atonement coming alive in modern terms.

In newspaper accounts of murder trials, relatives of the victim in the case are often quoted as saying something such as 'you can't begin to talk about forgiveness for the perpetrator of this outrageous crime. What we want to see is the all-important demand for justice to be done on behalf of our son/daughter...' In countless situations like that or in other situations and different

---

356. NRSV

357. Rider. Random House.

contexts, the gulf between forgiveness, or compassion, and justice can seem to be over and over again unbridgeable.

It is here that, for many of us, Archbishop Tutu's book will seem to be the great book to read, and indeed perhaps one of the great books of the twentieth century. (It was published in 1999, as mentioned.) The process followed by the Commission clearly had its critics, who said 'It is an immoral process...' 'Amnesty is being given at the cost of justice'... 'Amnesty for the perpetrators is not made conditional on prior remorse', and so on. But the Commission pressed on with its task without being deflected.

Traditional biblical and theological language about justice and compassion has used as central such related couplets as 'judgement and mercy' or 'law and grace'. St Paul in his complex but magnificent *Letter to the Romans* uses another related phrase when he writes 'Observe the kindness and the severity of God', in the later part of his letter to sum up 'God's way of righting wrong', [358] in a paradox that he sees as alone able to express twin aspects of the truth.[359] But the language of wounding and brokenness is not far away from any of these phrases, and it is the language that the 'Truth and Reconciliation Commission', and witnesses before the Commission, were using. Under Tutu's leadership they were led into a process of shared humiliation, acknowledged vulnerability and costliness. Echoing, as it were, the way of the Wounded healer on Calvary, Tutu's book has on its cover the phrase 'The Commissioners were "the wounded healers" of the whole situation'. There is no pretence in the book that Tutu himself could escape great personal anguish in the process: at one point

---

358. The *New English Bible's* masterly yet clear translation of the original Greek word in *Romans* 1.17 – a translation which gathers up the word's many nuances, especially 'being right' and 'seeing right done,' as found in that Greek word and the corresponding *Old Testament* Hebrew word.

359. *Romans* 11.22 (REB)

he writes 'I could not hold back my tears', about one occasion, and elsewhere 'I have been close to breaking down many times'.

The wounding and the cost to victims and to perpetrators which the process caused were clearly immense. The wounding and cost of the process for the perpetrators of apartheid was perhaps more obvious and easily stated. They were having to endure the humiliation of the public exposure of their cruelty to and torturing of others, and were to receive no compassion offered to themselves in this. The wounding and cost to the victims had several aspects to it. They felt deep anguish at not being allowed under the terms of the process to press criminal charges or civil damages in compensation for loss. Then there was the pain of having to meet those who had violated their persons and their rights, and not being able to express their own bitterness and hatred. Added to that was the wounding fact that no punishment was to be meted out to the perpetrators: also the fact that these additional woundings to their dignity were being added to the already existing hardships of their poverty and bad living conditions. All sorts of old wounds were to be opened up again for them.

All these deep grievances were indeed, agonisingly, brought into the open, it seems. Tutu's book makes clear that his own underlying conviction throughout was that 'God created us to belong to one another'. Although he says that for him what had happened in apartheid had been 'part of a radical brokenness in all of existence', yet the overwhelming impression left by the book is its conviction that the loving power of God's original purpose in creating humanity to belong to one another would prevail always, with renewal and life-giving. The utter integrity of the process is indeed overwhelming. There is no impression given of any quick or glib expectations of an easy closure to the dilemma, or closure or total forgetting of the difficulties and complexities passed through. But it is clear that some closure, with reality to it, had been achieved, widely recognised, and marvelled over. My own understanding of what happened has to be that 'the Nazareth route', with its marks of vulnerability and authoritativeness, had in a new form been glimpsed at and found surfacing yet again.

The justice-compassion dilemma confronts us in many other contexts and areas of life. Here two of such aspects of it are looked at. First in the world of prisons, prisoners and penal reform, where penal reform is currently much discussed, including debates in church-bodies and synods. Dr Duncan Forrester, in his essay 'Priorities for Social Theology Today',[360] has described how attitudes on penal policy have presented society in Scotland with a major dilemma: 'Our society remains highly punitive and former prisoners rarely experience real forgiveness and reconciliation at the hands of their neighbours and colleagues'. The discussion has centred much on the distinction between reparative justice which focuses on the offender and punishment, and restorative justice which focuses more on the future and recovery-related issues.

It seems that a group called the 'Penal Policy Group' in Scotland has placed particular emphasis on restorative justice and the perceived need for any Christian account of punishment to be directed towards the good of society and of the offender. Also that in the group most of those in the penal system and academic criminology appeared to find the notion of forgiveness 'a fresh and exciting and challenging idea'. But between such explorations and statements of popular opinion on the treatment of criminals a big gulf clearly exists and presents an undoubted dilemma. Issues concerning capital punishment are obviously related to all the above, and must loom large not least in the USA where the numbers in prison and in the 'death-cells' are so large.

A second 'justice-compassion' challenge and aspect of the dilemma is this. In achieving justice, are we going to use physical

---

360. in *Vision and Prophecy* ed. Michael Northcott. Edinburgh Centre for Theology and Public Issues. 1991.

military force or non-physical force? This does not refer to policing but to the so-called 'pacifist' question. (The word 'pacifism' clearly describes the negative, 'opting-out-of-violence' side of those who disagree with military violence, but does not touch on their search for a non-violent way of resisting injustice. The great pioneer Mahatma Gandhi always refused the label 'pacifist' and said he was a 'non-violent resister' against injustice and wrong.)

During the twentieth century and more recently, in addition to a big majority who have seen military, violent resistance as necessary and right in many situations in the last resort, there have been others who have searched, or worked for, alternative and non-violent ways of resisting injustice or aggression. In times of war, most have joined armed services, finding it impossible to leave to others the risks and responsibilities of defending their country, their family and themselves against an unjust aggressor. But those exploring alternative routes, while recognising, probably agonisingly, the full force of the points of the majority just mentioned, may have joined a Friends Ambulance or an American Peace Corps unit; or others, more compromisingly, and in an army-navy-related way, may have manoeuvred to get into a naval 'minesweeper' (a far from passive First World War route for some), or into an army mobile surgical unit in Europe or Burma in the Second World War, one of the sort of units which spent two or three weeks at a time with whatever part of a brigade happened to be active at any given time. Feeble alternatives perhaps, some would say, when at the same time relatives in Britain might be being bombed in air raids on civilians in cities such as London, but these alternatives were undertaken as 'at least something', that was not a complete opting out. Also something that at least a minority ought to do.

And the 'alternative-routes' explorers, in what were always acknowledged to be more long-term forms of resistance, often continued after the world wars their endeavours in thorough and effective ways – endeavours in tackling the causes of war and division across the world. Recent responses to world-wide injustices – responses made by some politicians, following the method of instant military action and with a result predictably that has often proved counterproductive – have shown that ventures of violent sorts sometimes have their difficulties of achievement. Rosemary Hartill, the Quaker worker, has described some non-violent approaches, in international action against flagrant injustices in which participation is and has been possible in very recent years: briefly summarised these are: involvement in negotiating structures aimed at a treaty to reduce arms sales, encouraging the handing in of guns in exchange for food vouchers, as in El Salvador in 1995-1997; the training of civilians to check and report on ethnic violence; articulating and addressing the roots of terrorism; helping to work towards a just Israeli-Palestinian settlement; work on sanctions as a method in difficult situations; work on the closing off of the supply of fissile material to many Middle Eastern countries; the backing of a convention on biological and toxin weapons; and the raising of money for conflict resolution. The above provides us with one example, which is detailed, and not just vague, of alternative ways of approach [361]to issues of justice and compassionate understanding.

Such examples, reminders of the sorts of approach that can be attempted, will, for Christians, also naturally be a reminder of some of Jesus' penetrating words in the Gospels, such as: 'You have heard that our forefathers were told, "An eye for an eye, a tooth for a tooth," but what I tell you is this: "Do not resist those who wrong you".'[362] Like all biblical verses these words need interpreting, and have to be seen alongside other verses in the Gospels, as

---

361. *The Guardian*. Dec 30th 2002, published Rosemary Hartill's description.

362. *Matthew* 5. 38 and 39 (REB)

when Jesus on one occasion overturned the tables of the Temple money-changers; and also have to be worked out in relation to distinctions between policing force and major armed force, as far as corporate bodies and not just individuals are concerned. But the impact in general of Jesus' words there remains supremely strong and gives us a pointer towards some of the priorities of Jesus' Nazareth route. Jesus' words about 'resisting' can hardly be interpreted by us today without making us think hard about their relevance concerning such facts about major armed force, as that Britain, we are told, has 200 nuclear warheads, each 8 times more powerful than the Hiroshima bomb.

4. The Apparent Contradiction Between Competition and Sharing.

To many of us in Britain it may come as a surprise to learn that some of the most forthright opposition to the prominent place of competition in the modern world of market-economies has come not just from the USA, but from a leading top business-executive in the USA.

Thirty years ago, Robert Greenleaf was the executive in charge of all management development for what was then the largest corporation in the world, American Telephone and Telegraph, as it then was. A Quaker in his upbringing, and with a training in engineering, he had then had a full life in business. But in his retirement he wrote in 1974 a thirty-four-page booklet called *The Servant as Leader,* which reflected trenchantly his long-growing disillusionment with conventional and top-down ideas of how business-companies should be managed; and with prevailing principles at the time, for the running of a society's economy which continued to centre on competition. About ten years later, a professor in the University of Texas backed up Greenleaf's views strongly and wrote: 'people often say that they enjoy competing, but then change their minds when they learn firsthand what it's like to work or play in a setting that does not require winners and losers.' Work in a business corporation was not seen by him as such a non-competitive setting. But 'salaries go up as competitiveness goes down', was an experience cited. Greenleaf looked forward to a 'relational' pattern of leading rather than a 'top-down' one, a 'networks' pattern of power rather than a 'pyramid one'. But he admitted that so far such proposals had been greeted by admiring comments, but refused in practice as a viable system of American management philosophy. Progress would be difficult. Other people prominent in different areas of life and work, however, backed Greenleaf , including Bennett Sims, Bishop of the Diocese of Atlanta in the Episcopal Church for eleven years, who later wrote that he had found that Greenleaf's ideas must surely change the pattern of relationship between a diocesan bishop and his clergy. Perhaps the bishop, who refers to Jesus' words to his disciples as found in the Gospels – 'among you, whoever wants to be first must be the willing slave of all' – was in effect saying 'Greenleaf drives home Jesus' words powerfully for us'.[363] Bishop Sims adds that competition in life is like 'spice' in food, and has its uses. But, he adds, we need above all something more substantial, 'the real "food" of life', which is co-operation and sharing.

The phrase used above about 'winners and losers' seems to point us usefully towards other areas of life than the business world or the world of church dioceses. Stewart Dakers who has worked in the world of handicapped people for over twenty years, and has himself a handicapped son, wrote a very striking newspaper article in 1997 with the title 'Christ's losers as role

---

363. *Mark* 10. 43. in the *New English Bible*. Bishop Sims' book, from which I have gratefully taken the information above about Robert Greenleaf, is *Why Bush Must Go.* Continuum. 2004. New York and London. Chapter 2: 'Competition Superseded'.

models'.[364] It seemed to be a remarkable spelling out in a modern setting of the Nazareth route of Jesus, the wounded healer for a broken world. Dakers comments that the people whom Jesus is recorded as healing were nearly all of them the handicapped: the blind, the crippled and the epileptics: and that their healing can surely be for us 'a focus for contemporary celebration'. In effect he implies that Jesus came to them to bring strength; but what sort of strength? Not the sort of strengths that 'competition' could do much, or anything, to foster. Bringing up a handicapped person, he implies, one tries to create an atmosphere of 'co-operation' and sharing, round him or her. Jesus, as pictured in the Gospels, could perhaps be said (and here I am tempted to use, as in earlier pages, a phrase that slides into 'technical' theological terms) to have developed the redemptive potential of his own times of adversity, and of his having been rejected and 'made weak'. So gradually, in a modern century, an atmosphere of co-operation and sharing could be seen developing, and causing to emerge, in a handicapped person, 'unusual human qualities such as humour, balance, tolerance, patience, persistence, accommodation and modesty', the realising of a modern potential inspired.

We need now, however, to return here to 'competition' in the market-economy setting. Is the central place given to competition currently in that setting a true and just policy in theory and practice? Is Robert Greenleaf's call a generation ago (he died in 1990) for a non-competitive, non-top-down pattern of leadership to be welcomed and as something at which to aim? Three different viewpoints on the issues raised seem to be current in the western world.

In some quarters, continuing and strong support for a competitive capitalist system of the modern sort is found. A

---

364. *The Guardian 'Face to Faith'* section. June 1997

leading article in *The Economist*[365] recently was very critical of some qualifications in that system suggested in recent years as being needed.

Articles in the journal were published, which were dismissive of the qualifying, less competitive proposals, describing them as just a false search for 'a kinder, gentler form of capitalism'. The leading article said that such proposals were 'based on a faulty, and dangerously faulty, analysis of the capitalist system'. Pro-competition supporters along those lines tend to make much of the argument that, although critics of the market-economy focus their criticisms on capitalism's 'shareholder profits', in fact capitalism's emphases and strengths go far wider than that, and its benefits by way of public service to government and country lie also in wealth-creation, the maintaining of employment and boosting of the national economy budget.

Secondly, there are the viewpoints of theologians and the staff of aid-agencies and charities, whose words, such as the following, are often crystal clear and need no spelling out, in their criticisms of the market-economy. Rowan Williams, the present Archbishop of Canterbury, spoke in a sermon in front of judges in Chester some years ago:

> 'At a time of rampant dishonourableness – the slick, evasive marketing and massaging of the egos of the powerful that so threatens our public life and discourse, and that has its nemesis and negative image in a prurient, trivial, malicious culture in so much of our media – we ask a great deal of those who do justice. But that we ask it reveals us as beings who, in spite of all, remain obstinately hungry for the bread of truth; and that's a thought to nourish failing hope.'[366]

---

365. *The Economist*. January 22. 2005.

366. *Open to Judgement*. DLT. 1994. p.246.

Thirdly, there is the viewpoint that may perhaps be said to be concerned to express a middle position between the pro-competition and anti-competition stances, though not in any 'woolly' manner. This viewpoint reminds us that many business executives quite widely, and many managers of multinational companies, would see their companies as working for service to the community generally, and not just in terms of profits to shareholders, and could cite education programmes, websites and newsletters in their organisations to further that end. What is called 'corporate social responsibility' is the phrase used to sum up this conviction. But those with this viewpoint tend to want to uphold some proper place for competition. A book and a report from the ecumenical Churches Together in Britain and Ireland in 2005,[367] with expertise from its social responsibility staff behind it, may be found to have some surprising statements in it for many of us, in its far-reaching policy recommendations. It is obviously well aware of the much-reported payment to directors themselves, by top companies' non-executive directors, of huge annual increases, and so on: it issues an 'invitation to business to serious moral choice' in the hugely increased range of choices, saying that currently many use their wealth in a hedonism that degrades humanity and the natural order. But it also says that while it is in its approach 'hard on business', it is 'in favour of the market'. Then adds 'competition restrains, and it is our contention that an unfettered market suppresses competition rather than encourages it. To be of benefit to the society around them, market players need to be backed between the shafts of competition... A key feature of competition is that it brings innovation into the market-place'. Recent words of Jürgen Moltmann are relevant: 'One step on the way would be to stop making the global market either into

---

367. *Prosperity with a Purpose: Exploring the Ethics of Affluence* by Clifford Longley. *Churches together in Britain and Ireland.* CTBI, Inter-Church House, 35-41 Lower Marsh, London SE1 7RL. 2005.

an idol which has to have its victims, or into a demon which has to be feared, and to cut it down to human size. Another stage in society's maturity is undoubtedly conceivable, a stage in which we would move from the principle of competition to co-operation, and grow as human beings beyond anything which the market can conceive.'[368]

The above varied viewpoints seem to be useful pointers in relation to business for the modern Christian exploration of the relation of faith to everyday life, and may perhaps help us to glimpse at where the Nazareth route is leading. The inclusion of fairly extended details such as the above has been made because that issue concerning the competitive principle does not always receive so much coverage in the press as it might. As a result, that has left very little space for some other huge issues that come under the very wide subject of 'sharing'. Happily on the subject of sharing of resources between wealthy Western countries and developing countries, the press coverage has often been good on matters such as debt, aid and trade; and progress has often been made. So I conclude with only just one particularly outstanding problem, connected with trade, where there is work especially waiting to be done, and where (one could say) there seems to be a section of the Nazareth route ahead waiting to be explored. That is, the area of work given prominence notably by Tax Justice Network, and such aid-agencies and charities as Christian Aid, from about 2005.

The tax-problem being tackled relates to the following situations. Say in the case of a donor-agency, such as a multinational firm, or donations given as a result of a G8 financial summit, in a trade-deal with an African country which produces diamonds. The donor may follow the procedure of using an off-shore 'tax-haven'

---

368. Jürgen Moltmann. *God for a Secular Society (The Public Relevance of Theology)*. SCM. London.1999. (German original 1997). P.163-164.

and this can have drastic results with huge amounts of money involved, and with the African country and government certainly receiving western aid, but having that receipt offset by a loss of a very large amount of money because of the tax-haven procedure. The total procedure would be: the donor buys the diamonds at falsely cheap prices much below the diamonds' real value; and the profits accruing to the multinational through the deal are shifted, with the African country cheated of its rightful tax-gains on profits made in its country, since the diamonds will then be sold at their real high value rate by the multinational, and will be put in a tax-haven bank whose dealings are not made publicly available. In an article 'Plug the leaks or waste the aid' in 2005, two senior advisers to the Tax Justice Network and Christian Aid[369] urged that the following action be taken internationally: action aimed towards the shutting down of tax havens, the elimination of banking secrecy, and the automatic exchange of information between tax jurisdictions.

All the above complexity of detail shows that the route being urged and travelled there is certainly a Nazareth-type route with countless complex turnings. But one undoubtedly being travelled in sure hope.

---

369. Sony Kapoor and John Christiansen in *The Guardian*

EPILOGUE: LOOKING AHEAD

The 'looking ahead' phrase in a way gathers up, for me, three points, supplementing the many scriptural passages and truths about death and eternity in the Gospels and the New Testament passages looked at in earlier parts of this book.

Looking ahead here, in this part of the book, takes me back to Bunyan's Pilgrim's Progress, with all its pilgrim-perspectives about life. Although there has already been a brief reference to Bunyan's book in Chapter 8, here the following parts come to mind. At one stage in the dangerous journey Christian and his companion Hopeful arrived at the crossing of the river which, in Bunyan's allegory, represented human beings encountering death. Christian was apprehensive at the prospect, but Hopeful, going ahead into the water, turned back towards Christian and cried out 'Be of good cheer, my brother; I feel the bottom and it is sound!' And they both went forward. Then, towards the end of the journey, Bunyan inserts the now-well-known poem to show the spirit of the travellers on their way at a later stage:-

'He who would valiant be
'Gainst all disasters,
Let him in constancy
        Follow the master.
There's no discouragement
Shall make him once relent
His first avowed intent
        To be a pilgrim.'

And then, when they came near to their goal, the Holy City, 'there came out… to meet them several of the King's trumpeters…, who… saluted Christian and his fellow with ten thousand welcomes from the world; and this they did with shouting, and the sound of the trumpet.' There are those whose background and classic favourite is The Dark Night of the Soul and not The Pilgrim's Progress, but the two need not be seen as mutually exclusive: and for some of us Bunyan's story is a good helper in 'looking ahead'.

'Looking ahead', secondly, can also bring to mind some of what the scientist-priest Teilhard de Chardin wrote in the middle of the 20th century.[370] de Chardin's vision is couched in similar sort of language to that used by a somewhat more modern priest-scientist who has already been mentioned in Chapter 9, Arthur Peacocke. Peacocke has written that Jesus' 'imperative "Follow me"' to his disciples, as we saw, constituted a call for the transformation of humanity into a new kind of human being and a new kind of 'becoming'. de Chardin was a priest and a specialist in geology and palaeontology. Out of his work he came to issue a challenging Christian call to all Christians to look ahead with a growing expectancy to realise the significance for the future of Christ's life on earth in the incarnation, fully divine, fully human; and the significance of the promise of the Second Coming. In Le Milieu Divin in 1957 he wrote of how 'For us God is eternal discovery', and how God's evolving presence, for us all and with us all, should stimulate us far more than it does to discern the surrounding presence of God in Christ in life on earth, for the present and the future that lies ahead.

'Only twenty centuries,' he wrote, 'have passed since the Ascension. What have we made of our expectancy? We have allowed the flame to die down in our sleeping hearts. No doubt we

---

370. *Le Milieu Divin*. English translation. Collins. 1960

see with greater or less distress the approach of individual death. No doubt, again, our prayers and actions are conscientiously directed to the bringing about of the coming of God's Kingdom. But in fact how many of us are genuinely moved in our hearts by the wild hope that <u>our</u> earth will be recast?' de Chardin's intense longing and conviction was that, as the Kingdom's 'force' and thrust has as its 'role' to transform nature and human nature, so disciples of Christ should be eager to realise and to work to harness this force 'which needs us, and which we need', in his words. He describes how, all over the modern world, people are 'toiling in laboratories, in studios, in deserts, in factories, in the vast social crucible', and says that 'this ferment' through art and science and thought should be focussed on more eagerly by Christians. 'Accept it, tend it and back it up with your interest and help,' he says. 'We shall never know all that the Incarnation still expects of the world's potentialities.' The implications of de Chardin's call clearly has environmental challenges, but wider and more general implications of varied kinds, which scientists can help us to explore, obviously underlie the call deep down.

Finally, a third manner of understanding the phrase 'looking ahead' will be moving at a different level, and be thinking of what looking ahead means for our personal lives in an immediate sense, and what message it brings to our hearts through treasured, small-scale language. I close with three examples of this out of what has come to be treasured by me, in addition to so many biblical verses, and in phrases from prayers.

G.K. Chesterton, a long time ago, began a poem, which is mainly about Christmas, with these four lines:

> 'To an open house in the evening
> Home shall all men come,
> To an older place than Eden
> And a taller town than Rome...'

Catherine Bramwell-Booth, a granddaughter of William Booth, founder of the Salvation Army, said these words at the time of her 100th birthday in 1983:

> 'I don't want to die….I'm in love with life…But
> I'm full of thankfulness, and faith for the future.
> God has always helped me when my best wasn't
> good enough…Let us declare more clearly some
> of God's surprises we have known…'

Eric Treacy was a parson and also a lifelong steam-railway enthusiast. He worked at one time in inner-city Liverpool, and after a life in parish work became Bishop of Wakefield. When preaching at funerals, he would often use the following words:

> 'Death is not a terminus; it is a junction, which
> leads on to the way ahead.'

MELROSE BOOKS

If you enjoyed this book you may also like:

India: Past Glimpses of Country Life
Canon C. M. Copland

India: Past Glimpses of Country Life provides an in-depth account of the Christian Mission sent from Scotland to Chanda, India, in 1870. The information is derived from the first-hand knowledge of those who took part as well as a range of other sources. In addition, readers will find interesting accounts of jungle life.

The book describes how missionaries, forced to live in simple conditions, came to reside in Chanda and gradually became accepted. They were confronted with an almost impossible task; village families had been worshipping their own gods and had been dedicated to their own religions for countless centuries. The people had nothing to gain except salvation and had literally everything to lose. Yet in December 1945, in the face of all the world, four families of Sakerwai publicly accepted Christ as their Saviour, renounced Hinduism and promised to learn the Christian ways of worship and life.

Size: 210 mm x 148 mm	Pages: 128	
Binding: Hardback with dust jacket	ISBN: 978-1-905226-56-6	£12.99

Imaginative Contemplations
Ronald S. Davies

Imaginative Contemplations is a series of short meditations based on different incidents of the life of Christ, as recorded in the four gospels. Starting with the visit of the angel Gabriel to Mary, the meditations take in some of the key events including Christ's baptism, his temptation in the wilderness, some of the healings and other miracles, as well as his death, resurrection and the gathering of his disciples.

The meditations are based upon the method of study and reflection recommended by St. Ignatius of Loyola, the founder of the Jesuits, in his book Spiritual Exercises. The idea is to prepare for the time of reflection and meditation by properly preparing oneself by sitting comfortably and relaxing. Once prepared the reader is then encouraged to read each study slowly and carefully and imagine that they are actually present at the scene being described, hearing the sounds, seeing the sights and feeling the emotions; hence Imaginative Contemplation. This type of study then helps the reader to enter in to the scenes rather than just viewing them from a 'distance'. Encouragements to aid the reader in the exercise are included in the text, for example by suggesting that the heat of the sun can be felt or the softness of the sand under the feet or by hearing the children playing nearby in a village.

Size: 210 mm x 148 mm	Pages: 200	
Binding: Paperback	ISBN: 978-1-905226-90-0	£9.99

On the Edge
Andy Bown

On the Edge is the autobiography of Andy Bown's life. Andy writes passionately about how he found Jesus and how the Holy Spirit entered his body and flowed through him.

He wanted the world to know how he felt about God and decided to be baptised in September 1993. He describes how the first warning signs of Ulcerative Colitis appeared in February 1996 when Andy was training to be a primary school teacher. Andy Bown leads us through his life story and with details of how his faith gave him direction and helped him essentially survive his life-controlling illness.

Size: 234 mm x 156 mm	Pages: 49
Binding: Hardback	ISBN: 978-1-906050-41-2 £12.99

St Thomas' Place, Ely, Cambridgeshire CB7 4GG, UK

www.melrosebooks.com   sales@melrosebooks.com